Pioneer Potpourri

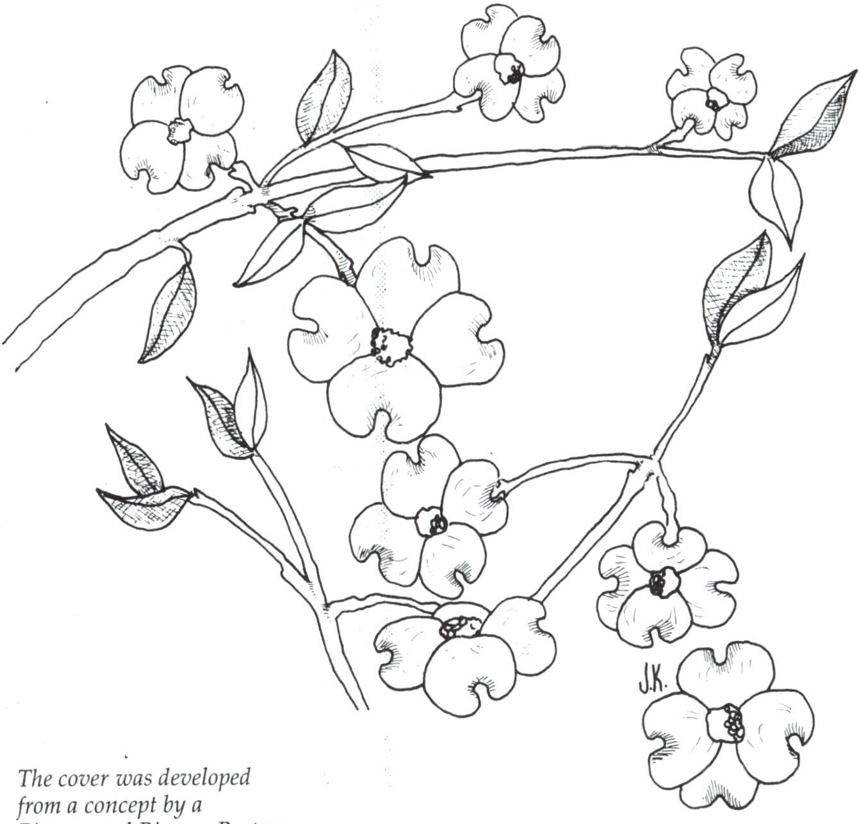

The cover was developed from a concept by a Pioneer and Pioneer Partner and from a sketch by J. W. (Jake) Jacobs.

George Washington Chapter 102

Acknowledgements

When I accepted the job of Project Chairperson for this cookbook, I did not realize the enormity of the task; however, with the dedication of my committee and the Pioneer Administrator, ***Pioneer Potpourri*** became a reality. My heartfelt thanks to committee members:

Constance Billings
Frances Burton
Linda Clarke
W. C. (Dave) Davenport
Wilma Eilenberger
Emerson (Hutch) Hutchings
Tijuan Neal
Sandra Whiteman

And a special thanks to *Terry Rothenberg*, our Pioneer Administrator who came on board after the project started and to our recently retired Administrator, *Bruce Sykes.*

We thank those Pioneers, their families and friends, and their co-workers who contributed their favorite recipes. Our sincere wish is that ***Pioneer Potpourri*** will give you many years of pleasure.

Lucille

Lucille T. King

This cookbook is a collection of our favorite recipes
which are not necessarily original recipes.

Published by: Favorite Recipes® Press
P.O. Box 305142
Nashville, TN 37230

Printed in the United States of America
First Printing: 1990, 12,500 copies

Library of Congress Number: 90-44080
ISBN: 0-87197-286-7

Foreword

Pioneer Potpourri is a collection of favorite recipes from members of George Washington Chapter Telephone Pioneers of America, their families, friends and co-workers.

Profits from this cookbook will be used to continue our many projects such as building gazebos at Veterans hospitals and nursing homes, hug-a-bears to the police, rescue squads and hospitals, aiding battered women, literacy programs, gifts to hospital and nursing home patients, our involvement with the handicapped, environmental projects such as planting trees and seedlings and donations to the "Save the Bay" Foundation, donations to "All Night Long," a drug and alcohol-free prom night and hand-operated tricycles to little ones who are unable to use their legs.

Telephone Pioneers number over 800,000 across the United States and Canada. We are the largest volunteer organization in the world. The Pioneers are here to serve their communities and everyday, somewhere, you will find them doing just that.

The Telephone Pioneers of America were established in 1911 by men and women who were dedicated Pioneers of the telephone industry. The George Washington Chapter is comprised of employees and retirees of AT&T and covers Virginia, West Virginia, the District of Columbia and Maryland.

List of Contributors

Sandra L. Aiker
Mary Glenna Alt
Joann C. Anders
Sheila Anderson
Connie Attisano
Denise J. Babbitt
R. K. Barnes
Joyce Barnett
Vernis Barr
Katharine Bestracky
Constance A. Billings
Kathryn L. Blankenship
Elizabeth J. Blanks
Mary P. Bolen
Virginia Bolling
Jill Bonafield
Ed Bostedo
Barbara Bosworth
Bobbi Bosworth
Frances Bowen
Barbara Breen
Joan Broome
Allison Brown
Dave Brown
Dorothy D. Brown
Frances Burton
Jay E. Callison
Willie Carter
William P. Cecil, Jr.
Grace B. Charlesworth
S. M. Charney
Chris Clark
Linda Clarke
Wanda B. Clemons
Dane R. Cochran
Florence E. Coffey
Lena Cox
Sandra L. Cox
Sylvia Crouch
Linda Crow
Marion F. Daly
Alice Davenport
Brenda Davenport
Dave Davenport
Shirley E. Davis
Mary Di Prima
Marge Dove
Bob Dunlap
Betsy Dye
Bob Eilenberger
Wilma Eilenberger
Henrietta F. Falls
Joan Ferguson
Betsy Bell Figueroa
Mary C. Fletcher
Sherri Fogleman-Williams
Alice Forrest
Anna H. Francis
Doris G. Francis
Patricia Freeman
Ms. Frances H. Geiser
Elizabeth F. Glorio
Mary Ann Goodrich
Mrs. Fran Hannah
Dorothy Hargreaves
Ardell Holden
Rita Howell
Terry Hrezo
Sherry Hughart
Mrs. Arthur W. Hughes, Jr.
Ann B. Hunter
E. V. Hutchings
Susan K. Irvin
J. W. Jacobs
Elizabeth Jacobson
Hazel Jenkins
Elizabeth Johnson
Ruby Frances Johnson
Warren Johnson
Patricia W. Jones
Sherry Kaspar
Joan Keller
Jeanne Kemp
Katherine Ann Kent
Diane Kerr
Janet C. King
Janet E. King
Lucille T. King
Jean Kinney
Lynn R. Kito
Toni Kolling
Jo Kruchten
Mrs. Leon Lambrechts
Bonnie S. Lane
Shelby S. Lewis
Susan Anderson Lewis
Judy Lichman
Elaine Liddle
Tom Liddle
Donna L. Lindblad
Catherine L. Lockwood
P. L. Marshall
Mrs. W. L. Martin
Lorraine McCoy
Linda E. McDonnell
Gail McGee
John W. McMullin, Jr.
Shirley McNanny
Carol Meadows
James L. Mecum
Linda Miles
Joyce Misener
Harry Moran
Phyllis Nelson
Eric W. Nyman
Mrs. Terrie Offer
William H. Parrish
Stephanie A. Pazur
Alice Pointer
Katherine Pruitt
Mrs. Mickey Pugh
Dea Raisanen
Mrs. Kenneth Rhyne
Dolores Riego de Dios
Brenda Sue Robertson
Rita A. Rogers
Georgia Romas
Terry Rothenberg
Faye Rowe
Beverly Rubenstien
Bruce Rubenstien
Mary Etta Sage
Susie Sang
Libby Sauls
John R. Saunders
Joyce Savoy
Bob Schindler
Barbara Schott
William Skey 3rd
Gloria Sladek
Sharon Slater
Charles H. Smith
Marlene Speak
Frances Stapp
Leila B. Stone
Ray "Rocky" Stone
Vicki C. Stone
Judy T. Stoots
Janice Stottlemuer
Bruce Sykes
Glen Sykes
Bonita Thomas
Ivan Thompson
Cynthia Timberman
Sally Topping
John E. Tubbs
Thelma W. Turner
Mary C. Unglesbee
Trish Varnell
Joyce M. Walker
Kay Wall
Sue Walls
Nancy L. Wetter
Virginia White
Sandra Whiteman
Wendy Whiteman
Mrs. Alexander P. Wild
Carroll Williams
Gwendolyn N. Williams
Launna Williams
Sam Winn
Allyson A. Wolford
Margie Worrell
Alice Wright
Kathryn Yarnell

Contents

Nutritional Guidelines

The editors have attempted to present these family recipes in a form that allows approximate nutritional values to be computed. Persons with dietary or health problems or whose diets require close monitoring should not rely solely on the nutritional information provided. They should consult their physician or a registered dietitian for specific information.

Abbreviations for Nutritional Analysis

Cal — Calories	Fiber — Dietary Fiber	Sod — Sodium
Prot — Protein	T Fat — Total Fat	g — gram
Carbo — Carbohydrates	Chol — Cholesterol	mg — milligram

Nutritional information for these recipes is computed from information derived from many sources, including materials supplied by the United States Department of Agriculture, computer databanks and journals in which the information is assumed to be in the public domain. However, many specialty items, new products and processed foods may not be available from these sources or may vary from the average values used in these analyses. More information on new and/or specific products may be obtained by reading the nutrient labels.

Unless otherwise specified, the nutritional analysis of these recipes is based on all measurements being level.

- Artificial sweeteners vary in use and strength so should be used "to taste," using the recipe ingredients as a guideline.
- Artificial sweeteners using aspertame (NutraSweet and Equal) should not be used as a sweetener in recipes involving prolonged heating which reduces the sweet taste. For further information on the use of these sweeteners, refer to package information.
- Alcoholic ingredients have been analyzed for the basic ingredients, although cooking causes the evaporation of alcohol thus decreasing caloric content.
- Buttermilk, sour cream, and yogurt are commercial types.
- Cake mixes using package directions include 3 eggs and 1/2 cup oil.
- Chicken, cooked for boning and chopping, has been roasted; this method yields the lowest caloric values.
- Cottage cheese is cream-style with 4.2% creaming mixture. Dry-curd cottage cheese has no creaming mixture.
- Eggs are all large.
- Flour is unsifted all-purpose flour.
- Garnishes, serving suggestions and other optional additions and variations are not included in the analysis.
- Margarine and butter are regular, not whipped or presoftened.
- Milk is whole milk, 3.5% butterfat. Lowfat milk is 1% butterfat. Evaporated milk is whole milk with 60% of the water removed.
- Oil is any type of vegetable cooking oil. Shortening is hydrogenated vegetable shortening.
- Salt and other ingredients to taste as noted in the method have not been included in the nutritional analysis.

Children's Kitchen

Virginia Walker

Egg in a Frame

Ingredients

1 slice bread
1 teaspoon butter
1 egg
1 teaspoon butter

Cut . . . . hole in center of bread with rim of drinking glass.

Melt . . . . 1 teaspoon butter in small skillet over low heat.

Place . . . . bread in skillet. Break egg into small bowl; slide into hole in bread. Don't worry if the yolk breaks.

Cook . . . . until bread is golden brown on the bottom and egg is partially set.

Lift . . . . egg and bread very carefully using pancake turner. Place remaining 1 teaspoon butter in skillet. Turn egg and bread uncooked side down in skillet.

Cook . . . . for 1 to 2 minutes longer or until egg is cooked the way you like it.

Yield . . . . 1 serving.

Hot Diggety Dogs

Ingredients

1 8-count can crescent rolls
8 hot dogs
4 slices American cheese

Preheat .... oven to 400 degrees.
Unroll .... and separate crescent roll dough.
Place .... 1 hot dog and 1/2 slice cheese on wide end of each roll.
Roll .... up hot dog and cheese in roll dough.
Place .... point side down on lightly greased baking sheet.
Bake .... for 10 minutes or until golden brown.
Serve .... rolls hot with mustard, mayonnaise and pickles or relish.
Yield .... 8 servings.

Miniature Pizzas

Ingredients

3/4 cup catsup
48 Melba rounds
2 ounces thinly sliced pepperoni
1 cup shredded mozzarella cheese
Oregano to taste

Preheat .... oven to 400 degrees.
Spread .... catsup thinly over each cracker.
Top .... each cracker with a pepperoni slice.
Sprinkle .... cheese over pepperoni; sprinkle oregano over cheese.
Place .... on ungreased baking sheet.
Bake .... for 3 minutes or until cheese is melted.
Yield .... 48 small pizzas.

These really taste like pizza!

Peanut Butter-Stuffed Apples

Ingredients

4 apples
1/2 cup peanut butter
2 tablespoons raisins
2 tablespoons granola
1 tablespoon oats
2 tablespoons honey

Remove .... cores from apples carefully. Do not cut apples into halves.

Combine .... peanut butter with any or all of the remaining ingredients in small bowl; mix well.

Spoon .... 2 tablespoons peanut butter mixture into apples. Wrap in foil.

Yield .... 4 servings.

These are great for camping. Eat them whole or sliced.

ABC Pancakes

Ingredients

1 1/4 cups sifted flour
1 1/2 teaspoons baking powder
3/4 teaspoon salt
1 tablespoon sugar
1 egg, beaten
1/2 cup milk
3 tablespoons oil

Preheat .... griddle over medium heat.
Sift .... flour, baking powder, salt and sugar together onto waxed paper.
Combine .... egg, milk and oil in bowl; mix well.
Add .... flour mixture to egg mixture; stir just until mixed.
Drizzle .... 1 teaspoonful batter at a time onto hot greased griddle to form letters.
Cook .... until golden brown on bottom. Turn pancakes over carefully. Cook until golden brown.
Ladle .... remaining batter carefully over and around letters, making pancakes of desired size.
Cook .... until golden brown on both sides, turning pancakes over once.
Serve .... with butter and pancake syrup.
Yield .... 12 pancakes.

Hawaiian Toast

Ingredients

8 slices white bread
8 slices pineapple
8 1/8 inch slices ham
8 slices Cheddar cheese

Preheat . . . . broiler.
Place . . . . bread slices on baking sheet.
Layer . . . . 1 slice pineapple, 1 slice ham and 1 slice cheese over each bread slice.
Place . . . . under broiler. Broil until cheese is melted.
Yield . . . . 4 servings.

This recipe came from an exchange student from Germany.

Angels on Horseback

Ingredients

8 large graham crackers
4 small milk chocolate candy bars
12 marshmallows

Preheat .... broiler.
Place .... 4 graham crackers on baking sheet.
Top .... each graham cracker with 1 candy bar.
Place .... under broiler. Broil until candy bar is slightly melted.
Remove .... from oven. Place 3 marshmallows on chocolate on each graham cracker.
Broil .... until marshmallows are slightly browned and puffed.
Remove .... from oven. Place remaining graham crackers over top.
Serve .... warm with glass of cold milk.
Yield .... 4 servings.

Coconut Snowballs

Ingredients

$1\frac{1}{3}$ cups coconut
Several drops of food coloring
$\frac{1}{2}$ teaspoon milk
1 quart favorite ice cream

Place .... coconut in bowl.
Mix .... several drops of any desired food coloring with milk.
Sprinkle .... tinted milk over coconut; toss with fork until coconut is tinted evenly.
Scoop .... ice cream into balls. Roll each ice cream ball in tinted coconut until coated.
Place .... ice cream balls in dessert dishes to serve right away.
May .... place ice cream balls in 9x13-inch pan, cover tightly and store in freezer until ready to serve.
Yield .... 8 to 10 servings.

Cupcake Cones

Ingredients

1 2-layer package cake mix
1 16-ounce can frosting
24 flat-bottomed cones
Candy sprinkles

Select .... your favorite flavor of cake mix and frosting go-togethers.
Preheat .... oven using cake mix package directions.
Prepare .... cake mix according to the package directions.
Spoon .... enough batter into ice cream cones to fill 1/3 full. Arrange cones on baking sheet.
Bake .... for 20 to 25 minutes or until cake tests done when toothpick inserted in center comes out clean.
Remove .... to wire rack to cool.
Spread .... each cupcake with frosting; swirl frosting into point at center of top.
Decorate .... with candy sprinkles.
Yield .... 2 dozen.

Ice Cream Banana Puddings

Ingredients

1 4-ounce package vanilla instant pudding mix
2 cups milk
1 12-ounce package vanilla wafers
3 or 4 bananas, sliced
1 pint vanilla ice cream
8 ounces whipped topping

Prepare .... the pudding mix with the milk using package directions.
Place .... several vanilla wafers in the bottom and around edge of 6 dessert dishes.
Spoon .... pudding into dishes.
Add .... layer of bananas and 1 scoop ice cream to each dish.
Top .... with whipped topping.
Yield .... 6 servings.

Peanut Butter Candy

Ingredients

1/2 cup cold water
1 1-pound package confectioners' sugar
1 1/2 cups peanut butter
1 7-ounce jar marshmallow creme
1/8 teaspoon vanilla extract

Combine .... cold water and confectioners' sugar in saucepan; mix well.
Boil .... sugar mixture for 5 minutes, stirring very fast.
Remove .... from heat.
Add .... peanut butter, marshmallow creme and vanilla. Stir very fast to keep mixture from sticking to pan.
Spread .... in buttered baking dish.
Chill .... in refrigerator until firm.
Cut .... into squares and serve.
Yield .... 20 servings.

Edible Play Dough

Ingredients

1 cup peanut butter
1 cup corn syrup
$1^1/_4$ cups confectioners' sugar
$1^1/_4$ cups nonfat dry milk

Combine .... peanut butter and corn syrup in large bowl; mix until smooth.

Mix .... confectioners' sugar and dry milk in small bowl.

Add .... confectioners' sugar mixture to peanut butter mixture; mix well. May add enough additional confectioners' sugar to make of consistency of play dough.

Let .... kids create yummy sculptures and then gobble them up.

Yield .... $2^1/_2$ to 3 cups.

Play Dough for Children

Ingredients

1 cup salt
4 to 5 cups flour
Several drops of food coloring
1 cup (about) water

Combine .... salt, flour and food coloring in large bowl; mix well.

Stir .... in a small amount of water at a time until mixture becomes smooth and elastic. Don't worry if you need more or less than 1 cup water.

Yield .... 5 to 6 cups.

This is a Vacation Bible School recipe.

Appetizers and Soups

Virginia Walker

Bacon-Wrapped Water Chestnuts

Yield:
16 servings

Utensil:
9x13-inch dish

Approx Per Serving:
Cal 40
Prot 2 g
Carbo 5 g
Fiber <1 g
T Fat 2 g
Chol 3 mg
Sod 244 mg

1 8-ounce can whole water chestnuts, drained
1/4 cup light soy sauce
1/4 cup sugar
8 slices bacon, cut into halves

Marinate water chestnuts in soy sauce in bowl for 2 hours; drain. Roll in sugar. Wrap each with 1 piece of bacon; secure with toothpicks. Place on wire rack in 9x13-inch baking dish. Bake at 400 degrees for 30 minutes or until golden brown.

Spicy Cheese Ball

Yield:
64 servings

Utensil:
serving plate

Approx Per Serving:
Cal 39
Prot 1 g
Carbo <1 g
Fiber <1 g
T Fat 4 g
Chol 8 mg
Sod 33 mg

8 ounces sharp Cheddar cheese, cut into pieces
8 ounces cream cheese, softened
1 tablespoon chopped pimento
1 teaspoon grated onion
1 1/2 teaspoons Tabasco sauce
Hot sauce to taste
1 cup finely chopped pecans

Combine Cheddar cheese, cream cheese, pimento, onion, Tabasco sauce and pepper sauce in mixer bowl. Beat until smooth. Shape into large ball. Roll in pecans. Chill until serving time.

Appetizers

Pineapple and Pecan Cheese Ball

Yield:
48 servings

Utensil:
serving plate

Approx Per Serving:
Cal 36
Prot 1 g
Carbo 1 g
Fiber <1 g
T Fat 3 g
Chol 5 mg
Sod 57 mg

8 ounces cream cheese, softened
1 8-ounce can crushed pineapple, drained
1/4 cup chopped green bell pepper
2 tablespoons chopped onion
1 teaspoon garlic salt
1 cup chopped pecans

Combine cream cheese, pineapple, green pepper, onion, garlic salt and half the pecans in bowl; mix well. Shape into large ball. Sprinkle with remaining pecans. Chill for 6 hours.

Cheese Crispies

Yield:
80 servings

Utensil:
baking sheet

Approx Per Serving:
Cal 32
Prot 1 g
Carbo 2 g
Fiber <1 g
T Fat 2 g
Chol 3 mg
Sod 51 mg

1/2 cup margarine, softened
8 ounces extra-sharp Cheddar cheese, shredded
1 1/2 cups flour
1/2 teaspoon salt
1/4 teaspoon red pepper
1 1/2 cups crisp rice cereal
Salt to taste

Combine margarine and cheese in bowl; mix well. Stir in flour, 1/2 teaspoon salt and red pepper. Add cereal; mix well. Shape into 1-inch balls. Place on ungreased baking sheet. Flatten with fork. Bake at 375 degrees for 10 minutes or until lightly browned. Sprinkle with remaining salt. Store in tightly covered container.

Cheese Pennies

Yield:
48 servings

Utensil:
baking sheet

Approx Per Serving:
Cal 46
Prot 1 g
Carbo 2 g
Fiber <1 g
T Fat 4 g
Chol 10 mg
Sod 81 mg

1/2 cup butter, softened
8 ounces medium-sharp Cheddar cheese, shredded
1 cup flour
1 envelope onion soup mix
1/2 teaspoon salt
Red pepper to taste

Combine butter and cheese in large bowl; mix well. Stir in flour, soup mix, salt and red pepper. Shape into 1-inch rolls; wrap in plastic wrap. Freeze until firm. Remove from freezer; unwrap rolls. Cut into thin slices. Place on ungreased baking sheet. Bake at 400 degrees for 8 minutes or until lightly browned.

Melt-A-Way Cheese Rounds

Yield:
40 servings

Utensil:
baking sheet

Approx Per Serving:
Cal 85
Prot 3 g
Carbo 4 g
Fiber <1 g
T Fat 6 g
Chol 18 mg
Sod 82 mg

3/4 cup butter, softened
3 cups shredded sharp Cheddar cheese
1 3/4 cups flour
Dash of salt
1 tablespoon poppy seed
Paprika to taste

Cream butter in mixer bowl until light and fluffy. Add cheese, flour, salt and poppy seed; mix well. Chill dough for 2 hours. Shape into small balls. Place on greased baking sheet. Sprinkle with paprika. Bake at 400 degrees for 10 minutes; do not brown. Cool. Remove carefully. Store in airtight containers. May substitute paprika for poppy seed. These make nice gifts packed in tins.

California Bean Dip

Yield:
16 servings

Utensil:
2-quart casserole

Approx Per Serving:
Cal 232
Prot 11 g
Carbo 9 g
Fiber 3 g
T Fat 17 g
Chol 50 mg
Sod 552 mg

1 16-ounce can refried beans
8 ounces cream cheese, softened
1 cup sour cream
1 envelope taco seasoning mix
1/2 onion, minced
8 ounces Cheddar cheese, shredded
8 ounces Monterey Jack pepper cheese, shredded

Combine beans, cream cheese, sour cream, seasoning mix and onion in bowl; mix well. Layer bean mixture and cheeses 1/2 at a time in 2-quart casserole. Bake at 350 degrees for 30 minutes or until bubbly.

Chili con Queso

Yield:
15 servings

Utensil:
double boiler

Approx Per Serving:
Cal 248
Prot 14 g
Carbo 5 g
Fiber 1 g
T Fat 20 g
Chol 58 mg
Sod 916 mg

1 1/2 teaspoons oil
1 cup chopped onion
1 16-ounce can chopped tomatoes
2 4-ounce cans chopped green chilies
1 tablespoon paprika
1 tablespoon cayenne pepper
32 ounces Velveeta cheese, cut into small pieces

Combine oil, onion, tomatoes and chilies in double boiler. Cook for 45 minutes or until onion is tender. Stir in paprika and cayenne pepper. Add cheese gradually. Cook until cheese is melted, stirring constantly. Serve with chips. May store in refrigerator and reheat in microwave at serving time.

Hot Crab Meat Cocktail

Yield:
32 servings

Utensil:
saucepan

Approx Per Serving:
Cal 39
Prot 2 g
Carbo <1 g
Fiber <1 g
T Fat 4 g
Chol 12 mg
Sod 53 mg

2 tablespoons lemon juice
1 6-ounce can crab meat, drained
1/4 cup half and half
1/4 cup mayonnaise
6 ounces cream cheese, softened
1 teaspoon minced onion
1/2 teaspoon minced chives
1/4 teaspoon Worcestershire sauce
1/8 teaspoon garlic
1/8 teaspoon salt
3 drops of Tabasco sauce

Pour lemon juice over crab meat in bowl. Combine half and half, mayonnaise, cream cheese, onion, chives, Worcestershire sauce, garlic, salt and Tabasco sauce in saucepan; mix well. Stir in crab meat mixture; mix well. Cook over low heat until heated through. Spoon into fondue pot or chafing dish. Serve with crackers.

Hot Crab Dip

Yield:
30 servings

Utensil:
1-quart dish

Approx Per Serving:
Cal 33
Prot 2 g
Carbo <1 g
Fiber <1 g
T Fat 3 g
Chol 13 mg
Sod 42 mg

1 6-ounce can crab meat, drained
8 ounces cream cheese, softened
1 tablespoon milk
2 tablespoons chopped fresh onion
1/2 teaspoon prepared horseradish

Combine crab meat, cream cheese, milk, onion, and horseradish in bowl; mix well. Spoon into baking dish. Bake at 375 degrees for 15 minutes or until bubbly. Serve hot with bite-sized fresh vegetables or crackers.

Tangy Crab Dip

Yield:
48 servings

Utensil:
saucepan

Approx Per Serving:
Cal 59
Prot 3 g
Carbo <1 g
Fiber 0 g
T Fat 5 g
Chol 19 mg
Sod 82 mg

16 ounces cream cheese
1/2 cup margarine
1 pound crab meat
Salt and pepper to taste
Worcestershire sauce to taste

Combine cream cheese and margarine in saucepan. Cook over low heat until margarine is melted. Stir in crab meat, salt and pepper and Worcestershire sauce. Cook until heated through. Serve with crackers.

Herb Curry Dip

Yield:
24 servings

Utensil:
serving bowl

Approx Per Serving:
Cal 76
Prot <1 g
Carbo 1 g
Fiber <1 g
T Fat 8 g
Chol 8 mg
Sod 78 mg

1 cup mayonnaise
1/2 cup sour cream
1 tablespoon snipped parsley
1 tablespoon grated onion
2 teaspoons capers, drained
1 1/2 teaspoons lemon juice
1 teaspoon mixed herbs
1/2 teaspoon Worcestershire sauce
1/4 teaspoon salt
1/8 teaspoon curry powder

Combine mayonnaise, sour cream, parsley, onion, capers, lemon juice, mixed herbs, Worcestershire sauce, salt and curry powder in bowl; mix well. Chill until serving time. Serve with bite-sized fresh vegetables.

Mexican Dip

Yield:
64 servings

Utensil:
serving bowl

Approx Per Serving:
Cal 24
Prot 1 g
Carbo 1 g
Fiber <1 g
T Fat 2 g
Chol 6 mg
Sod 61 mg

1 16-ounce can stewed tomatoes
1 4-ounce can chopped green chilies, drained
1/2 green bell pepper, minced
1 small onion, minced
1/2 teaspoon cumin
1/4 teaspoon pepper
1/4 teaspoon garlic salt
1/4 teaspoon salt
12 ounces Cheddar cheese, shredded

Drain and chop tomatoes. Drain again. Combine tomatoes, green chilies, green pepper and onion in bowl; mix well. Stir in cumin, pepper, garlic salt and salt. Add cheese; mix well. Serve with tortilla chips.

Shrimp Dip

Yield:
56 servings

Utensil:
serving bowl

Approx Per Serving:
Cal 34
Prot 1 g
Carbo <1 g
Fiber <1 g
T Fat 3 g
Chol 13 mg
Sod 52 mg

1/2 cup mayonnaise
8 ounces cream cheese, softened
1/4 medium onion, grated
Juice of 1/2 lemon
1 tablespoon catsup
1/2 teaspoon seasoned salt
8 ounces cooked salad shrimp

Cream mayonnaise and cream cheese in mixer bowl until light and fluffy. Add onion, lemon juice, catsup and seasoned salt; mix well. Stir in shrimp. Chill until serving time. Serve with chips or crackers.

Spinach Dip

Yield:
64 servings

Utensil:
serving bowl

Approx Per Serving:
Cal 28
Prot <1 g
Carbo 1 g
Fiber <1 g
T Fat 3 g
Chol 2 mg
Sod 27 mg

2 10-ounce packages frozen spinach
1 cup mayonnaise
1 cup sliced scallions
2 teaspoons Salad Supreme seasoning
1 teaspoon dillseed

Thaw spinach; squeeze dry. Combine spinach, mayonnaise, scallions, seasoning and dillseed in bowl; mix well. Chill until serving time. Serve with crackers or as a spread for tea sandwiches.

Nutritional information for this recipe does not include Salad Supreme seasoning.

Ham Rolls

Yield:
20 servings

Utensil:
serving plate

Approx Per Serving:
Cal 181
Prot 12 g
Carbo <1 g
Fiber <1 g
T Fat 14 g
Chol 44 mg
Sod 633 mg

10 slices crisp-fried bacon, crumbled
8 ounces cream cheese, softened
1 tablespoon mayonnaise
Worcestershire sauce to taste
Tabasco sauce to taste
1/4 cup parsley
10 thick slices cooked ham

Combine bacon and cream cheese in bowl; mix well. Stir in mayonnaise. Add enough Worcestershire sauce to make mixture beige. Stir in Tabasco sauce and parsley. Mix with fork until smooth and creamy; do not use blender or mixer. Spread over ham slices. Roll lengthwise. Chill for 45 to 60 minutes or until firm. Cut ham rolls into slices. May substitute roast beef or other cold cuts for ham. May be prepared ahead and frozen.

Mushrooms in Wine

Yield:
24 servings

Utensil:
saucepan

Approx Per Serving:
Cal 30
Prot 1 g
Carbo 1 g
Fiber <1 g
T Fat 2 g
Chol 5 mg
Sod 103 mg

1 pound small mushrooms
1 cup red wine
1/4 cup butter
2 tablespoons soy sauce

Rinse mushrooms; leave stems intact. Combine mushrooms, wine, butter and soy sauce in saucepan. Simmer until mushrooms are tender. Serve warm or cold. May store in refrigerator for 1 week.

Olive Cheese Balls

Yield:
36 servings

Utensil:
baking sheet

Approx Per Serving:
Cal 40
Prot 2 g
Carbo 2 g
Fiber <1 g
T Fat 3 g
Chol 6 mg
Sod 174 mg

3/4 cup flour
1 8-ounce jar processed bacon-cheese spread
Dash of Worcestershire sauce
Dash of hot pepper sauce
2 tablespoons butter, softened
36 olives

Combine flour, cheese spread, Worcestershire sauce, pepper sauce and butter in bowl; mix well. Wrap a small amount of mixture around each olive. Place on baking sheet. Bake at 350 degrees for 20 minutes.

Oyster Cracker Party Snack

Yield:
32 servings

Utensil:
baking sheet

Approx Per Serving:
Cal 107
Prot 1 g
Carbo 11 g
Fiber <1 g
T Fat 7 g
Chol 0 mg
Sod 238 mg

1 16-ounce package oyster crackers
1 envelope ranch salad dressing mix
1/2 teaspoon dillweed
1/4 teaspoon lemon pepper
1/4 teaspoon garlic powder
3/4 cup oil

Combine crackers, salad dressing mix, dillweed, lemon pepper, garlic powder and oil in bowl; mix well. Spread on baking sheet. Bake at 200 degrees for 20 minutes, stirring once. Let stand until cool. Store in tightly covered container.

Cold Pizza

Yield:
14 servings

Utensil:
baking sheet

Approx Per Serving:
Cal 302
Prot 4 g
Carbo 16 g
Fiber 1 g
T Fat 25 g
Chol 27 mg
Sod 577 mg

2 8-count cans crescent rolls
1 envelope ranch salad dressing mix
1 cup mayonnaise
8 ounces cream cheese, softened
1 teaspoon Worcestershire sauce
1 bunch green onions, chopped
1/2 cup chopped broccoli
1/2 cup chopped tomatoes
1/4 cup chopped celery
1/4 cup chopped cucumber
1/4 cup chopped carrots
1/4 cup chopped green bell pepper
1/4 cup chopped red bell pepper
1/4 cup sliced black olives

Unroll crescent roll dough. Press thinly over baking sheet; seal perforations. Bake at 400 degrees for 6 to 8 minutes or until golden brown. Let stand until cool. Combine salad dressing mix, mayonnaise, cream cheese, Worcestershire sauce and green onions in bowl; mix well. Spread over crust. Sprinkle with vegetables. Chill, covered, for 8 hours to overnight. Cut into squares. May use any combination of vegetables.

Salmon Mousse

Yield:
48 servings

Utensil:
mold

Approx Per Serving:
Cal 49
Prot 2 g
Carbo <1 g
Fiber <1 g
T Fat 4 g
Chol 12 mg
Sod 111 mg

1 envelope unflavored gelatin
1/4 cup cold water
1/2 cup boiling water
1/2 cup mayonnaise
2 tablespoons finely chopped fresh dill
1 tablespoon lemon juice
1 tablespoon finely grated onion
1 teaspoon salt
1/4 teaspoon paprika
Dash of Tabasco sauce
2 cups finely flaked salmon
1 cup whipping cream, whipped

Soften gelatin in cold water in bowl. Add boiling water; stir until gelatin is dissolved. Cool to room temperature. Add mayonnaise, dill, lemon juice, onion, salt, paprika and Tabasco sauce; mix well. Chill for 20 minutes or until partially set. Fold in salmon. Fold in whipped cream gently. Pour into mold. Chill for 4 hours. Unmold onto serving plate. Serve on toast, black bread or crackers.

Hot Ham Sandwiches

Yield:
50 servings

Utensil:
baking sheet

Approx Per Serving:
Cal 112
Prot 5 g
Carbo 11 g
Fiber 1 g
T Fat 5 g
Chol 26 mg
Sod 273 mg

1 pound baked or boiled ham, shredded
8 ounces Velveeta cheese, shredded
2 hard-boiled eggs, chopped
1 small onion, grated
1/2 cup chili sauce
2 tablespoons mayonnaise
50 small party rolls

Combine ham, cheese, eggs, onion, chili sauce and mayonnaise in bowl; mix well. Split rolls; spread with filling. Replace tops to form sandwiches. Wrap in foil. Place on baking sheet. Bake at 400 degrees for 10 minutes. Serve warm.

Overnight Sandwich

Yield:
6 servings

Utensil:
9x13-inch dish

Approx Per Serving:
Cal 562
Prot 24 g
Carbo 29 g
Fiber 4 g
T Fat 40 g
Chol 213 mg
Sod 1496 mg

8 slices whole wheat bread, crusts trimmed
8 ounces ham, finely chopped
4 hard-boiled eggs, finely chopped
1 4-ounce can chopped mushrooms, drained
1/2 cup mayonnaise
3/4 teaspoon dillweed
1 can cream of celery soup
1/2 cup sour cream
1/2 cup milk
2 tablespoons minced parsley
1 tablespoon minced chives
4 ounces Cheddar cheese, shredded

Arrange half the bread slices in lightly greased 9x13-inch baking dish. Combine ham, eggs, mushrooms, mayonnaise and dillweed in bowl; mix well. Spread over bread. Top with remaining bread slices. Combine soup, sour cream, milk, parsley and chives in bowl; mix well. Spoon over bread. Sprinkle with cheese. Chill, covered, overnight. Bake at 375 degrees for 25 to 30 minutes or until browned and bubbly. Cut into squares.

Vegetable Sandwich Spread

Yield:
48 servings

Utensil:
serving plate

Approx Per Serving:
Cal 70
Prot <1 g
Carbo 1 g
Fiber <1 g
T Fat 7 g
Chol 5 mg
Sod 100 mg

1 envelope unflavored gelatin
1 teaspoon cold water
1 cucumber, finely chopped
1 onion, finely chopped
1 cup finely chopped celery
1 green bell pepper, finely chopped
2 small carrots, finely chopped
1 teaspoon salt
2 cups mayonnaise

Soften gelatin in cold water. Combine gelatin, vegetables, salt and mayonnaise in bowl; mix well. Chill, covered, overnight. Serve with bread cut into party shapes.

Sauerkraut Balls

Yield:
96 servings

Utensil:
skillet

Approx Per Serving:
Cal 34
Prot 1 g
Carbo 3 g
Fiber <1 g
T Fat 2 g
Chol 6 mg
Sod 107 mg

1 pound hot sausage
1 large onion, finely chopped
4 cups sauerkraut, drained, squeezed dry
8 ounces cream cheese, softened
2 tablespoons prepared mustard
1/4 cup parsley
1/2 teaspoon garlic
1/4 teaspoon pepper
1 cup flour
1 egg, beaten
2 cups Italian bread crumbs
Oil for frying

Brown sausage with onion in skillet, stirring frequently; drain. Combine sausage mixture, sauerkraut, cream cheese, mustard, parsley, garlic and pepper in bowl; mix well. Chill for 2 hours to overnight. Shape into small balls; roll in flour. Dip into egg; roll in bread crumbs. Cook in hot oil in skillet until golden brown.

Nutritional information for this recipe does not include oil for frying.

Sausage Balls

Yield:
75 servings

Utensil:
baking sheet

Approx Per Serving:
Cal 49
Prot 2 g
Carbo 3 g
Fiber 0 g
T Fat 3 g
Chol 6 mg
Sod 106 mg

1 pound hot sausage
10 ounces sharp Cheddar cheese, shredded
3 cups baking mix
4 drops of Tabasco sauce (optional)

Brown sausage in skillet; drain. Combine sausage, cheese, baking mix and Tabasco sauce in bowl; mix well. Shape into walnut-sized balls. Place on baking sheet. Bake at 375 degrees for 15 minutes. May freeze before baking.

Sausage Cookies

Yield:
48 servings

Utensil:
baking sheet

Approx Per Serving:
Cal 72
Prot 2 g
Carbo 5 g
Fiber 0 g
T Fat 5 g
Chol 8 mg
Sod 160 mg

1 pound sausage
3 cups baking mix
1/2 cup water
8 ounces Cheddar cheese, shredded

Brown sausage in skillet; drain. Combine sausage, baking mix, water and cheese in bowl; mix well. Drop by teaspoonfuls onto nonstick baking sheet. Bake at 350 degrees for 20 to 25 minutes or until golden brown.

Spinach Bites

Yield:
96 servings

Utensil:
baking sheet

Approx Per Serving:
Cal 28
Prot 1 g
Carbo 2 g
Fiber <1 g
T Fat 2 g
Chol 13 mg
Sod 89 mg

2 10-ounce packages frozen chopped spinach
3 cups herb-seasoned stuffing
1 large onion, grated
4 eggs, beaten
3/4 cup melted butter
1/2 cup Parmesan cheese
1 1/2 teaspoons garlic salt
1 teaspoon pepper
1/2 teaspoon thyme

Thaw and drain spinach. Combine spinach, stuffing, onion, eggs, butter, cheese, garlic salt, pepper and thyme in bowl; mix well. Shape into bite-sized balls. Bake at 350 degrees for 20 minutes.

Pineapple Cheese Spread

Yield:
48 servings

Utensil:
serving plate

Approx Per Serving:
Cal 41
Prot 1 g
Carbo 1 g
Fiber <1 g
T Fat 4 g
Chol 10 mg
Sod 73 mg

16 ounces cream cheese, softened
1 8-ounce can crushed pineapple, drained
1/3 cup chopped pecans
1/4 cup chopped green bell pepper
2 tablespoons chopped green onions
1 teaspoon seasoned salt

Combine cream cheese, pineapple, pecans, green pepper, green onions and salt in bowl; mix well. Chill for several hours to overnight. May shape into large ball and roll in additional 1 cup chopped pecans.

Spanakopita (Spinach Pie)

Yield:
48 servings

Utensil:
10x15-inch pan

Approx Per Serving:
Cal 111
Prot 5 g
Carbo 8 g
Fiber 1 g
T Fat 7 g
Chol 47 mg
Sod 233 mg

1 1-pound package phyllo dough
3 10-ounce packages frozen chopped spinach, thawed
16 ounces small curd cottage cheese
16 ounces feta cheese, rinsed, crumbled
6 eggs, beaten
Dillweed to taste
Pepper to taste
1 cup melted butter

Thaw phyllo using package directions. Squeeze spinach dry. Combine spinach, cheeses and eggs in bowl; mix well. Stir in dillweed and pepper. Brush sides and bottom of 10x15-inch baking pan with a small amount of butter. Layer half the phyllo sheets 1 at a time in baking pan, brushing each sheet with butter. Spread with spinach mixture. Layer remaining phyllo sheets 1 at a time over spinach mixture, brushing each sheet with butter. Tuck in sides. Brush top and sides with butter. Cut into small squares, cutting to but not through bottom. Brush cuts with melted butter. Bake at 325 degrees for 45 to 60 minutes or until lightly browned. May refrigerate or freeze before baking. This dish is very popular among the Greek people. This version was given to me by my mother, who was born and raised in Greece.

Broiled Zucchini Slices

Yield:
36 servings

Utensil:
baking sheet

Approx Per Serving:
Cal 18
Prot <1 g
Carbo <1 g
Fiber <1 g
T Fat 2 g
Chol 2 mg
Sod 25 mg

1/3 cup mayonnaise
1/3 cup Parmesan cheese
1/2 teaspoon basil
1 large zucchini, cut into 1/4-inch slices

Combine mayonnaise, cheese and basil in bowl; mix well. Spread on zucchini slices. Place on baking sheet. Broil for 1 minute or until cheese is bubbly. Serve immediately.

Light Batter-Fried Whatever

Yield:
30 servings

Utensil:
electric skillet

Approx Per Serving:
Cal 21
Prot 1 g
Carbo 4 g
Fiber <1 g
T Fat <1 g
Chol 7 mg
Sod 38 mg

3/4 cup cornstarch
1/4 cup flour
1 teaspoon baking powder
1/2 teaspoon salt (optional)
1/2 teaspoon pepper
1/2 cup water
1 egg, slightly beaten
4 cups (about) corn oil
4 cups sliced zucchini, carrots, mushrooms and onions

Combine cornstarch, flour, baking powder, salt, pepper, water and egg in bowl; mix well. Pour enough oil into skillet to fill no more than 1/3 full. Heat to 375 degrees. Dip several vegetable slices at a time into batter. Add to hot oil. Cook on each side for 3 to 5 minutes or until golden brown and crisp; drain. Keep batter stirred. May substitute 1/3 to 1/2 cup cold beer for water or add 1 teaspoon basil and garlic salt for herb batter. May use beef, chicken or pork cut into 2-inch strips.

Chuck Wagon Red Bean Soup

Yield:
6 servings

Utensil:
stockpot

Approx Per Serving:
Cal 366
Prot 32 g
Carbo 48 g
Fiber 17 g
T Fat 5 g
Chol 43 mg
Sod 54 mg

1 pound dried red beans
10 cups water
1 pound chopped beef
2 stalks celery, chopped
1 onion, chopped
Chili powder, salt, pepper and other seasonings to taste
1/4 cup beer

Bring beans and water to a boil in stockpot. Add beef, celery, onion and seasonings to taste; reduce heat. Simmer, covered, for 3 to 4 hours, stirring frequently. Stir in beer 30 minutes before end of cooking time.

Cream of Broccoli Soup

Yield:
8 servings

Utensil:
heavy saucepan

Approx Per Serving:
Cal 267
Prot 9 g
Carbo 19 g
Fiber 2 g
T Fat 18 g
Chol 56 mg
Sod 755 mg

2 cups water
1 16-ounce package frozen broccoli cuts
1/2 cup chopped onion
1/2 cup butter
1/2 cup flour
6 cups milk
4 chicken bouillon cubes
1 teaspoon white pepper

Bring water to a boil in saucepan. Add broccoli; reduce heat. Simmer, covered, for 5 minutes; do not drain. Sauté onion in butter in heavy saucepan for 10 minutes or until tender. Stir in flour. Cook for 1 minute, stirring constantly. Add milk and bouillon cubes. Cook over medium heat until thickened, stirring constantly. Add broccoli with cooking liquid and white pepper. Simmer for 20 to 30 minutes or to desired consistency, stirring occasionally. Ladle into soup bowls.

Brunswick Stew

Yield:
6 servings

Utensil:
heavy saucepan

Approx Per Serving:
Cal 388
Prot 31 g
Carbo 52 g
Fiber 10 g
T Fat 8 g
Chol 69 mg
Sod 403 mg

2 slices bacon
2 pounds cut-up chicken
1 16-ounce can tomatoes, chopped
3 cups cold water
1 onion, chopped
1/2 cup sliced celery
1 tablespoon brown sugar
Salt, pepper and cayenne pepper to taste
1 10-ounce package frozen lima beans
1 12-ounce can corn
1 10-ounce package frozen okra
2 carrots, sliced
2 potatoes, chopped

Cook bacon in heavy saucepan until crisp; remove bacon. Rinse chicken and pat dry. Brown on both sides in bacon drippings in saucepan. Add tomatoes, water, onion, celery, brown sugar, salt, pepper and cayenne pepper; mix well. Cook, covered, over medium heat for 1 to 1 1/2 hours or until chicken is tender. Remove and bone chicken; return to saucepan. Add lima beans, corn, okra, carrots, potatoes and crumbled bacon. Cook for 30 minutes. Chill overnight and reheat to improve flavor. Serve with bread and salad.

Brunswick Stew in a Hurry

Yield:
8 servings

Utensil:
saucepan

Approx Per Serving:
Cal 377
Prot 28 g
Carbo 47 g
Fiber 13 g
T Fat 10 g
Chol 65 mg
Sod 1528 mg

3 6-ounce cans boned chicken
3 19-ounce cans tomatoes, chopped
2 16-ounce cans butter beans
2 cans cream of celery soup
1 16-ounce can corn
1 chicken bouillon cube
1 tablespoon butter
1 teaspoon sugar
Salt, pepper and red pepper to taste

Combine chicken, tomatoes, butter beans, soup, corn, bouillon cube, butter, sugar, salt, pepper and red pepper in saucepan; mix well. Simmer for 1 1/2 to 1 3/4 hours or to desired consistency.

Dragon's Breath Chili

Yield:
12 servings

Utensil:
large saucepan

Approx Per Serving:
Cal 244
Prot 25 g
Carbo 22 g
Fiber 4 g
T Fat 7 g
Chol 64 mg
Sod 701 mg

3 pounds lean ground beef
10 ounces green bell peppers, chopped
1 pound red onions, chopped
1/2 teaspoon salt
1/2 teaspoon ground black pepper
1/2 teaspoon garlic salt
1/2 teaspoon white pepper
30 ounces tomato sauce
18 ounces tomato paste
1 teaspoon ground hot mustard
2 teaspoons crushed red peppers
2 teaspoons chopped chervil
1 teaspoon curry powder
1 tablespoon Worcestershire sauce
1 tablespoon chili powder
1 ounce Tabasco sauce
1/4 cup sugar

Brown 1/2 of the ground beef with 1/4 of the green peppers, 1/4 of the onions, salt and black pepper in skillet, stirring frequently. Remove ground beef mixture to large heavy saucepan; drain skillet. Brown remaining ground beef with 1/4 of the green peppers, 1/4 of the onions, garlic salt and white pepper in skillet, stirring frequently. Drain; remove to saucepan. Add tomato sauce, tomato paste and remaining green peppers and onions. Bring just to the boiling point; reduce heat to medium. Add mustard, red peppers, chervil, curry powder, Worcestershire sauce, chili powder, Tabasco sauce and sugar. Simmer for 1 1/2 hours or to desired consistency, adding water as needed. Serve with cheese or sour cream. This is the mild version of Dragon's Breath Chili.

To continue on toward Dragon's Breath status: add one 12-ounce jar chopped peppers, 2 teaspoons steak sauce, 5 whole hot chili peppers, 1 teaspoon white pepper, 1 teaspoon ground black pepper and two 4-ounce bottles of pepper sauce. Increase Worcestershire sauce to 5 teaspoons, chili powder to 4 teaspoons, Tabasco sauce to 2 ounces and sugar to 1/2 cup.

CHILI SOUP

Yield:
10 servings

Utensil:
saucepan

Approx Per Serving:
Cal 633
Prot 49 g
Carbo 36 g
Fiber 12 g
T Fat 34 g
Chol 130 mg
Sod 1029 mg

1 pound round steak, cut into 1/2-inch cubes
1 teaspoon olive oil
2 pounds lean ground beef
2 medium onions, finely chopped
2 medium cloves of garlic, minced
2 large stalks celery, finely chopped
2 teaspoons olive oil
4 medium Anaheim chilies, seeded, chopped
2 large green bell peppers, finely chopped
2 28-ounce cans whole tomatoes, chopped
4 cups beef broth
1/4 cup chili powder
2 tablespoons oregano
1 tablespoon baking cocoa
2 teaspoons cumin
1/4 teaspoon salt
1/4 teaspoon freshly ground pepper
1/2 teaspoon cayenne pepper
1 16-ounce can kidney beans, drained, rinsed
1 16-ounce can black beans, drained, rinsed
2 tablespoons finely chopped fresh cilantro
2 cups shredded Cheddar cheese
3/4 cup sliced black olives
3/4 cup low-fat yogurt
Corn Bread Croutons

Brown steak cubes in 1 teaspoon olive oil in saucepan; remove steak. Add ground beef to 8-quart saucepan. Cook until brown and crumbly, stirring constantly; remove with slotted spoon. Drain saucepan. Sauté onions, garlic and celery in 2 teaspoons olive oil in saucepan for 5 minutes or until tender. Stir in chilies and green peppers. Sauté for 2 minutes. Stir in beef cubes, ground beef, tomatoes, beef broth, chili powder, oregano, cocoa, cumin, salt, pepper and cayenne pepper. Bring to a boil; reduce heat. Simmer for 1 hour, stirring occasionally. Stir in kidney beans, black beans and cilantro. Simmer for 15 minutes. Ladle into soup bowls. Top with cheese, olives, yogurt and Corn Bread Croutons (page 42).

Nutritional information for this recipe does not include Corn Bread Croutons.

Corn Bread Croutons

Yield:
10 servings

Utensil:
9x13-inch pan

Approx Per Serving:
Cal 169
Prot 4 g
Carbo 22 g
Fiber 1 g
T Fat 7 g
Chol 25 mg
Sod 190 mg

1 cup yellow cornmeal
1 cup flour
2 teaspoons baking powder
1/2 teaspoon salt
1 cup milk
1 egg
1/4 cup oil
2 medium cloves of garlic, pressed

Mix cornmeal, flour, baking powder and salt in bowl. Add milk, egg, oil and garlic; whisk until smooth. Pour into buttered 9x13-inch baking pan. Bake at 425 degrees for 20 minutes. Remove to wire rack to cool. Cut into 1-inch cubes. Place on baking sheet. Toast at 350 degrees for 10 minutes. Store in plastic bag.

Cioppino

Yield:
10 servings

Utensil:
saucepan

Approx Per Serving:
Cal 363
Prot 48 g
Carbo 10 g
Fiber 2 g
T Fat 12 g
Chol 197 mg
Sod 872 mg

1 1/2 cups chopped onions
1 cup chopped green bell pepper
3 cloves of garlic, crushed
1/4 cup olive oil
1 tablespoon sugar
1 small bay leaf
1/4 teaspoon each thyme, oregano, basil, marjoram, paprika and pepper
1/4 cup chopped parsley
1 teaspoon salt
1 8-ounce bottle of clam juice
1 28-ounce can tomatoes, crushed
1 8-ounce can tomato sauce
1 cup red wine
1 pound shrimp, shelled
2 pounds firm fish filets, cut into bite-sized pieces
1 pound crab meat
36 clams in shells

Sauté onions, green pepper and garlic in olive oil in 8-quart saucepan for 10 minutes. Add next 10 ingredients; mix well. Cook until heated through. Add clam juice, tomatoes, tomato sauce and wine. Simmer for 30 minutes or until thickened to desired consistency, stirring occasionally. Add shrimp, fish, crab meat and clams. Cook until clam shells open. Discard bay leaf. Serve with green salad, sour dough bread and red wine.

Lazy Manhattan Clam Chowder

Yield:
10 servings

Utensil:
saucepan

Approx Per Serving:
Cal 207
Prot 18 g
Carbo 22 g
Fiber 3 g
T Fat 5 g
Chol 40 mg
Sod 166 mg

1/2 medium onion, chopped
2 large stalks celery, chopped
3 tablespoons olive oil
3 7-ounce cans minced clams
3 large potatoes, peeled, chopped
1 16-ounce can whole tomatoes, chopped
1 16-ounce package frozen mixed vegetables
2 teaspoons thyme
2 teaspoons Old Bay seasoning
1/8 teaspoon cayenne pepper
1 bay leaf

Sauté onion and celery in olive oil in 6-quart saucepan until tender. Drain clams, reserving liquid. Add enough water to reserved liquid to measure 4 cups. Add to saucepan. Simmer for several minutes. Bring potatoes to a boil in water to cover in small saucepan. Cook for 5 minutes; rinse with cold water. Add potatoes, tomatoes and mixed vegetables to chowder. Stir in seasonings. Simmer for 20 minutes. Add clams. Simmer for 10 minutes longer. Remove bay leaf. Serve with fresh bread or crackers.

New England Clam Chowder

Yield:
6 servings

Utensil:
heavy saucepan

Approx Per Serving:
Cal 596
Prot 41 g
Carbo 96 g
Fiber 5 g
T Fat 4 g
Chol 69 mg
Sod 688 mg

3 slices bacon, chopped
1 large onion, chopped
4 medium potatoes, chopped
2 cups water
1 teaspoon salt
1/4 teaspoon pepper
2 10-ounce cans minced clams
1 8-ounce bottle of clam juice
1 cup water
1 1/3 cups dry milk powder
3 tablespoons flour
2 tablespoons chopped parsley

Cook bacon in heavy saucepan until crisp; remove bacon. Add onion. Sauté in bacon drippings until tender. Add potatoes, 2 cups water, salt and pepper. Simmer, covered, for 15 minutes; remove from heat. Drain clams, reserving liquid. Combine reserved liquid, bottled clam juice, 1 cup water, dry milk powder and flour in bowl; mix until smooth. Stir into chowder. Cook over medium heat until thickened, stirring constantly. Stir in clams. Heat to serving temperature. Ladle into serving bowls. Sprinkle with bacon and parsley.

Corn Chowder

Yield:
6 servings

Utensil:
large saucepan

Approx Per Serving:
Cal 337
Prot 13 g
Carbo 32 g
Fiber 2 g
T Fat 19 g
Chol 35 mg
Sod 793 mg

6 slices bacon
1 small onion, chopped
3 tablespoons flour
2 cups water
1 cup chopped potato
3/4 teaspoon sage
1 large bay leaf
1 cup instant nondairy creamer
1 cup boiling water
1 1/2 cups shredded Cheddar cheese
2 cups whole kernel corn
1 teaspoon salt
1/8 teaspoon pepper

Fry bacon with onion in large saucepan until bacon is crisp and onion is tender, stirring frequently. Stir in flour. Cook for 1 minute. Add 2 cups water, potato, sage and bay leaf. Simmer, covered, for 10 to 15 minutes or just until potatoes are tender. Remove bay leaf. Add creamer, 1 cup boiling water, cheese, corn, salt and pepper. Heat just to the boiling point, stirring until cheese is melted. Ladle into soup bowls. Sprinkle with crumbled bacon. Garnish with parsley and chives.

Cream of Crab Soup

Yield:
6 servings

Utensil:
saucepan

Approx Per Serving:
Cal 257
Prot 21 g
Carbo 11 g
Fiber <1 g
T Fat 14 g
Chol 110 mg
Sod 652 mg

1 quart milk
3 tablespoons flour
1/4 cup butter
2 tablespoons chopped parsley
Tabasco sauce to taste
Celery seed and curry powder to taste
1/2 teaspoon onion salt
1/4 teaspoon salt
1 pound fresh crab meat

Shake milk and flour in jar until smooth. Melt butter in saucepan. Stir in flour mixture, parsley, Tabasco, celery seed, curry powder, onion salt and salt. Simmer until thickened, stirring constantly. Stir in crab meat. Heat to serving temperature.

Seafood Chowder

Yield:
10 servings

Utensil:
saucepan

Approx Per Serving:
Cal 176
Prot 16 g
Carbo 23 g
Fiber 3 g
T Fat 3 g
Chol 72 mg
Sod 571 mg

1 red onion, chopped
1 large carrot, chopped
1 large green bell pepper, chopped
1 medium clove of garlic, minced
1 tablespoon olive oil
2 28-ounce cans whole tomatoes
1 cup tomato juice
1 8-ounce bottle of clam juice
1/4 teaspoon salt
1/4 teaspoon freshly ground pepper
3/4 cup rice
1 1/2 cups water
8 ounces tiny bay scallops
8 ounces cooked small shrimp
8 ounces crab meat
1 1/4 teaspoons Tabasco sauce
1 1/3 cups finely chopped parsley

Sauté first 4 ingredients in olive oil in 6-quart saucepan for 5 minutes. Purée undrained tomatoes 1 can at a time in food processor. Add puréed tomatoes, tomato juice, clam juice, salt and pepper to soup. Bring to a boil; reduce heat. Simmer for 30 minutes. Cook rice in water in saucepan until level of water just covers rice; reduce heat to low. Simmer, covered, for 20 minutes. Add scallops to boiling water to cover in medium saucepan. Cook for 2 minutes; drain. Add scallops and remaining ingredients to soup. Simmer for 10 minutes; do not boil.

Gazpacho

Yield:
8 servings

Utensil:
large bowl

Approx Per Serving:
Cal 55
Prot 1 g
Carbo 10 g
Fiber 1 g
T Fat 2 g
Chol 0 mg
Sod 515 mg

1/2 cup chopped celery
1/2 cup chopped green bell pepper
1/2 cup chopped onion
1/2 cup thinly sliced cucumber
1 cup chopped tomato
1 can tomato soup
1 soup can water
1 tablespoon wine vinegar
1 1/2 cups mixed vegetable juice cocktail
1 tablespoon Italian salad dressing
Worcestershire sauce and hot sauce to taste
Garlic salt to taste
1/4 teaspoon salt
1/8 teaspoon pepper

Combine celery, green pepper, onion, cucumber, tomato, soup, water, vinegar, vegetable juice, salad dressing, Worcestershire sauce, hot sauce, garlic salt, salt and pepper in bowl; mix gently. Chill, covered, for 4 hours or longer. Mix well before serving. Serving in chilled bowls or mugs.

French Onion Soup

Yield:
4 servings

Utensil:
large saucepan

Approx Per Serving:
Cal 255
Prot 12 g
Carbo 19 g
Fiber 2 g
T Fat 14 g
Chol 37 mg
Sod 812 mg

3 cups sliced onions
2 tablespoons butter
2 cans beef broth
1½ cups water
1 teaspoon Worcestershire sauce
1 tablespoon parsley flakes
1½ ounces sweet Sherry
2 thin slices French bread
⅓ cup shredded Swiss cheese
⅓ cup shredded mozzarella cheese
⅓ cup Parmesan cheese

Sauté onions in butter in saucepan over very low heat for 25 minutes. Add broth, water and Worcestershire sauce. Bring to a boil; reduce heat. Add parsley flakes and Sherry. Simmer, covered, for 30 minutes. Cut bread slices into halves. Place each piece in ovenproof bowl. Spoon soup into bowls; sprinkle with cheeses. Bake at 350 degrees for 20 to 25 minutes or until cheeses melt.

Florentine Veal Stew

Yield:
4 servings

Utensil:
heavy saucepan

Approx Per Serving:
Cal 504
Prot 53 g
Carbo 5 g
Fiber 1 g
T Fat 25 g
Chol 218 mg
Sod 1014 mg

2 pounds veal, cubed
⅓ cup olive oil
1 tablespoon chopped parsley
2 cloves of garlic, minced
½ teaspoon thyme
1 bay leaf
1 cup dry white wine
1 teaspoon salt
½ teaspoon pepper
1 8-ounce can tomato sauce
½ cup boiling water

Brown veal on all sides in olive oil in heavy saucepan. Add parsley, garlic, thyme, bay leaf, wine, salt and pepper. Simmer until wine has nearly evaporated. Add tomato sauce and water. Cook, covered, for 1½ hours or until veal is tender. Discard bay leaf. Serve over rice.

Beverages

Virginia Walker

Amaretto

Yield:
32 servings

Utensil:
glass jar

Approx Per Serving:
Cal 72
Prot 0 g
Carbo 6 g
Fiber 0 g
T Fat 0 g
Chol 0 mg
Sod <1 mg

1 cup sugar
1/2 cup water
3 cups vodka
1 teaspoon almond extract

Bring sugar and water to a boil in saucepan. Cook until sugar dissolves. Combine with vodka and almond extract in glass jar with lid. Let stand, covered, for 3 days to age. May tint with food coloring if desired.

Hot Apple Cider

Yield:
8 servings

Utensil:
saucepan

Approx Per Serving:
Cal 109
Prot <1 g
Carbo 28 g
Fiber <1 g
T Fat <1 g
Chol 0 mg
Sod 2 mg

1/4 cup whole cloves
1 teaspoon chopped candied ginger
1 cinnamon stick, broken
2/3 cup sugar
1 cup water
2 cups apple cider
1 cup orange juice
2 tablespoons lemon juice

Place cloves, ginger and cinnamon in tea ball or tie in cheesecloth. Bring sugar and water to a boil in saucepan. Boil for 10 minutes. Add spices; remove from heat. Let stand for 1 hour. Add apple cider, orange juice and lemon juice. Heat just to the boiling point. Remove spices. May serve cold if preferred.

Bourbon Slush

Yield:
10 servings

Utensil:
freezer container

Approx Per Serving:
Cal 108
Prot <1 g
Carbo 21 g
Fiber <1 g
T Fat <1 g
Chol 0 mg
Sod 1 mg

1 cup water
2 small tea bags
1/2 cup sugar
1/3 cup thawed frozen lemonade concentrate
1 6-ounce can frozen orange juice concentrate, thawed
1/2 cup Bourbon
3 1/2 cups water

Bring 1 cup water to a boil in saucepan; remove from heat. Add tea bags. Let stand for several minutes; remove tea bags. Stir in sugar. Combine with lemonade concentrate, orange juice concentrate, Bourbon and 3 1/2 cups water in freezer container; mix well. Freeze for 24 to 48 hours. Scoop into glasses with ice cream scoop.

Hot Cranberry Cider

Yield:
32 servings

Utensil:
percolator

Approx Per Serving:
Cal 111
Prot <1 g
Carbo 20 g
Fiber 1 g
T Fat <1 g
Chol 0 mg
Sod 3 mg

3 quarts apple cider
1 quart cranberry juice cocktail
1/4 cup sugar
3 oranges
16 whole cloves
6 cinnamon sticks
1 teaspoon whole allspice
2 cups rum
1 teaspoon bitters
1/4 cup sugar

Combine cider, cranberry juice and 1/4 cup sugar in 30-cup percolator. Pierce oranges with fork. Place oranges, cloves, cinnamon and allspice in percolator basket. Perk as for coffee. Add rum, bitters and 1/4 cup sugar. Serve hot.

Hot Cranberry Tea

Yield:
20 servings

Utensil:
saucepan

Approx Per Serving:
Cal 89
Prot <1 g
Carbo 23 g
Fiber 1 g
T Fat <1 g
Chol 0 mg
Sod 1 mg

3 cups cranberries
$3^1/_2$ quarts water
12 whole cloves
4 cinnamon sticks
Juice of 2 lemons
Juice of 2 oranges
2 cups sugar

Combine cranberries, water, cloves and cinnamon in large saucepan. Bring to a boil, stirring frequently; reduce heat. Simmer, covered, for 12 minutes. Strain through several thicknesses of cheesecloth, squeezing gently. Combine with lemon juice, orange juice and sugar in saucepan. Heat to serving temperature, stirring to dissolve sugar. Serve hot.

Eggnog

Yield:
6 servings

Utensil:
bowl

Approx Per Serving:
Cal 452
Prot 10 g
Carbo 42 g
Fiber 0 g
T Fat 24 g
Chol 218 mg
Sod 122 mg

4 egg yolks
1 cup sugar
1 teaspoon vanilla extract
1 cup cream, chilled
1 quart milk, chilled
4 egg whites
6 tablespoons Bourbon
Nutmeg to taste

Beat eggs yolks with sugar in bowl until thick and lemon-colored. Add vanilla, cream and milk; mix well. Place in freezer until chilled. Beat egg whites in mixer bowl until stiff peaks form. Fold gently into milk mixture. Pour into chilled glasses. Add 1 tablespoon Bourbon to each glass; mix well. Garnish with nutmeg. May substitute rum for Bourbon if preferred.

Chocolate Eggnog

Yield:
24 servings

Utensil:
punch bowl

Approx Per Serving:
Cal 276
Prot 6 g
Carbo 29 g
Fiber <1 g
T Fat 16 g
Chol 95 mg
Sod 88 mg

3 quarts eggnog, chilled
1¼ cups chocolate syrup
¼ cup rum
3 tablespoons sugar
1½ cups whipping cream, chilled
1 tablespoon baking cocoa
1 ounce semisweet chocolate, shaved

Combine eggnog, chocolate syrup and rum in large punch bowl; mix well. Beat sugar, whipping cream and cocoa at high speed in small mixer bowl until soft peaks form. Spoon onto eggnog. Sprinkle with shaved chocolate.

Classic Eggnog

Yield:
38 servings

Utensil:
punch bowl

Approx Per Serving:
Cal 118
Prot 3 g
Carbo 8 g
Fiber 0 g
T Fat 5 g
Chol 81 mg
Sod 37 mg

12 egg yolks
1 cup sugar
1½ cups Bourbon
½ cup Brandy
6 cups milk
1¼ teaspoons nutmeg
12 egg whites
1 cup whipping cream

Combine egg yolks and sugar in large mixer bowl; beat at low speed until well blended. Beat at high speed for 15 minutes or until thick and lemon-colored, scraping frequently. Beat in Bourbon and Brandy 1 tablespoon at a time. Chill, covered, for 2 hours or longer. Combine with milk and nutmeg in punch bowl; mix well. Beat egg whites at high speed in mixer bowl until soft peaks form. Beat whipping cream at medium speed in small bowl until soft peaks form. Fold egg whites and whipped cream gently into eggnog with rubber spatula or wire whisk. Garnish with additional nutmeg. Serve in punch cups.

Florida Fling

Yield:
10 servings

Utensil:
pitcher

Approx Per Serving:
Cal 100
Prot 1 g
Carbo 12 g
Fiber <1 g
T Fat <1 g
Chol 0 mg
Sod 5 mg

1 quart freshly squeezed orange juice
1 fifth of Champagne, chilled

Chill orange juice in pitcher in refrigerator. Add Champagne at serving time; mix gently. Pour into tall stemmed glasses.

Kahlua

Yield:
40 servings

Utensil:
saucepan

Approx Per Serving:
Cal 89
Prot 0 g
Carbo 13 g
Fiber 0 g
T Fat 0 g
Chol 0 mg
Sod 4 mg

1 cup sugar
1½ cups packed brown sugar
2 cups water
½ cup instant coffee
3 cups vodka
1 vanilla bean, split

Bring sugar, brown sugar and water to a boil in 2-quart saucepan; reduce heat. Simmer for 5 minutes. Whisk in instant coffee powder. Add vodka and vanilla bean. Pour into jar with lid. Let stand, covered, for 2 weeks or longer. Remove vanilla bean. May substitute 2 tablespoons vanilla extract for vanilla bean if preferred.

Piña Colada

Yield:
6 servings

Utensil:
blender

Approx Per Serving:
Cal 158
Prot 1 g
Carbo 7 g
Fiber <1 g
T Fat 8 g
Chol 14 mg
Sod 7 mg

3/4 cup light rum
1 cup unsweetened pineapple juice
1/4 cup whipping cream
1/2 cup cream of coconut
2 cups crushed ice

Combine rum, pineapple juice, whipping cream, cream of coconut and 2 cups crushed ice in blender container; process until smooth. Pour over additional crushed ice in glasses. Garnish glasses with pineapple spears.

Pink Smoothie

Yield:
2 servings

Utensil:
blender

Approx Per Serving:
Cal 221
Prot 3 g
Carbo 37 g
Fiber 1 g
T Fat 7 g
Chol 30 mg
Sod 61 mg

1 cup vanilla ice cream
1 cup cranberry juice, chilled
1/4 cup orange juice, chilled

Combine ice cream, cranberry juice and orange juice in blender container; process until smooth. Serve immediately.

Tropical Champagne Punch

Yield:
20 servings

Utensil:
pitcher

Approx Per Serving:
Cal 80
Prot <1 g
Carbo 13 g
Fiber 0 g
T Fat <1 g
Chol 0 mg
Sod 17 mg

1 46-ounce can Hawaiian Punch
1/4 cup sugar
1/2 cup Brandy
1 fifth of Champagne, chilled

Combine Hawaiian Punch and sugar in large pitcher; stir until sugar dissolves. Add Brandy; mix well. Chill until serving time. Add Champagne at serving time; mix gently. Serve over ice. Garnish with orange slices and strawberries.

Hot Grape Punch

Yield:
12 servings

Utensil:
punch bowl

Approx Per Serving:
Cal 111
Prot <1 g
Carbo 28 g
Fiber <1 g
T Fat <1 g
Chol 0 mg
Sod 2 mg

1 cup water
2 tea bags
1 cup sugar
1 cup orange juice
1/2 cup lemon juice
1 24-ounce bottle of grape juice
5 cups hot water

Bring 1 cup water to a boil in saucepan; remove from heat. Add tea bags; let stand for several minutes. Remove tea bags. Add sugar, stirring until completely dissolved. Combine with orange juice, lemon juice, grape juice and 5 cups hot water in punch bowl; mix well.

Ice Cream Punch

Yield:
40 servings

Utensil:
punch bowl

Approx Per Serving:
Cal 124
Prot 2 g
Carbo 17 g
Fiber 0 g
T Fat 6 g
Chol 24 mg
Sod 51 mg

1 gallon vanilla ice cream
1 32-ounce bottle of 7-Up
1 32-ounce bottle of ginger ale

Let ice cream stand at room temperature for 25 to 30 minutes or until softened. Combine with 7-Up and ginger ale in punch bowl; mix gently.

Hot Spiced Percolator Punch

Yield:
10 servings

Utensil:
percolator

Approx Per Serving:
Cal 99
Prot <1 g
Carbo 25 g
Fiber <1 g
T Fat <1 g
Chol 0 mg
Sod 60 mg

2 1/4 cups pineapple juice
2 cups cranberry juice
1 3/4 cups water
1 tablespoon whole cloves
3 cinnamon sticks, broken
1 1/2 teaspoons whole allspice
1/2 cup packed brown sugar
1/4 teaspoon salt

Combine pineapple juice, cranberry juice and water in 8-cup percolator. Place cloves, cinnamon, allspice, brown sugar and salt in basket of percolator. Perk for 10 minutes.

Tropical Pineapple Punch

Yield:
30 servings

Utensil:
punch bowl

Approx Per Serving:
Cal 163
Prot 1 g
Carbo 39 g
Fiber <1 g
T Fat 1 g
Chol 4 mg
Sod 32 mg

1 cup sugar
2 small packages lemon-lime drink mix
2 cups hot water
1 46-ounce can pineapple juice, chilled
1 2-liter bottle of lemon-lime soda, chilled
1/2 gallon pineapple sherbet

Combine sugar, drink mix and hot water in large bowl; stir until sugar dissolves. Let stand until cool. Combine with pineapple juice and soda in punch bowl; mix well. Spoon sherbet into punch.

Whiskey Sour Punch

Yield:
25 servings

Utensil:
punch bowl

Approx Per Serving:
Cal 118
Prot <1 g
Carbo 14 g
Fiber <1 g
T Fat <1 g
Chol 0 mg
Sod 9 mg

3 6-ounce cans frozen lemonade concentrate, thawed
3 cups orange juice, chilled
1 32-ounce bottle of club soda, chilled
2 trays ice cubes
1 fifth of Bourbon
1 small orange

Combine lemonade concentrate, orange juice, club soda, ice cubes and Bourbon in punch bowl; mix well. Cut orange into thin slices, discarding end slices. Flute edges of slices with sharp knife. Place in punch bowl.

Hot Buttered Rum

Yield:
50 servings

Utensil:
freezer container

Approx Per Serving:
Cal 352
Prot <1 g
Carbo 37 g
Fiber 0 g
T Fat 9 g
Chol 25 mg
Sod 77 mg

1 1-pound package brown sugar
1 1-pound package confectioners' sugar
1 quart vanilla ice cream
1 pound butter
1 teaspoon allspice
1 teaspoon cinnamon
1 teaspoon nutmeg
9 cups rum
9 cups Brandy

Combine brown sugar, confectioners' sugar, ice cream, butter, allspice, cinnamon and nutmeg in saucepan. Heat over very low heat until consistency of thin cake batter, stirring constantly. Let stand until cool. Place in freezer container. Freeze, covered, until firm. Place 2 teaspoons frozen mixture in mug for each serving. Add 1½ ounces rum and 1½ ounces Brandy to each mug. Fill mug with hot water, stirring to melt frozen mixture. Garnish with additional nutmeg.

Sangria

Yield:
8 servings

Utensil:
pitcher

Approx Per Serving:
Cal 131
Prot <1 g
Carbo 18 g
Fiber <1 g
T Fat <1 g
Chol 0 mg
Sod 11 mg

½ cup lemon juice
½ cup orange juice
½ cup sugar
1 7-ounce bottle of club soda, chilled
4/5 quart dry red wine
¼ cup chopped orange
¼ cup chopped pineapple

Combine lemon juice, orange juice, sugar, club soda, wine, orange and pineapple in pitcher; mix well. Pour over ice in tall glasses.

STRAWBERRY DAIQUIRIS

Yield:
8 servings

Utensil:
blender

Approx Per Serving:
Cal 140
Prot <1 g
Carbo 24 g
Fiber 1 g
T Fat <1 g
Chol 0 mg
Sod 1 mg

1 10-ounce package frozen strawberries
6 ounces rum
1 12-ounce can frozen limeade concentrate
5 cups crushed ice

Combine strawberries, rum, limeade concentrate and crushed ice in blender container. Process until smooth. Serve immediately or store in freezer.

STRAWBERRY SPARKLERS

Yield:
12 servings

Utensil:
pitcher

Approx Per Serving:
Cal 57
Prot <1 g
Carbo 1 g
Fiber 0 g
T Fat 0 g
Chol 0 mg
Sod 11 mg

1 quart low-calorie lemon-lime soda, chilled
1 quart strawberry wine, chilled

Combine soda and wine in pitcher; mix gently. Serve immediately. May vary quantities, using equal amounts of soda and wine.

Instant Russian Tea

Yield:
80 servings

Utensil:
1-quart jar

Approx Per Serving:
Cal 43
Prot 0 g
Carbo 11 g
Fiber 0 g
T Fat 0 g
Chol 0 mg
Sod 4 mg

1 18-ounce jar instant orange breakfast drink mix
1/2 cup instant tea
1 cup sugar
1 teaspoon cinnamon
1/2 teaspoon cloves

Combine orange drink mix, instant tea powder, sugar, cinnamon and cloves in large jar; mix well. Dissolve 1 tablespoonful mix in 1 cup hot water for each serving.

Spiced Tea

Yield:
10 servings

Utensil:
saucepan

Approx Per Serving:
Cal 341
Prot 1 g
Carbo 87 g
Fiber 0 g
T Fat <1 g
Chol 0 mg
Sod 1 mg

2 cinnamon sticks
1 1/2 cups sugar
1 1/2 cups water
1/2 cup red hot cinnamon candies
1/2 cup honey
1 46-ounce can pineapple juice
1 46-ounce can orange juice
1 pint strong tea

Tie cinnamon sticks in cheesecloth. Combine sugar, water and candies in saucepan. Add cinnamon sticks. Simmer for 30 minutes or until candies are melted. Stir in honey, pineapple juice and orange juice. Pour into large container. Let stand overnight. Stir in tea before serving. May add 2 tablespoons rum flavoring if desired.

Tomato Toddy

Yield:
4 servings

Utensil:
saucepan

Approx Per Serving:
Cal 93
Prot 2 g
Carbo 10 g
Fiber <1 g
T Fat 5 g
Chol 11 mg
Sod 885 mg

1 can tomato soup
1 14-ounce can beef broth
1 broth can water
1/4 teaspoon marjoram
1/4 teaspoon thyme
4 teaspoons butter

Combine soup, beef broth, water, marjoram and thyme in saucepan; mix well. Bring to a boil; reduce heat. Simmer for 2 minutes. Spoon into mugs. Dot with butter. Garnish with croutons.

Wassail

Yield:
16 servings

Utensil:
saucepan

Approx Per Serving:
Cal 159
Prot 1 g
Carbo 40 g
Fiber 0 g
T Fat <1 g
Chol 0 mg
Sod 5 mg

2 quarts sweet apple cider
2 cups orange juice
1 cup lemon juice
5 cups pineapple juice
1 cinnamon stick
1 teaspoon whole cloves
1 cup sugar

Combine cider, orange juice, lemon juice, pineapple juice, cinnamon, cloves and sugar in saucepan; mix well. Bring just to the boiling point. Remove from heat; strain hot mixture into cups.

Salads

Virginia Walker

Blueberry Salad

Yield:
12 servings

Utensil:
9x13-inch dish

Approx Per Serving:
Cal 262
Prot 4 g
Carbo 42 g
Fiber 2 g
T Fat 10 g
Chol 22 mg
Sod 112 mg

1 20-ounce can crushed pineapple
2 3-ounce packages black raspberry gelatin
2 cups boiling water
1 16-ounce can blueberries, drained
1 envelope whipped topping mix
8 ounces cream cheese, softened
1/2 cup sugar
1/4 cup chopped pecans

Drain pineapple, reserving 1 cup juice. Dissolve gelatin in boiling water in bowl. Add reserved pineapple juice; mix well. Chill until partially set. Add pineapple and blueberries; mix well. Pour into 9x13-inch glass serving dish. Chill until firm. Prepare whipped topping mix using package directions. Beat cream cheese and sugar in mixer bowl until light and fluffy. Fold in whipped topping. Spread over gelatin. Chill until serving time. Sprinkle with pecans.

Blueberry and Pineapple Salad

Yield:
12 servings

Utensil:
9x13-inch dish

Approx Per Serving:
Cal 308
Prot 4 g
Carbo 45 g
Fiber 1 g
T Fat 14 g
Chol 29 mg
Sod 126 mg

2 3-ounce packages black cherry gelatin
2 cups boiling water
1 20-ounce can crushed pineapple
1 20-ounce can blueberry pie filling
1 cup sour cream
8 ounces cream cheese, softened
1/2 cup sugar
1 teaspoon vanilla extract
1/2 cup chopped pecans

Dissolve gelatin in boiling water in bowl. Add undrained pineapple and pie filling; mix well. Pour into 9x13-inch glass serving dish. Chill, covered, for 4 to 6 hours or until firm. Mix sour cream, cream cheese and sugar in small bowl until smooth. Stir in vanilla. Spread over gelatin; sprinkle with pecans. Chill until serving time.

Coca-Cola Salad

Yield:
12 servings

Utensil:
9x13-inch dish

Approx Per Serving:
Cal 257
Prot 4 g
Carbo 33 g
Fiber 1 g
T Fat 13 g
Chol 21 mg
Sod 104 mg

1 16-ounce can dark sweet cherries
1 16-ounce can crushed pineapple
1 6-ounce package cherry gelatin
1 12-ounce can Coca-Cola
8 ounces cream cheese, softened
1/2 to 1 cup chopped pecans

Drain cherries and pineapple, reserving juices. Bring reserved juices to a boil in saucepan. Add gelatin; stir until dissolved. Add Coca-Cola; mix well. Cut cream cheese into small cubes. Add cherries, pineapple, pecans and cream cheese to gelatin mixture, stirring until cream cheese melts. Pour into 9x13-inch glass serving dish. Chill in refrigerator until firm.

Cranberry Salad

Yield:
12 servings

Utensil:
9x13-inch dish

Approx Per Serving:
Cal 236
Prot 3 g
Carbo 33 g
Fiber 1 g
T Fat 11 g
Chol 12 mg
Sod 112 mg

1 6-ounce package cherry gelatin
2 cups boiling water
2 tablespoons lemon juice
1 16-ounce can whole cranberry sauce
1 envelope whipped topping mix
3 ounces cream cheese
1/4 cup confectioners' sugar
1/4 cup mayonnaise
1/2 cup chopped pecans

Dissolve gelatin in boiling water in bowl. Stir in lemon juice. Let stand until cool. Add cranberry sauce; mix well. Pour into 9x13-inch glass serving dish. Chill until firm. Prepare whipped topping mix using package directions. Beat cream cheese in small mixer bowl until smooth. Add confectioners' sugar and mayonnaise; beat until fluffy. Fold in whipped topping. Spread over gelatin; sprinkle with pecans. Chill until serving time.

Fast and Easy Fruit Salad

Yield:
4 servings

Utensil:
salad bowl

Approx Per Serving:
Cal 466
Prot 17 g
Carbo 60 g
Fiber 2 g
T Fat 19 g
Chol 16 mg
Sod 521 mg

2 cups cottage cheese
1 3-ounce package raspberry gelatin
1 16-ounce can fruit cocktail, drained
8 ounces whipped topping
1 cup miniature marshmallows
1/4 cup chopped pecans

Place cottage cheese in salad bowl. Sprinkle with gelatin; mix well. Stir in fruit cocktail. Fold in whipped topping, marshmallows and pecans. Chill until serving time.

Lazy Day Salad

Yield:
8 servings

Utensil:
salad bowl

Approx Per Serving:
Cal 320
Prot 1 g
Carbo 57 g
Fiber 2 g
T Fat 11 g
Chol 0 mg
Sod 204 mg

1 11-ounce can mandarin oranges
1 20-ounce can crushed pineapple
1 4-ounce package lemon instant pudding mix
1 4-ounce package vanilla instant pudding mix
12 ounces whipped topping

Combine undrained oranges and pineapple in salad bowl; mix well. Add pudding mixes; mix well. Fold in 3/4 of the whipped topping. Spread remaining whipped topping over top. Chill until firm. Garnish with coconut if desired.

Lime Gelatin Salad

Yield:
12 servings

Utensil:
9x13-inch dish

Approx Per Serving:
Cal 123
Prot 2 g
Carbo 23 g
Fiber 1 g
T Fat 3 g
Chol 27 mg
Sod 67 mg

1 3/4 cups crushed pineapple
1 3-ounce package lime gelatin
1 cup boiling water
1 cup lemon-lime soda
1 banana, sliced
1 tablespoon flour
1/4 cup sugar
1 egg, beaten
1/2 cup whipped cream
1/4 cup shredded American cheese

Drain pineapple, reserving juice. Dissolve gelatin in boiling water in bowl. Add lemon-lime soda; mix well. Chill until mixture will coat spoon. Stir in pineapple and banana. Pour into 9x13-inch glass serving dish. Chill until firm. Combine reserved pineapple juice, flour, sugar and egg in saucepan; mix well. Cook until thickened and smooth, stirring constantly. Cool completely. Fold in whipped cream. Spread over gelatin; sprinkle with cheese. Chill until serving time. Cut into squares.

Cheesy Lime Salad

Yield:
8 servings

Utensil:
8x8-inch dish

Approx Per Serving:
Cal 148
Prot 5 g
Carbo 25 g
Fiber 1 g
T Fat 4 g
Chol 6 mg
Sod 154 mg

1 3-ounce package lime gelatin
1 cup boiling water
1 cup cottage cheese
1 16-ounce can crushed pineapple
1 envelope whipped topping mix

Dissolve gelatin in boiling water in bowl. Cool. Prepare whipped topping mix using package directions, omitting vanilla. Add cottage cheese and pineapple to gelatin; mix well. Fold in whipped topping. Pour into 8-inch square serving dish. Chill until firm. Cut into squares. May add 1/4 cup each chopped celery and pecans if desired.

Congealed Orange Salad

Yield:
4 servings

Utensil:
salad mold

Approx Per Serving:
Cal 362
Prot 5 g
Carbo 62 g
Fiber 2 g
T Fat 12 g
Chol 26 mg
Sod 105 mg

1 11-ounce can mandarin oranges
1 8-ounce can crushed pineapple
1 3-ounce package orange gelatin
1 6-ounce can frozen orange juice concentrate
1 cup sour cream

Drain oranges and pineapple, reserving juice. Add enough water to reserved juice to measure 1 cup. Bring just to the boiling point in saucepan; remove from heat. Add gelatin, stirring to dissolve well. Add orange juice; mix well. Stir in sour cream. Fold in oranges and pineapple. Chill until partially set. Pour into oiled 6-cup salad mold. Chill overnight. Unmold onto serving plate.

Mandarin Orange Salad

Yield:
8 servings

Utensil:
salad mold

Approx Per Serving:
Cal 207
Prot 3 g
Carbo 49 g
Fiber 1 g
T Fat 1 g
Chol 4 mg
Sod 93 mg

1 6-ounce package orange gelatin
2 cups boiling water
1 pint orange sherbet
1 11-ounce can mandarin oranges, drained
1 20-ounce can crushed pineapple, drained

Dissolve gelatin in boiling water in bowl. Add orange sherbet; whisk until melted and smooth. Add oranges and crushed pineapple; mix well. Pour into salad mold. Chill until firm. Unmold onto serving plate.

Orange and Pear Mold

Yield:
8 servings

Utensil:
salad mold

Approx Per Serving:
Cal 160
Prot 2 g
Carbo 40 g
Fiber 2 g
T Fat <1 g
Chol 0 mg
Sod 123 mg

1 29-ounce can pears
2 3-ounce packages orange gelatin
1 3/4 cups boiling water
2 tablespoons lemon juice
2 tablespoons vinegar
2 tablespoons prepared horseradish
1/8 teaspoon salt
1 cup finely chopped celery

Drain pears, reserving juice. Chop pears. Dissolve gelatin in boiling water in medium bowl. Add lemon juice, vinegar, horseradish and salt; mix well. Add enough water to pear juice to measure 1 1/4 cups. Stir into gelatin mixture. Chill until partially set. Fold in pears and celery. Pour into slightly oiled 1 1/2-quart salad mold. Chill until firm. Unmold onto serving plate. May use 8 individual 2/3-cup molds if preferred. This is particularly good with pork.

Party Salad

Yield:
12 servings

Utensil:
large bowl

Approx Per Serving:
Cal 361
Prot 4 g
Carbo 49 g
Fiber 2 g
T Fat 18 g
Chol 11 mg
Sod 70 mg

16 ounces whipped topping
1 14-ounce can sweetened condensed milk
1 15-ounce can crushed pineapple, drained
1 21-ounce can cherry pie filling
1/2 cup chopped pecans
1 cup coconut
1 cup miniature marshmallows

Blend whipped topping and condensed milk in bowl. Chill for 2 hours. Fold in pineapple, pie filling, pecans, coconut and marshmallows. Chill overnight. Serve on lettuce-lined salad plates.

Pineapple and Cheese Salad

Yield:
10 servings

Utensil:
salad mold

Approx Per Serving:
Cal 455
Prot 5 g
Carbo 37 g
Fiber 1 g
T Fat 34 g
Chol 115 mg
Sod 162 mg

2½ tablespoons unflavored gelatin
1 cup cold water
1 20-ounce can crushed pineapple
Juice of 1 lemon
1 cup sugar
16 ounces cream cheese, softened
2 cups whipping cream, whipped

Soften gelatin in cold water in large saucepan. Add pineapple, lemon juice and sugar; mix well. Cook until sugar and gelatin dissolve, stirring constantly. Do not boil. Let stand until cool. Add cream cheese; mix well. Fold in whipped cream. Pour into 10-cup salad mold. Chill overnight. Unmold onto serving plate. Garnish with strawberries, pineapple chunks or parsley. May serve as a light dessert.

Pistachio and Coconut Frozen Salad

Yield:
6 servings

Utensil:
loaf pan

Approx Per Serving:
Cal 349
Prot 3 g
Carbo 37 g
Fiber 3 g
T Fat 22 g
Chol 34 mg
Sod 172 mg

2 cups sour cream
1 4-ounce package pistachio instant pudding mix
1½ cups coconut
1 8-ounce can crushed pineapple

Combine sour cream and pudding mix in bowl; mix well. Add coconut and undrained pineapple; mix well. Spoon into 5x9-inch loaf pan. Freeze for 4 hours to overnight or until firm. Unmold onto serving plate. May be prepared and served immediately or chilled instead of frozen if preferred.

PRETZEL SALAD

Yield:
12 servings

Utensil:
9x13-inch dish

Approx Per Serving:
Cal 446
Prot 4 g
Carbo 49 g
Fiber 1 g
T Fat 27 g
Chol 21 mg
Sod 438 mg

2 cups crushed pretzels
1 cup melted margarine
3 tablespoons sugar
8 ounces cream cheese, softened
1 cup sugar
8 ounces whipped topping
1 6-ounce package strawberry gelatin
2 cups boiling water
2 10-ounce packages frozen strawberries

Combine pretzels, margarine and 3 tablespoons sugar in bowl; mix well. Pat into 9x13-inch baking dish. Bake at 375 degrees for 10 minutes. Cool in refrigerator. Beat cream cheese, remaining 1 cup sugar and whipped topping in mixer bowl until smooth. Spread over baked layer. Chill in refrigerator. Dissolve gelatin in boiling water in large bowl. Stir in frozen strawberries. Pour over cream cheese layer. Chill until firm.

LAYERED STRAWBERRY SALAD

Yield:
12 servings

Utensil:
9x13-inch dish

Approx Per Serving:
Cal 254
Prot 4 g
Carbo 30 g
Fiber 2 g
T Fat 15 g
Chol 17 mg
Sod 67 mg

2 3-ounce packages strawberry gelatin
1 cup boiling water
1 20-ounce can crushed pineapple
2 10-ounce packages frozen strawberries, thawed
1 cup chopped pecans
2 cups sour cream

Dissolve gelatin in boiling water in large bowl. Stir in pineapple, strawberries and pecans. Reserve half the gelatin mixture. Let stand at room temperature. Pour remaining gelatin mixture into 9x13-inch glass serving dish. Chill until firm. Spread with sour cream. Pour reserved gelatin mixture over sour cream. Chill until firm.

Strawberry Delight

Yield:
12 servings

Utensil:
salad bowl

Approx Per Serving:
Cal 165
Prot 1 g
Carbo 27 g
Fiber 3 g
T Fat 7 g
Chol 9 mg
Sod 38 mg

2 cups frozen sweetened strawberries, thawed, drained
1 cup miniature marshmallows
1 cup mandarin oranges
1 cup pineapple chunks
1 cup coconut
1 cup sour cream

Combine strawberries, marshmallows, oranges, pineapple and coconut in salad bowl; toss to mix. Stir in sour cream. Chill until serving time.

Chicken Salad

Yield:
8 servings

Utensil:
salad bowl

Approx Per Serving:
Cal 499
Prot 28 g
Carbo 8 g
Fiber 1 g
T Fat 40 g
Chol 98 mg
Sod 345 mg

5 cups finely chopped cooked chicken
1/2 cup chopped celery
1 cup cashew halves
1 cup mayonnaise
3/4 cup sour cream
2 tablespoons lemon juice
Salt and pepper to taste
Sugar to taste

Combine chicken, celery and cashew halves in salad bowl; mix well. Mix mayonnaise, sour cream, lemon juice, salt, pepper and sugar in small bowl until smooth. Pour over chicken mixture; toss to coat. Chill until serving time.

GRILLED CHICKEN CAESAR SALAD

Yield:
4 servings

Utensil:
salad bowl

Approx Per Serving:
Cal 350
Prot 24 g
Carbo 9 g
Fiber 2 g
T Fat 24 g
Chol 55 mg
Sod 537 mg

1 tablespoon extra-virgin olive oil
2 slices rye bread, crusts trimmed, cut into 1/2-inch cubes
1 pound chicken breast filets
1/4 teaspoon salt
1/4 teaspoon pepper
4 anchovy filets, chopped
2 teaspoons minced garlic
1/4 teaspoon salt
1/4 teaspoon pepper
2 tablespoons fresh lemon juice
1 tablespoon Dijon mustard
2 dashes of red pepper sauce
1/3 cup extra-virgin olive oil
1 large head romaine lettuce, torn into bite-sized pieces
3 tablespoons freshly grated Parmesan cheese

Preheat broiler. Heat 1 tablespoon olive oil in large skillet over medium-high heat. Add bread cubes. Cook for 5 minutes or until light brown, stirring constantly; drain on paper towels. Rinse chicken and pat dry. Sprinkle with 1/4 teaspoon salt and 1/4 teaspoon pepper. Place on lightly oiled rack in broiler pan. Broil 3 inches from heat source for 5 to 6 minutes or until tender, turning once. Cool for 5 minutes. Cut cross grain into 1/4-inch thick slices. Mash anchovy filets with garlic and 1/4 teaspoon salt in large salad bowl until of paste consistency. Add remaining 1/4 teaspoon pepper, lemon juice, mustard and red pepper sauce; mix well. Whisk in remaining 1/3 cup olive oil. Add chicken; toss to coat. Add lettuce, Parmesan cheese and bread cubes; toss to mix.

Grill chicken breast filets over coals for a char-broiled flavor. Serve over salad greens tossed with pineapple chunks and mandarin oranges.

Crab Meat Salad

Yield:
4 servings

Utensil:
salad bowl

Approx Per Serving:
Cal 212
Prot 19 g
Carbo 7 g
Fiber 2 g
T Fat 12 g
Chol 84 mg
Sod 365 mg

12 ounces crab meat
1 cucumber, chopped
1 medium onion, chopped
1 green bell pepper, chopped
1/4 cup mayonnaise
Salt and pepper to taste

Combine crab meat, cucumber, onion and green pepper in salad bowl; toss to mix. Add mayonnaise, salt and pepper; mix well. Chill, covered, for 1 hour before serving. Serve with favorite snack crackers.

Macaroni Salad

Yield:
8 servings

Utensil:
salad bowl

Approx Per Serving:
Cal 327
Prot 8 g
Carbo 25 g
Fiber 2 g
T Fat 22 g
Chol 30 mg
Sod 577 mg

1 8-ounce package spiral macaroni, cooked, drained
1 green bell pepper, chopped
1 red bell pepper, chopped
1 cup shredded Cheddar cheese
1/3 cup sliced pimento-stuffed olives
1/2 cup chopped onion
2/3 cup mayonnaise
1/3 cup sour cream
1 teaspoon salt
Dash of pepper
1 tablespoon lemon juice

Combine macaroni, green pepper, red pepper, cheese, olives and onion in salad bowl. Mix mayonnaise, sour cream, salt, pepper and lemon juice in small bowl until smooth. Pour over macaroni mixture; toss to mix. Chill until serving time.

Pasta Salad

Yield:
8 servings

Utensil:
salad bowl

Approx Per Serving:
Cal 739
Prot 32 g
Carbo 42 g
Fiber 4 g
T Fat 50 g
Chol 86 mg
Sod 1240 mg

1 16-ounce package spiral trio vegetable pasta
2 tablespoons virgin olive oil
1/2 6-ounce can large pitted black olives, drained
1 10-ounce jar Progresso olive salad
8 ounces feta cheese, crumbled
8 ounces Monterey Jack pepper cheese, cut into 1/4-inch cubes
1 pound ham, cut into 1/4-inch cubes
2 tablespoons Italian seasoning
4 dashes of Wye River spicy black pepper seasoning
1/2 cup virgin olive oil

Cook pasta using package directions adding 2 tablespoons olive oil; drain. Combine olives, olive salad, feta cheese, Monterey Jack cheese, ham, pasta, Italian seasoning, black pepper and remaining 1/2 cup olive oil in large salad bowl; toss to mix. Chill for 1 hour or longer. May substitute Progresso pepper salad and 1/2 cup salad olives for olive salad and 1 pound sliced pepperoni for ham.

Nutritional information for this recipe does not include olive salad.

Taco Salad

Yield:
4 servings

Utensil:
salad bowl

Approx Per Serving:
Cal 1121
Prot 40 g
Carbo 57 g
Fiber 13 g
T Fat 83 g
Chol 137 mg
Sod 1517 mg

1 pound ground beef
1 head lettuce, torn into bite-sized pieces
1 medium onion, chopped
1 16-ounce can red kidney beans, drained
1 cup shredded sharp Cheddar cheese
1 cup mayonnaise
1 cup taco sauce
1 teaspoon lemon juice
1 7-ounce package tortilla chips, crushed

Brown ground beef in medium skillet, stirring until crumbly; drain. Combine ground beef, lettuce, onion, beans and cheese in salad bowl; toss to mix. Mix mayonnaise, taco sauce and lemon juice in small bowl. Pour over salad; toss to mix well. Reserve 1/4 cup chips. Add remaining chips to salad; toss gently. Sprinkle with reserved chips. This is a fast and easy summer dish.

Baco Salad

Yield:
8 servings

Utensil:
9x13-inch dish

Approx Per Serving:
Cal 381
Prot 10 g
Carbo 24 g
Fiber 6 g
T Fat 27 g
Chol 41 mg
Sod 868 mg

1 medium head lettuce, chopped
1 red onion, finely chopped
1/2 cup chopped celery
1 cup chopped green bell pepper
1 10-ounce package frozen green peas, thawed, drained
1 1/2 cups mayonnaise-type salad dressing
4 teaspoons sugar
2 cups shredded Cheddar cheese
1 3-ounce jar bacon bits

Combine lettuce, onion, celery, green pepper and peas in large bowl; toss to mix. Spoon into 9x13-inch glass serving dish. Mix salad dressing and sugar in small bowl. Spread over vegetables. Do not stir. Sprinkle with cheese and bacon bits. Chill, covered, overnight. May store in refrigerator for several days.

Four-Bean Salad

Yield:
12 servings

Utensil:
salad bowl

Approx Per Serving:
Cal 218
Prot 5 g
Carbo 30 g
Fiber 7 g
T Fat 9 g
Chol 0 mg
Sod 500 mg

1 16-ounce can green beans, rinsed, drained
1 16-ounce can wax beans, rinsed, drained
1 16-ounce can kidney beans, rinsed, drained
1 16-ounce can lima beans, rinsed, drained
1 green bell pepper, thinly sliced
1 large onion, thinly sliced, separated into rings
3/4 cup sugar
1/2 cup vinegar
1/2 cup oil
1/2 teaspoon salt
1/2 teaspoon pepper
1 tablespoon minced parsley

Combine green beans, wax beans, kidney beans, lima beans, green pepper and onion in large salad bowl; toss to mix. Combine sugar, vinegar, oil, salt, pepper and parsley in saucepan; mix well. Cook until sugar dissolves, stirring constantly. Pour over vegetables. Chill, covered, for 5 hours to overnight.

BROCCOLI AND CHEDDAR SALAD

Yield:
8 servings

Utensil:
salad bowl

Approx Per Serving:
Cal 293
Prot 5 g
Carbo 11 g
Fiber 1 g
T Fat 27 g
Chol 28 mg
Sod 285 mg

3 cups broccoli flowerets
6 slices crisp-fried bacon, crumbled
1 cup chopped red onion
1/2 cup shredded Cheddar cheese
1 cup mayonnaise
2 tablespoons vinegar
1/4 cup sugar

Combine broccoli, bacon, onion and cheese in salad bowl; toss to mix. Mix mayonnaise, vinegar and sugar in small bowl until smooth. Pour over broccoli mixture; toss to coat. Chill, covered, until serving time.

BROCCOLI SALAD

Yield:
6 servings

Utensil:
salad bowl

Approx Per Serving:
Cal 179
Prot 6 g
Carbo 18 g
Fiber 3 g
T Fat 10 g
Chol 20 mg
Sod 314 mg

1/2 cup mayonnaise-type salad dressing
1/4 cup sugar
3 tablespoons vinegar
1/4 cup bacon bits
1 large bunch broccoli
1 large onion, thinly sliced, separated into rings
1/2 to 3/4 cup shredded Cheddar cheese

Mix salad dressing, sugar, vinegar and bacon bits in small bowl until smooth. Rinse broccoli; drain. Trim flowerets; chop stems. Combine broccoli, onion rings and cheese in salad bowl; toss to mix. Chill until serving time. Drizzle with salad dressing; toss to coat. May garnish with additional bacon bits.

Broccoli and Raisin Salad

Yield:
12 servings

Utensil:
salad bowl

Approx Per Serving:
Cal 186
Prot 4 g
Carbo 23 g
Fiber 3 g
T Fat 10 g
Chol 10 mg
Sod 257 mg

Flowerets of 2 bunches broccoli
1 large red onion, thinly sliced, separated into rings
1/2 cup golden raisins
12 slices crisp-fried bacon, crumbled
1 cup mayonnaise-type salad dressing
1/2 cup sugar
2 tablespoons vinegar

Combine broccoli, onion, raisins and bacon in large salad bowl; toss to mix. Mix salad dressing, sugar and vinegar in small bowl until smooth. Pour over broccoli mixture. Chill in refrigerator for 4 hours.

Coleslaw Mold

Yield:
6 servings

Utensil:
salad mold

Approx Per Serving:
Cal 195
Prot 2 g
Carbo 16 g
Fiber 1 g
T Fat 15 g
Chol 11 mg
Sod 245 mg

1 3-ounce package lemon gelatin
1 cup boiling water
1/2 cup cold water
2 tablespoons vinegar
1/2 cup mayonnaise
1/4 teaspoon salt
Dash of pepper
2 cups finely chopped cabbage
2 tablespoons minced green bell pepper
1 tablespoon minced onion
1/4 teaspoon celery seed
1/2 cup shredded carrot

Dissolve gelatin in boiling water in large mixer bowl. Add cold water, vinegar, mayonnaise, salt and pepper; beat until smooth. Chill in freezer until firm around edge. Beat until fluffy. Fold in cabbage, green pepper, onion, celery seed and carrots. Pour into salad mold. Chill until firm. Unmold onto serving plate.

Salads

Green and White Salad

Yield:
12 servings

Utensil:
salad bowl

Approx Per Serving:
Cal 117
Prot 4 g
Carbo 10 g
Fiber 4 g
T Fat 8 g
Chol 7 mg
Sod 123 mg

1 10-ounce package frozen green peas
1 head cauliflower, chopped
1 bunch broccoli, chopped
3 small zucchini, sliced
1 cup sliced mushrooms
1 cup chopped pimento
1/2 cup sliced purple onion
1 8-ounce bottle of creamy cucumber salad dressing
Salt and pepper to taste
Paprika to taste

Thaw peas in cold water in colander; drain. Combine cauliflower, broccoli, zucchini, mushrooms, pimento, onion and peas in large salad bowl; toss to mix. Pour salad dressing over vegetables; toss to coat. Stir in salt and pepper; sprinkle with paprika. Chill for 2 hours or longer. May use any fresh vegetables as desired.

Tomato Aspic Salad

Yield:
9 servings

Utensil:
8x8-inch dish

Approx Per Serving:
Cal 92
Prot 17 g
Carbo 4 g
Fiber 4 g
T Fat 1 g
Chol 0 mg
Sod 478 mg

2 envelopes unflavored gelatin
1/2 cup cold water
2 8-ounce cans tomato sauce
1 1/2 cups water
2 tablespoons grated onion
1/2 cup thinly sliced celery
1/4 cup sliced stuffed olives

Soften gelatin in 1/2 cup cold water. Combine tomato sauce, remaining 1 1/2 cups water and onion in saucepan; mix well. Cook over low heat until heated through, stirring constantly. Stir in gelatin, celery and olives. Let stand until cool. Pour into lightly oiled 8-inch square glass serving dish. Chill until firm. Cut into squares. Serve on lettuce-lined salad plates. Garnish with mayonnaise.

Layered Vegetable Salad

Yield:
8 servings

Utensil:
salad bowl

Approx Per Serving:
Cal 523
Prot 8 g
Carbo 10 g
Fiber 3 g
T Fat 51 g
Chol 49 mg
Sod 516 mg

1 head lettuce, shredded
1/2 cup chopped red onion
1/2 cup chopped celery
1 10-ounce package frozen peas, cooked, drained, cooled
1/2 cup chopped green bell pepper
2 cups mayonnaise
1 tablespoon sugar
3/4 cup shredded Swiss cheese
10 slices crisp-fried bacon, crumbled

Layer lettuce, onion, celery, peas and green pepper in salad bowl. Spread with mayonnaise, sealing to edge. Sprinkle with sugar, cheese and bacon. Chill, tightly covered, for up to 24 hours. Toss just before serving. May substitute sharp Cheddar cheese for Swiss cheese.

Marinated Vegetables

Yield:
10 servings

Utensil:
salad bowl

Approx Per Serving:
Cal 375
Prot 5 g
Carbo 43 g
Fiber 5 g
T Fat 23 g
Chol 0 mg
Sod 286 mg

1 16-ounce can green peas, drained
1 16-ounce can bean sprouts, drained
1 16-ounce can whole kernel corn, drained
2 5-ounce cans chopped water chestnuts, drained
1 4-ounce jar pimento, drained, chopped
1 6-ounce can sliced mushrooms, drained
1 large green bell pepper, thinly sliced
1 large red onion, thinly sliced
1 cup water
1 cup oil
1 cup sugar
1/2 to 1 cup vinegar
Salt and pepper to taste

Combine peas, bean sprouts, corn, water chestnuts, pimento, mushrooms, green pepper and onion in large salad bowl; toss to mix. Mix water, oil, sugar, vinegar, salt and pepper in small bowl until smooth. Pour over vegetables; toss to coat. Marinate, covered, in refrigerator overnight up to 24 hours. Drain just before serving.

MARINATED VEGETABLE SALAD

Yield:
12 servings

Utensil:
salad bowl

Approx Per Serving:
Cal 150
Prot 3 g
Carbo 16 g
Fiber 3 g
T Fat 10 g
Chol 0 mg
Sod 507 mg

1 16-ounce can tiny peas, drained
1 16-ounce can French-style green beans
1 16-ounce can Shoe Peg corn
1 4-ounce jar chopped pimento, drained
1/2 cup chopped onion
1/2 cup chopped green bell pepper
1/2 cup chopped celery
1 teaspoon salt
1 teaspoon pepper
1 cup plus 1 tablespoon water
1/2 cup oil
3/4 cup white vinegar

Combine peas, green beans, corn, pimento, onion, green pepper and celery in large salad bowl; toss to mix. Mix salt, pepper, water, oil and vinegar in small bowl until blended. Pour over vegetables. Marinate in refrigerator for 12 hours to overnight. Drain just before serving.

SEVEN-LAYER SALAD

Yield:
10 servings

Utensil:
8x12-inch dish

Approx Per Serving:
Cal 419
Prot 10 g
Carbo 13 g
Fiber 3 g
T Fat 37 g
Chol 49 mg
Sod 483 mg

1 head lettuce, shredded
1 8-ounce can sliced water chestnuts, drained
1 10-ounce package frozen peas, cooked, drained, cooled
1 cup chopped celery
1 cup chopped onion
1 1/2 cups mayonnaise
2 tablespoons sugar
2 cups shredded Cheddar cheese
8 ounces bacon, crisp-fried, crumbled

Layer lettuce, water chestnuts, peas, celery and onion in 8x12-inch glass serving dish. Spread with mayonnaise, sealing to edge. Sprinkle with sugar, cheese and bacon. Chill, covered, for 24 hours. May substitute chopped green bell pepper for onion or use a combination.

Sweet and Sour Vegetables

Yield:
8 servings

Utensil:
salad bowl

Approx Per Serving:
Cal 194
Prot 2 g
Carbo 51 g
Fiber 4 g
T Fat <1 g
Chol 0 mg
Sod 1617 mg

2 carrots, shredded
1 medium head cabbage, shredded
4 cucumbers, chopped
1/2 red bell pepper, chopped
2 large green bell peppers, chopped
2 tablespoons salt
2 cups vinegar
1 1/2 cups sugar

Combine carrots, cabbage, cucumbers, red pepper and green pepper in large salad bowl; toss to mix. Sprinkle with salt; mix well. Let stand for 24 hours; drain well. Mix vinegar and sugar in small bowl until sugar dissolves. Pour over vegetables; mix well. Chill for 24 hours longer.

French Salad Dressing

Yield:
64 servings

Utensil:
blender

Approx Per Serving:
Cal 46
Prot <1 g
Carbo 4 g
Fiber <1 g
T Fat 3 g
Chol 0 mg
Sod 56 mg

1 cup sugar
1 teaspoon salt
1/4 teaspoon pepper
1/2 teaspoon paprika
1 small onion, grated
1 cup oil
1/2 cup catsup
Juice of 1 lemon
1/3 cup vinegar

Combine sugar, salt, pepper, paprika, onion, oil, catsup, lemon juice and vinegar in blender container. Process until smooth. Pour into glass container with lid. Store in refrigerator. Mix well before serving. Serve over vegetable or fruit salad.

Meat, Poultry and Seafood

Linda Crow

Barbecued Chuck Roast

Yield:
10 servings

Utensil:
pressure cooker

Approx Per Serving:
Cal 382
Prot 44 g
Carbo 21 g
Fiber 2 g
T Fat 13 g
Chol 128 mg
Sod 2075 mg

1 5-pound chuck roast
3 cups water
4 onions, chopped
1 1/4 cups catsup
1 1/4 cups vinegar
2 cups water
3 tablespoons brown sugar
3 tablespoons Worcestershire sauce
4 1/2 teaspoons paprika
4 1/2 teaspoons dry mustard
1 tablespoon barbecue spice
1 1/4 teaspoons chili powder
1 tablespoon onion salt
4 1/2 teaspoons salt
1/2 teaspoon red pepper
1 tablespoon black pepper

Cook roast in 3 cups water in pressure cooker for 30 minutes using manufacturer's directions; drain. Let beef stand until cool. Cut into 1-inch cubes. Combine with onions, catsup, vinegar, 2 cups water, brown sugar, Worcestershire sauce, paprika, dry mustard, barbecue spice, chili powder, onion salt, salt, red pepper and black pepper in pressure cooker. Cook for 20 minutes longer.

Busy-Day Pot Roast

Yield:
8 servings

Utensil:
roasting pan

Approx Per Serving:
Cal 582
Prot 49 g
Carbo 53 g
Fiber 5 g
T Fat 20 g
Chol 128 mg
Sod 1671 mg

1 4-pound beef roast
2 cans cream of mushroom soup
1 envelope onion soup mix
8 potatoes, peeled
8 carrots
2 tablespoons water

Place roast on large sheet of foil in roasting pan. Spread with cream of mushroom soup. Sprinkle with dry onion soup mix. Arrange potatoes and carrots around roast. Sprinkle with water. Seal foil tightly. Roast at 300 degrees for 3 to 4 hours or until beef is tender. Skim pan juices if necessary. Serve with roast. Serve with salad and garlic bread. Serve leftovers on open-faced sandwiches.

Crock•Pot Beef Burgundy

Yield:
8 servings

Utensil:
Crock•Pot

Approx Per Serving:
Cal 313
Prot 10 g
Carbo 28 g
Fiber 3 g
T Fat 17 g
Chol 43 mg
Sod 1140 mg

6 slices bacon, chopped
4 pounds beef cubes
3 tablespoons butter
2 4-ounce cans mushrooms, drained
2 cloves of garlic, chopped
6 tablespoons butter
1 cup flour
1/2 cup Burgundy
3 14-ounce cans beef consommé
2 bay leaves, crushed
2 tablespoons chopped parsley
1 teaspoon thyme
1 teaspoon salt
1/8 teaspoon pepper

Fry bacon in skillet; place in Crock•Pot. Add beef to drippings in skillet. Cook until brown on all sides; add to Crock•Pot. Add 3 tablespoons butter, mushrooms and garlic to skillet. Sauté until mushrooms are tender; add to Crock•Pot. Add 6 tablespoons butter and flour to skillet, stirring to blend well. Cook until golden brown, stirring constantly. Stir in wine and consommé. Cook until thickened, stirring constantly. Add to Crock•Pot with bay leaves, parsley, thyme, salt and pepper; mix well. Cook on Medium for 7 to 8 hours or to desired consistency. May simmer in saucepan on top of stove for 2 hours if preferred.

Crock•Pot Roast Beef

Yield:
6 servings

Utensil:
Crock•Pot

Approx Per Serving:
Cal 452
Prot 47 g
Carbo 32 g
Fiber 1 g
T Fat 15 g
Chol 129 mg
Sod 2039 mg

1 3-pound sirloin tip roast
1/2 cup flour
1 envelope onion soup mix
1 envelope brown gravy mix
2 cups ginger ale

Coat roast with flour; place in Crock•Pot. Combine remaining flour with soup mix, gravy mix and ginger ale in bowl; mix well. Pour over roast. Cook on Low for 8 to 10 hours or until roast is tender. Cut beef into cubes. Serve with gravy over cooked noodles.

ITALIAN POT ROAST ≈MW≈

Yield:
8 servings

Utensil:
3-quart dish

Approx Per Serving:
Cal 336
Prot 34 g
Carbo 20 g
Fiber 2 g
T Fat 12 g
Chol 96 mg
Sod 254 mg

1 onion, chopped
3 carrots, chopped
1 stalk celery, chopped
1 cup cut green beans
2 cloves of garlic, finely chopped
1 tablespoon olive oil
2 tablespoons tomato paste
1 bay leaf
1/8 teaspoon thyme
1/2 cup beef stock
1/2 cup dry red wine
1/2 teaspoon salt
1/4 teaspoon pepper
1 3-pound rump roast
1 tablespoon tomato paste
2 cups cooked rice

Combine first 6 ingredients in glass 3-quart dish. Microwave, covered, on High for 3 to 4 minutes, stirring once. Stir in 2 tablespoons tomato paste, bay leaf, thyme, beef stock, wine, salt and pepper. Add roast to dish fat side up. Microwave, covered, on High for 15 minutes, turning dish once. Turn roast over and baste. Cook, covered, on Medium for 1 hour or until tender, turning roast over, basting and rotating dish halfway during cooking time. Place roast on serving platter. Let stand, covered, for 10 minutes. Stir 1 tablespoon tomato paste into cooking liquid in glass dish. Microwave on High for 5 minutes or until thickened, stirring every 2 minutes. Slice beef into thin slices. Serve with sauce and rice.

STEAK AND GRAVY

Yield:
4 servings

Utensil:
skillet

Approx Per Serving:
Cal 454
Prot 47 g
Carbo 24 g
Fiber 1 g
T Fat 18 g
Chol 133 mg
Sod 621 mg

2 pounds round steak
Garlic powder to taste
1 teaspoon salt
Pepper to taste
3/4 cup flour
1 tablespoon oil
1/4 cup water
2/3 cup milk
3 tablespoons flour
2 tablespoons instant coffee

Cut steak into serving pieces. Sprinkle with garlic powder, salt and pepper. Coat with 3/4 cup flour, pounding in with meat mallet; shake off excess flour. Repeat process with remaining flour. Brown steak on both sides in oil in skillet. Add water. Simmer, covered, for 20 to 25 minutes or until steak is tender and liquid is absorbed. Remove steak to platter. Blend milk and 3 tablespoons flour in small bowl. Stir into juices in skillet. Stir in coffee powder. Cook until thickened, stirring constantly. Adjust salt and pepper. Cook for 5 minutes longer. Serve over steak.

PEPPER STEAK

Yield:
4 servings

Utensil:
heavy saucepan

Approx Per Serving:
Cal 418
Prot 45 g
Carbo 13 g
Fiber 2 g
T Fat 20 g
Chol 128 mg
Sod 1551 mg

2 pounds round steak
2 tablespoons oil
1 clove of garlic, crushed
1/4 teaspoon ginger
1/4 teaspoon sugar
1/2 teaspoon salt
Pepper to taste
1/4 cup soy sauce
2 green bell peppers, chopped
1 medium onion, chopped
1 16-ounce can whole tomatoes
1 tablespoon cornstarch
1/2 cup water

Slice steak into strips. Brown in oil in heavy saucepan over low heat. Add garlic, ginger, sugar, salt and pepper; mix well. Cook, covered, for 20 minutes. Push to side of saucepan. Add soy sauce, green peppers and onion. Cook, covered, for 5 minutes; push to side of saucepan. Add tomatoes. Cook for 5 minutes. Add mixture of cornstarch and water; mix gently. Cook until thickened, stirring constantly.

BEEF STROGANOFF

Yield:
6 servings

Utensil:
covered skillet

Approx Per Serving:
Cal 680
Prot 61 g
Carbo 15 g
Fiber 1 g
T Fat 41 g
Chol 199 mg
Sod 1380 mg

1 medium onion, finely chopped
3 cloves of garlic, finely chopped
2 tablespoons butter
4 pounds round steak, thinly sliced
3 cans cream of mushroom soup
1/2 soup can water
1 cup sour cream
Salt and pepper to taste

Cook onion and garlic in butter in 12-inch covered skillet until transparent. Add steak. Cook over medium heat for 10 to 15 minutes or until evenly browned, stirring frequently. Add soup, water and sour cream; mix well. Stir in salt and pepper. Bring to a boil; reduce heat. Simmer, covered, for 1 hour, stirring every 15 minutes. Serve over rice, noodles or baked potatoes.

Swiss Bliss

Yield:
5 servings

Utensil:
9x13-inch pan

Approx Per Serving:
Cal 330
Prot 38 g
Carbo 19 g
Fiber 2 g
T Fat 12 g
Chol 102 mg
Sod 2115 mg

2 pounds 1-inch thick chuck steak
1 16-ounce can tomatoes
1 envelope onion soup mix
1 green onion, sliced
1 8-ounce can sliced mushrooms, drained
1/4 teaspoon salt
1/4 teaspoon pepper
3 tablespoons steak sauce
1 tablespoon cornstarch

Cut steak into 5 serving portions; place on buttered 20-inch piece of foil, overlapping portions. Drain tomatoes, reserving 1/2 cup juice. Chop tomatoes. Layer soup mix, green onion, tomatoes, mushrooms, salt and pepper over steak. Combine reserved tomato juice, steak sauce and cornstarch in bowl; mix well. Pour over steak and vegetables. Bring up edges of foil, sealing with double fold. Place in 9x13-inch baking pan. Bake at 375 degrees for 2 hours.

Company Casserole

Yield:
10 servings

Utensil:
9x13-inch dish

Approx Per Serving:
Cal 335
Prot 17 g
Carbo 23 g
Fiber 1 g
T Fat 20 g
Chol 63 mg
Sod 631 mg

1 pound ground beef
2 teaspoons butter
1 clove of garlic, finely chopped
2 8-ounce cans tomato sauce
1 tablespoon sugar
1 teaspoon salt
1 cup sour cream
3 ounces cream cheese, softened
1 medium onion, finely chopped
8 ounces uncooked medium noodles
1 cup shredded sharp Cheddar cheese

Brown ground beef in butter in saucepan, stirring until crumbly; drain. Add garlic, tomato sauce, sugar and salt; mix well. Simmer for 30 minutes. Combine sour cream, cream cheese and onion in mixer bowl; beat until well mixed. Cook noodles using package directions; drain. Layer cream cheese mixture, noodles and ground beef 1/2 at a time in 9x13-inch baking dish. Top with Cheddar cheese. Bake at 350 degrees for 20 minutes or until bubbly. May be prepared in advance and chilled or frozen until baking time.

Ground Beef and Cheese Casserole

Yield:
6 servings

Utensil:
2-quart dish

Approx Per Serving:
Cal 627
Prot 37 g
Carbo 40 g
Fiber 3 g
T Fat 36 g
Chol 118 mg
Sod 1171 mg

1½ pounds ground beef
1 tablespoon oil
2 8-ounce cans tomato sauce
1 6-ounce can tomato paste
½ cup shredded sharp Cheddar cheese
1 teaspoon Tabasco sauce
½ teaspoon oregano
½ cup water
1 teaspoon salt
1 8-ounce package uncooked noodles
1 cup cottage cheese
4 ounces cream cheese, softened
½ cup sour cream
¼ cup chopped green bell pepper
⅓ cup chopped onion

Brown ground beef in oil in skillet, stirring until crumbly; drain. Stir in tomato sauce, tomato paste, Cheddar cheese, Tabasco sauce, oregano, ½ cup water and salt; remove from heat. Cook noodles in boiling water in saucepan for 10 minutes; drain and rinse. Combine cottage cheese, cream cheese, sour cream, green pepper and onion in bowl; mix well. Layer half the noodles, all the cottage cheese mixture and remaining noodles in 2-quart baking dish. Spoon ground beef mixture over layers. Bake at 350 degrees for 30 minutes.

Mexican Hash

Yield:
6 servings

Utensil:
saucepan

Approx Per Serving:
Cal 371
Prot 27 g
Carbo 23 g
Fiber 2 g
T Fat 20 g
Chol 84 mg
Sod 422 mg

1½ pounds ground beef
1 16-ounce can tomatoes
½ green bell pepper, chopped
1 small onion, chopped
1 16-ounce can corn, drained
½ cup uncooked rice
Tabasco sauce to taste
½ cup shredded Cheddar cheese

Brown ground beef in saucepan, stirring until crumbly; drain. Add tomatoes, green pepper, onion, corn, rice and Tabasco sauce; mix well. Simmer until rice is tender. Spoon into baking dish. Sprinkle with cheese. Bake at 350 to 375 degrees until cheese melts.

Lasagna

Yield:
8 servings

Utensil:
9x13-inch dish

Approx Per Serving:
Cal 451
Prot 30 g
Carbo 33 g
Fiber 2 g
T Fat 22 g
Chol 84 mg
Sod 914 mg

1 cup chopped onion
1 clove of garlic, chopped
1 tablespoon oil
1 1/2 pounds ground beef
3/4 teaspoon rosemary
2 teaspoons salt
1 1/2 teaspoons pepper
1 32-ounce can tomatoes
1 6-ounce can tomato paste
8 ounces uncooked lasagna noodles
1 1/2 cups ricotta cheese
8 ounces mozzarella cheese, sliced

Sauté onion and garlic in oil in large skillet until tender. Add ground beef, rosemary, salt and pepper. Cook until beef is brown and crumbly; drain. Drain tomatoes, reserving juice. Add enough water to reserved juice to measure 2 1/4 cups. Add tomatoes, juice and tomato paste to ground beef; mix well. Simmer for 30 minutes. Cook noodles using package directions; drain. Spoon 1/3 of the sauce mixture into 9x13-inch baking dish. Layer noodles, ricotta cheese and remaining sauce 1/2 at a time in prepared dish. Top with mozzarella cheese. Bake at 350 degrees for 30 minutes.

Meatballs and Sauce

Yield:
8 servings

Utensil:
baking sheet

Approx Per Serving:
Cal 549
Prot 38 g
Carbo 40 g
Fiber 2 g
T Fat 27 g
Chol 142 mg
Sod 2028 mg

3 pounds ground beef
1 cup chopped onion
1 egg
1/2 cup bread crumbs
1/2 cup Parmesan cheese
1 teaspoon prepared horseradish
1 teaspoon salt
1 teaspoon pepper
2 12-ounce bottles of chili sauce
1 cup catsup
1 cup water
1 tablespoon Worcestershire sauce
1 tablespoon vinegar
2 tablespoons brown sugar
1 teaspoon dry mustard
1/4 teaspoon paprika
1/4 teaspoon chili powder
1/4 teaspoon red pepper

Combine ground beef, onion, egg, bread crumbs, cheese, horseradish, salt and pepper in bowl; mix well. Shape into balls. Place on baking sheet. Bake at 350 degrees for 15 minutes. Combine chili sauce, catsup, water, Worcestershire sauce, vinegar, brown sugar, dry mustard, paprika, chili powder and red pepper in saucepan; mix well. Add meatballs. Simmer for 20 minutes.

MEAT LOAF

Yield:
6 servings

Utensil:
loaf pan

Approx Per Serving:
Cal 410
Prot 36 g
Carbo 38 g
Fiber 2 g
T Fat 13 g
Chol 157 mg
Sod 2107 mg

2 pounds ground round
1 envelope onion soup mix
3/4 cup catsup
2 eggs
1 1/2 cups bread crumbs
1/4 cup warm water
1 8-ounce can tomato sauce

Combine ground round, soup mix, catsup, eggs, bread crumbs and water in bowl; mix well. Shape into loaf. Place in loaf pan. Bake at 350 degrees for 30 minutes. Pour tomato sauce over top. Bake for 30 minutes longer. Remove to serving plate; slice to serve

PIZZA MUFFINS

Yield:
8 servings

Utensil:
muffin pan

Approx Per Serving:
Cal 306
Prot 17 g
Carbo 23 g
Fiber 1 g
T Fat 16 g
Chol 50 mg
Sod 838 mg

1 pound ground beef
2 tablespoons minced onion
Chopped garlic to taste
1 cup barbecue sauce
2 cans biscuits
1 cup shredded mozzarella cheese

Brown ground beef in medium skillet, stirring until crumbly; drain. Add onion, garlic and barbecue sauce; mix well. Simmer for 5 minutes. Roll biscuits thin on floured surface. Fit into muffin cups. Spoon beef mixture into cups. Top with cheese. Bake at 350 degrees for 8 to 10 minutes or just until biscuits are brown.

Hamburger Pie

Yield:
6 servings

Utensil:
1 1/2-quart dish

Approx Per Serving:
Cal 413
Prot 22 g
Carbo 41 g
Fiber 4 g
T Fat 19 g
Chol 97 mg
Sod 1548 mg

1 medium onion, chopped
1 tablespoon oil
1 pound ground beef
3/4 tablespoon salt
Pepper to taste
1 16-ounce can cut green beans, drained
1 can tomato soup
5 medium potatoes, peeled, chopped
1/2 cup warm milk
1 egg, beaten
1/2 cup shredded American cheese

Sauté onion in oil in skillet until tender but not brown. Add ground beef, 3/4 tablespoon salt and pepper. Cook until ground beef is lightly browned and crumbly; drain. Add beans and soup; mix well. Spoon into 1 1/2-quart baking dish. Cook potatoes in water to cover in saucepan until tender; drain. Mash with milk, egg and salt and pepper to taste. Spoon in mounds over casserole. Sprinkle with cheese. Bake at 350 degrees for 25 to 30 minutes or until light brown.

Italian Meat Pie

Yield:
6 servings

Utensil:
quiche dish

Approx Per Serving:
Cal 569
Prot 41 g
Carbo 24 g
Fiber 4 g
T Fat 34 g
Chol 159 mg
Sod 1064 mg

1 1/2 pounds lean ground beef
3/4 cup oats
1 cup spaghetti sauce
1 egg, beaten
1/4 teaspoon garlic powder
2 teaspoons oregano
1/4 cup Parmesan cheese
1/2 teaspoon salt
1 10-ounce package frozen chopped spinach, cooked, drained
1 16-ounce can peeled tomatoes, drained, sliced
1/2 cup spaghetti sauce
1/4 cup Parmesan cheese
12 ounces mozzarella cheese, shredded

Brown ground beef in medium skillet, stirring until crumbly; drain. Add oats, 1 cup spaghetti sauce, egg, garlic powder, oregano, 1/4 cup Parmesan cheese and salt; mix well. Spread half the mixture in 10-inch quiche dish. Layer spinach, tomatoes, 1/2 cup spaghetti sauce and remaining meat sauce in prepared dish. Top with remaining 1/4 cup Parmesan cheese and mozzarella cheese. Bake at 350 degrees for 30 minutes.

Spaghetti Pie

Yield:
6 servings

Utensil:
pie plate

Approx Per Serving:
Cal 441
Prot 29 g
Carbo 32 g
Fiber 3 g
T Fat 22 g
Chol 147 mg
Sod 610 mg

6 ounces uncooked spaghetti
2 tablespoons butter
1/3 cup Parmesan cheese
2 eggs, beaten
1 cup cottage cheese
1 pound ground beef
1/4 cup chopped green bell pepper
1/2 cup chopped onion
1 8-ounce can tomatoes, cut up
1 6-ounce can tomato paste
1 teaspoon sugar
1 teaspoon oregano
1/2 teaspoon garlic salt
1/2 cup shredded mozzarella cheese

Cook spaghetti using package directions; drain. Stir in butter, Parmesan cheese and eggs. Place in 10-inch pie plate, shaping to form crust. Spread with cottage cheese. Cook ground beef with green pepper and onion in skillet, stirring until ground beef is crumbly; drain. Add undrained tomatoes, tomato paste, sugar, oregano and garlic salt; mix well. Cook until heated through. Spoon into spaghetti crust. Bake at 350 degrees for 20 minutes. Sprinkle with mozzarella cheese. Bake for 5 minutes longer or until cheese melts.

Fried Rice

Yield:
4 servings

Utensil:
skillet

Approx Per Serving:
Cal 405
Prot 25 g
Carbo 39 g
Fiber 2 g
T Fat 16 g
Chol 74 mg
Sod 1650 mg

1 pound ground beef
1 medium onion, chopped
2 large carrots, grated
1 1/2 teaspoons salt
1/2 teaspoon coarsely ground pepper
2 1/2 cups cooked rice
3 tablespoons soy sauce

Brown ground beef with onion, carrots, salt and pepper in 10-inch skillet, stirring until ground beef is crumbly. Simmer for 5 to 10 minutes. Stir in rice and soy sauce. Simmer for 5 minutes longer.

Spanish Rice

Yield:
8 servings

Utensil:
Crock•Pot

Approx Per Serving:
Cal 353
Prot 24 g
Carbo 27 g
Fiber 3 g
T Fat 17 g
Chol 74 mg
Sod 756 mg

2 pounds ground beef
2 cups chopped onions
2 pounds tomatoes, chopped
1 cup uncooked rice
2½ teaspoons chili powder
1 teaspoon Worcestershire sauce
2½ teaspoons salt

Brown ground beef in medium skillet, stirring until crumbly; drain. Combine with onions, tomatoes, rice, chili powder, Worcestershire sauce and salt in Crock•Pot; mix well. Cook on Low for 6 hours or until rice is tender.

Spaghetti Sauce for a Crowd

Yield:
28 servings

Utensil:
stockpot

Approx Per Serving:
Cal 247
Prot 20 g
Carbo 11 g
Fiber 3 g
T Fat 14 g
Chol 64 mg
Sod 240 mg

6 pounds ground beef
6 medium onions, chopped
6 green bell peppers, chopped
¼ cup garlic powder
¼ cup oregano
6 bay leaves
Salt to taste
4 16-ounce cans tomatoes
1 12-ounce can tomato paste
2 8-ounce cans mushroom stems and pieces, drained

Brown ground beef in stockpot, stirring until crumbly; drain. Add onions and green peppers. Simmer until vegetables are tender. Add garlic powder, oregano, bay leaves and salt; mix well. Drain tomatoes, reserving juice. Blend reserved juice with tomato paste in bowl. Add to sauce. Stir in tomatoes and mushrooms. Simmer for 2 hours, stirring frequently. Discard bay leaves. Serve over hot cooked spaghetti.

Ham Supper Casserole ≈MW≈

Yield:
6 servings

Utensil:
2-quart dish

Approx Per Serving:
Cal 252
Prot 15 g
Carbo 8 g
Fiber 1 g
T Fat 18 g
Chol 50 mg
Sod 1288 mg

1 can cream of chicken soup
1/2 cup sour cream
1 16-ounce can cut green beans, drained
2 cups chopped cooked ham
1/2 cup chopped American cheese

Mix soup and sour cream in 2-quart glass dish. Add beans and ham; mix well. Microwave on Medium-High for 12 to 14 minutes or until bubbly. Sprinkle with American cheese. Let stand, covered, for 5 minutes.

Rolled Lasagna

Yield:
6 servings

Utensil:
9x13-inch dish

Approx Per Serving:
Cal 490
Prot 24 g
Carbo 57 g
Fiber 2 g
T Fat 18 g
Chol 51 mg
Sod 812 mg

12 ounces uncooked lasagna noodles
1 cup chopped ham
1 cup chopped spinach
3/4 cup ricotta cheese
3/4 cup shredded mozzarella cheese
1 16-ounce jar spaghetti sauce

Cook noodles using package directions; drain. Combine ham, spinach and cheeses in small bowl; mix well. Spread on noodles; roll to enclose filling. Arrange rolls in 9x13-inch baking dish. Pour spaghetti sauce over rolls. Bake at 350 degrees for 20 minutes. Garnish with Parmesan cheese if desired.

Stromboli

Yield:
6 servings

Utensil:
baking sheet

Approx Per Serving:
Cal 452
Prot 22 g
Carbo 22 g
Fiber 1 g
T Fat 32 g
Chol 42 mg
Sod 1,477 mg

1 loaf frozen bread dough, thawed
1 tablespoon olive oil
Garlic powder and oregano to taste
1 8-ounce package sliced pepperoni
1 6-ounce can sliced mushrooms, drained
8 ounces provolone cheese, sliced
Garlic salt to taste
1/4 cup Parmesan cheese

Let dough rise using package directions. Press over lightly oiled baking sheet. Brush with olive oil. Sprinkle with garlic powder and oregano. Layer with pepperoni, mushrooms and provolone cheese. Roll as for jelly roll. Place seam side down on baking sheet. Sprinkle with garlic salt and Parmesan cheese. Bake at 400 degrees for 15 to 20 minutes or until brown. Slice stromboli. Serve sliced with spaghetti sauce.

Nutritional information for this recipe does not include spaghetti sauce.

Pork Chop Casserole

Yield:
4 servings

Utensil:
9x13-inch dish

Approx Per Serving:
Cal 335
Prot 35 g
Carbo 23 g
Fiber 1 g
T Fat 11 g
Chol 98 mg
Sod 312 mg

4 pork chops
Salt and pepper to taste
1/2 cup uncooked rice
1/2 cup chopped onion
4 onion slices
4 tomato slices
4 green bell pepper rings
Marjoram to taste
1 can consommé

Sprinkle pork chops with salt and pepper. Brown pork chops on both sides in skillet. Sprinkle rice and chopped onion in greased 9x13-inch baking dish. Arrange pork chops over rice. Top each with 1 onion slice, 1 tomato slice and 1 pepper ring. Sprinkle with salt. Add marjoram and consommé to skillet, stirring to deglaze. Bring to a boil. Pour into baking dish. Bake, covered with foil, at 350 degrees for 1 hour.

Cheese-Stuffed Pork

Yield:
2 servings

Utensil:
skillet

Approx Per Serving:
Cal 556
Prot 45 g
Carbo 13 g
Fiber 2 g
T Fat 35 g
Chol 231 mg
Sod 860 mg

2 thick pork chops
1 3-ounce can chopped mushrooms
1/2 cup chopped Swiss cheese
2 tablespoons chopped parsley
1/4 teaspoon salt
1/4 cup fine dry bread crumbs
1/8 teaspoon salt
Pepper to taste
1 egg, beaten
2 tablespoons oil

Trim pork chops. Cut pocket in each pork chop. Drain mushrooms, reserving liquid. Combine mushrooms, cheese, parsley and 1/4 teaspoon salt in bowl; mix well. Spoon into pockets in pork chops; secure with wooden picks and butcher's twine. Combine bread crumbs, 1/8 teaspoon salt and pepper in bowl; mix well. Dip pork chops in egg; coat with crumb mixture. Brown on both sides in oil in skillet over low heat. Add enough water to reserved mushroom liquid to measure 1/2 cup. Pour over pork chops. Simmer, covered, for 1 hour.

Italian Pork Chops

Yield:
6 servings

Utensil:
9x13-inch dish

Approx Per Serving:
Cal 371
Prot 41 g
Carbo 9 g
Fiber 2 g
T Fat 18 g
Chol 127 mg
Sod 676 mg

6 pork chops
1 onion, sliced
1 green bell pepper, cut into strips
2 8-ounce cans tomato sauce
1 8-ounce package sliced mozzarella cheese

Brown pork chops on both sides in skillet. Place in single layer in 9x13-inch baking dish. Top each with onion slice and green pepper strips. Pour tomato sauce over top. Bake at 350 degrees for 30 to 45 minutes or until pork chops are tender. Top with cheese. Bake until cheese melts.

Sweet and Sour Spareribs

Yield:
8 servings

Utensil:
roasting pan

Approx Per Serving:
Cal 807
Prot 55 g
Carbo 16 g
Fiber 1 g
T Fat 57 g
Chol 226 mg
Sod 776 mg

1 20-ounce can pineapple chunks
1/4 cup soy sauce
1 tablespoon teriyaki sauce
Ginger and pepper to taste
2 or 3 cloves of garlic, minced
5 pounds spareribs

Drain pineapple, reserving juice. Combine reserved juice, soy sauce, teriyaki sauce, ginger, pepper and garlic in bowl; mix well. Drizzle half the mixture over spareribs in roasting pan. Bake at 350 degrees for 30 minutes, turning ribs over and basting after 15 minutes. Drain pan juices into bowl with remaining basting sauce; mix well. Place spareribs on rack in broiler pan. Broil for 45 minutes or until tender, basting with sauce and turning ribs to glaze well. Add pineapple chunks. Broil for 5 minutes longer.

Bacon and Cheddar Quiche

Yield:
6 servings

Utensil:
pie plate

Approx Per Serving:
Cal 384
Prot 16 g
Carbo 18 g
Fiber 10 g
T Fat 27 g
Chol 179 mg
Sod 718 mg

1 unbaked 10-inch pie shell
10 slices bacon
3/4 medium onion, chopped
1 1/2 cups milk
1 cup shredded Cheddar cheese
4 eggs
2 teaspoons parsley flakes
1/4 teaspoon sugar
1/8 teaspoon nutmeg
1/2 teaspoon salt
1/4 teaspoon pepper
Red pepper to taste

Bake pie shell at 350 degrees for 5 minutes. Cook bacon in skillet until crisp. Remove and crumble bacon, reserving 2 teaspoons drippings. Sauté onion in reserved drippings in skillet. Combine with milk, cheese, eggs, bacon, parsley, sugar, nutmeg, salt, pepper and red pepper in bowl; mix well. Pour into prepared pie shell. Reduce oven temperature to 325 degrees. Bake for 40 minutes or until golden brown and set.

SAUSAGE CASSEROLE

Yield:
8 servings

Utensil:
9x13-inch dish

Approx Per Serving:
Cal 274
Prot 13 g
Carbo 7 g
Fiber <1 g
T Fat 21 g
Chol 197 mg
Sod 384 mg

1 pound sausage
3 slices bread, crumbled
1 cup shredded sharp Cheddar cheese
6 eggs, beaten
1 cup milk
Salt to taste
Pepper to taste

Cook sausage in skillet, stirring until crumbly; drain. Layer bread crumbs, sausage and cheese in 9x13-inch baking dish. Combine eggs, milk, salt and pepper in bowl; mix well. Pour over layers. Bake at 350 degrees for 30 to 40 minutes or until set. May prepare in advance and chill overnight.

HAWAIIAN SMOKES

Yield:
6 servings

Utensil:
9x13-inch dish

Approx Per Serving:
Cal 515
Prot 12 g
Carbo 41 g
Fiber 3 g
T Fat 34 g
Chol 49 mg
Sod 588 mg

2 pounds smoked sausage, sliced
1 16-ounce can sweet potatoes, drained, sliced 1/2 inch thick
1/2 cup cashews
1 16-ounce can pineapple chunks, drained
1 6-ounce can frozen orange juice concentrate, thawed

Combine sausage, sweet potatoes, cashews and pineapple in bowl; mix gently. Spoon into 9x13-inch baking dish. Spoon orange juice concentrate over top. Bake at 350 degrees for 20 to 30 minutes or until heated through.

Italian Delight

Yield:
6 servings

Utensil:
large saucepan

Approx Per Serving:
Cal 131
Prot 5 g
Carbo 21 g
Fiber 5 g
T Fat 5 g
Chol 3 mg
Sod 527 mg

1 clove of garlic
1 tablespoon oil
2 6-ounce cans tomato paste
2 8-ounce cans tomato sauce
2 cups water
1 teaspoon basil
1 teaspoon oregano
Salt to taste
1 tablespoon chopped parsley
1 bay leaf
2 pounds hot Italian sausage, sliced
8 ounces fresh mushrooms, sliced
3 green bell peppers, chopped

Sauté garlic in oil in large saucepan. Discard garlic. Add tomato paste, tomato sauce and water; mix well. Stir in basil, oregano, salt, parsley and bay leaf. Add sausage, mushrooms and green peppers. Simmer for 3 hours. Discard bay leaf. Serve on ranch bread or hard rolls.

Overnight Company Breakfast

Yield:
8 servings

Utensil:
9x16-inch dish

Approx Per Serving:
Cal 435
Prot 17 g
Carbo 17 g
Fiber 1 g
T Fat 33 g
Chol 230 mg
Sod 821 mg

1 pound sausage
8 slices bread
2 tablespoons butter, softened
1 1/2 cups shredded longhorn cheese
6 eggs
2 cups half and half
1 teaspoon dry mustard
1 teaspoon salt

Brown sausage in skillet, stirring until crumbly; drain. Spread bread with butter; cut into cubes. Layer bread, sausage and cheese in 9x16-inch baking dish. Combine eggs, half and half, dry mustard and salt in bowl; mix well. Pour over layers. Chill, covered, overnight. Bake at 350 degrees for 30 minutes or until brown and set.

Sausage and Peppers

Yield:
4 servings

Utensil:
skillet

Approx Per Serving:
Cal 135
Prot 2 g
Carbo 8 g
Fiber 2 g
T Fat 10 g
Chol 5 mg
Sod 50 mg

1 large green bell pepper
1 large red bell pepper
1 large yellow bell pepper
8 ounces lean mild link sausage
8 ounces lean hot link sausage
2 tablespoons oil
1 large Spanish onion, cut into 8 wedges
4 cloves of garlic
6 leaves fresh basil
Salt to taste
Red pepper to taste
1/4 cup red wine
Pepper to taste

Cut peppers into 1/2-inch strips. Blanch in boiling water in saucepan for 1 1/2 minutes. Drain and rinse with cold water. Cut thin sausages into 2 to 3-inch pieces or thick sausages into 1/2-inch slices. Stir-fry in hot oil in skillet or wok until brown. Add onion. Stir-fry until almost transparent. Add peppers and garlic. Stir-fry until color of peppers deepens. Add basil, salt and red pepper; mix well. Stir in wine. Cook, covered, for 1 minute. Discard garlic. Season with pepper to taste.

Hot Sausage on Italian Buns

Yield:
8 servings

Utensil:
saucepan

Approx Per Serving:
Cal 279
Prot 9 g
Carbo 47 g
Fiber 5 g
T Fat 8 g
Chol 3 mg
Sod 492 mg

3 pounds hot or mild sausage
8 Italian rolls
1 large green bell pepper, sliced lengthwise
1 medium onion, sliced
1 clove of garlic, chopped
1/4 teaspoon thyme
6 jalapeño peppers, chopped
1/4 teaspoon oregano
2 tablespoons olive oil
1 20-ounce can whole tomatoes
1 12-ounce can tomato paste

Cut sausage to length of Italian rolls. Cook in 2 to 3 inches of water in 3-quart saucepan for 35 to 40 minutes. Drain 3/4 of the water. Sauté green pepper, onion, garlic, thyme, jalapeño peppers and oregano in olive oil in skillet. Add sautéed vegetables, tomatoes and tomato paste to sausage in saucepan. Simmer for 20 to 30 minutes or to desired consistency. Serve on rolls.

Baked Parmesan Chicken

Yield:
6 servings

Utensil:
9x13-inch pan

Approx Per Serving:
Cal 504
Prot 37 g
Carbo 12 g
Fiber 1 g
T Fat 34 g
Chol 168 mg
Sod 496 mg

1 3-pound chicken, cut up
1 cup bread crumbs
1/3 cup Parmesan cheese
1/4 teaspoon oregano
Salt and pepper to taste
Garlic powder to taste
3/4 cup melted butter

Rinse chicken; pat dry. Combine crumbs, cheese, oregano, salt, pepper and garlic powder in shallow bowl; mix well. Dip chicken in melted butter in bowl; coat with crumbs. Arrange in single layer in 9x13-inch baking pan. Sprinkle with remaining crumbs; drizzle with remaining melted butter. Bake at 350 degrees for 55 minutes or until tender and brown. May cover with foil if necessary to prevent excessive browning. May use chicken breasts if preferred.

Champagne Chicken

Yield:
4 servings

Utensil:
skillet

Approx Per Serving:
Cal 278
Prot 24 g
Carbo 6 g
Fiber <1 g
T Fat 14 g
Chol 84 mg
Sod 394 mg

4 chicken breast filets
2 tablespoons flour
1/2 teaspoon salt
1/4 teaspoon pepper
2 tablespoons butter
1 tablespoon olive oil
3/4 cup Champagne
1/4 cup sliced fresh mushrooms
1/2 cup half and half

Rinse chicken; pat dry. Combine flour, salt and pepper in shallow bowl; mix well. Coat chicken with flour mixture. Sauté in butter and olive oil in skillet for 10 minutes, turning once. Add Champagne. Cook over medium heat for 12 to 15 minutes or until chicken is tender; remove to heated platter. Add mushrooms and half and half to skillet. Cook over low heat just until thickened, stirring constantly. Add chicken. Cook until heated through. Serve immediately. May serve over hot cooked rice or noodles. May substitute wine for Champagne.

Chicken Breasts Diane ≈MW≈

Yield:
4 servings

Utensil:
8x10-inch dish

Approx Per Serving:
Cal 244
Prot 24 g
Carbo 4 g
Fiber <1 g
T Fat 14 g
Chol 73 mg
Sod 461 mg

4 chicken breasts, boned
1/2 teaspoon salt
1/2 teaspoon pepper
2 tablespoons butter
2 tablespoons olive oil
3 tablespoons chopped fresh chives
Juice of 1/2 lime
2 tablespoons Brandy
3 tablespoons chopped parsley
2 teaspoons Dijon mustard
1/4 cup chicken broth

Rinse chicken; pat dry. Place between waxed paper; pound slightly. Sprinkle with salt and pepper. Microwave butter in 8x10-inch glass dish until melted. Add olive oil; mix well. Place chicken in olive oil mixture, turning to coat. Microwave on High for 3 minutes. Let stand for 1 minute. Turn chicken. Microwave for 3 minutes longer or until chicken is tender. Do not overcook. Drain, reserving pan drippings. Mix chives, lime juice, Brandy, parsley and mustard in small glass bowl. Microwave on High for 1 minute. Add reserved pan drippings and broth; mix well. Pour over chicken in serving dish. Serve with hot cooked noodles.

Breast of Chicken Magnifique

Yield:
8 servings

Utensil:
skillet

Approx Per Serving:
Cal 407
Prot 27 g
Carbo 34 g
Fiber 2 g
T Fat 18 g
Chol 78 mg
Sod 712 mg

4 whole chicken breasts
1/4 cup butter
2 cups sliced mushrooms
2 cans cream of chicken soup
1 large clove of garlic, crushed
1/4 teaspoon thyme
1/8 teaspoon rosemary, crushed
2/3 cup half and half
4 cups cooked rice
1/2 cup slivered almonds

Rinse chicken; pat dry. Brown in butter in large skillet; remove to warm platter. Sauté mushrooms in pan drippings in skillet until tender. Stir in soup, garlic, thyme and rosemary. Add chicken. Cook, covered, over low heat for 45 minutes. Stir in half and half. Cook until heated through. Serve over hot cooked rice. Sprinkle with almonds.

Chicken Breasts Supreme

Yield:
8 servings

Utensil:
9x13-inch dish

Approx Per Serving:
Cal 393
Prot 29 g
Carbo 11 g
Fiber <1 g
T Fat 25 g
Chol 81 mg
Sod 1610 mg

8 chicken breast filets
2 2-ounce jars chipped beef
8 slices bacon
3 cans cream of mushroom soup
2 cups sour cream

Rinse chicken filets; pat dry. Spread chipped beef in greased 9x13-inch baking dish. Wrap each chicken filet with 1 bacon slice. Arrange over chipped beef. Mix soup and sour cream in bowl. Pour over chicken. Bake at 275 degrees for 3 hours.

Crunchy Chicken Casserole

Yield:
8 servings

Utensil:
casserole

Approx Per Serving:
Cal 408
Prot 31 g
Carbo 16 g
Fiber 1 g
T Fat 24 g
Chol 93 mg
Sod 744 mg

1/4 cup margarine
1/4 cup flour
1 14-ounce can chicken broth
2 cups shredded Cheddar cheese
2 large carrots, sliced, cooked
4 cups chopped cooked chicken
1 2-ounce jar chopped pimento
2 tablespoons margarine
4 ounces herb-seasoned stuffing mix

Melt 1/4 cup butter in saucepan. Add flour, mixing until smooth. Stir in chicken broth. Cook until thickened, stirring constantly. Reduce heat. Add cheese, carrots, chicken and pimento; mix well. Spoon into 2-quart casserole. Mix remaining 2 tablespoons margarine and stuffing mix in small bowl. Sprinkle over casserole. Bake at 375 degrees for 30 minutes.

Poultry

Chicken Chow Mein

Yield:
6 servings

Utensil:
wok

Approx Per Serving:
Cal 666
Prot 46 g
Carbo 62 g
Fiber 8 g
T Fat 27 g
Chol 110 mg
Sod 2002 mg

2 quarts water
3 pounds chicken, coarsely chopped
4 large onions, chopped
1 bunch celery, sliced
1 head Napa cabbage, coarsely chopped
8 ounces bean sprouts
1 tablespoon salt
2 tablespoons cornstarch
1 pound chow mein noodles

Heat water in wok. Add chicken, onions, celery, cabbage, bean sprouts and salt; mix well. Bring to a boil. Cook over high heat for 10 minutes. Stir in mixture of cornstarch dissolved in small amount of cold water. Cook until thickened, stirring constantly. Place chow mein noodles on platter. Top with chicken mixture.

Chicken Cordon Bleu

Yield:
8 servings

Utensil:
9x13-inch dish

Approx Per Serving:
Cal 292
Prot 35 g
Carbo 6 g
Fiber <1 g
T Fat 14 g
Chol 95 mg
Sod 726 mg

8 chicken breast filets
8 slices ham
8 slices Swiss cheese
1 can cream of chicken soup
1 soup can milk

Rinse chicken; pat dry. Pound between waxed paper until thin. Place 1 ham slice and 1 cheese slice on each filet. Roll to enclose filling; secure with toothpick. Arrange in 9x13-inch baking dish. Mix soup and milk in bowl. Pour over chicken. Bake at 350 degrees for 45 minutes or until chicken is tender.

Chicken Creole

Yield:
4 servings

Utensil:
skillet

Approx Per Serving:
Cal 276
Prot 25 g
Carbo 10 g
Fiber 2 g
T Fat 15 g
Chol 57 mg
Sod 785 mg

2 whole chicken breasts, boned, skinned
1/2 teaspoon salt
1/4 teaspoon pepper
4 tablespoons oil
1 cup finely chopped onion
1/2 cup finely chopped celery
1/2 cup finely chopped green bell pepper
2 cloves of garlic, minced
1 15-ounce can whole peeled tomatoes
1/2 cup water
1 1/2 teaspoons paprika
1/2 teaspoon salt
1 bay leaf
1 teaspoon cornstarch
1 tablespoon cold water

Rinse chicken; pat dry. Cut into 1-inch pieces. Sprinkle with salt and pepper. Heat 1 tablespoon oil in large skillet. Add chicken. Sauté over medium-high heat for 5 minutes or until chicken is opaque and golden brown; remove with slotted spoon. Add remaining 3 tablespoons oil to skillet. Add onion, celery, green pepper and garlic. Sauté until vegetables are tender. Stir in undrained tomatoes; break apart with spoon. Stir in 1/2 cup water, paprika, salt and bay leaf. Bring to a boil. Simmer, covered, over medium-low heat for 10 minutes. Stir in chicken. Blend cornstarch with 1 tablespoon cold water. Stir into chicken mixture. Simmer, uncovered, over low heat for 10 to 15 minutes or until thickened, stirring constantly. Remove bay leaf.

Creole cooking blends many worlds: the French delicacy of touch and sense of economy; the Spanish taste for special foods and tendency to mix poultry and seafood and serve it over rice; the Choctaw thickening agent known as filé; and the African well-seasoned and patiently tended one-pot meal.

Chicken-Filled Biscuit Dumplings

Yield:
5 servings

Utensil:
saucepan

Approx Per Serving:
Cal 406
Prot 28 g
Carbo 30 g
Fiber 2 g
T Fat 18 g
Chol 78 mg
Sod 1536 mg

1 can cream of chicken soup
1 can golden mushroom soup
1¼ cups water
½ cup chopped green bell pepper
2 tablespoons chopped onion
¼ cup chopped celery
3 5-ounce cans boned chicken
2 tablespoons chopped onion
1 teaspoon parsley flakes
⅛ teaspoon pepper
1 10-count can buttermilk biscuits

Combine soups, water, green pepper and 2 tablespoons onion in 3-quart saucepan. Cook until bubbly, stirring occasionally. Combine celery, chicken, remaining 2 tablespoons onion, parsley and pepper in bowl; mix well. Separate biscuits; roll each biscuit into 4-inch circle on floured surface. Place ¼ cup chicken mixture on each circle. Wrap biscuit to enclose filling; seal edges. Place dumplings sealed side down in bubbling soup mixture; spoon soup mixture over dumplings. Cook, tightly covered, over medium heat for 15 to 20 minutes or until dumplings test done.

Old-Fashioned Chicken and Dumplings

Yield:
6 servings

Utensil:
saucepan

Approx Per Serving:
Cal 372
Prot 37 g
Carbo 33 g
Fiber 2 g
T Fat 9 g
Chol 101 mg
Sod 1613 mg

1 3-pound chicken, cut up
1 medium onion, cut into halves
1 tablespoon salt
¼ teaspoon pepper
7 cups water
2 cups self-rising flour
¼ teaspoon thyme
½ cup ice water

Rinse chicken; pat dry. Combine chicken, onion, salt, pepper and 7 cups water in large saucepan; mix well. Bring to a boil; reduce heat. Simmer, covered, for 2 hours. Remove chicken; let stand until cool. Bone and cut into bite-sized pieces. Return to broth. Bring to a boil. Combine flour, thyme and enough ice water in bowl to make soft dough. Knead on floured surface for 30 seconds. Roll ⅛ inch thick. Cut into ½x4-inch strips. Drop into boiling broth. Reduce heat. Simmer, covered, for 35 to 40 minutes or until dumplings test done.

Chicken Divan

Yield:
6 servings

Utensil:
8x12-inch dish

Approx Per Serving:
Cal 602
Prot 34 g
Carbo 39 g
Fiber 4 g
T Fat 35 g
Chol 98 mg
Sod 862 mg

2 10-ounce packages frozen broccoli spears
6 chicken breast filets
1 cup flour
2 tablespoons oil
1 can cream of chicken soup
1/2 cup mayonnaise
1/2 cup milk
1 teaspoon lemon juice
1/2 teaspoon curry powder
1 cup shredded Cheddar cheese
1 cup bread crumbs
2 tablespoons melted butter

Cook broccoli using package directions until tender-crisp; drain. Arrange in buttered 8x12-inch baking dish. Rinse chicken; pat dry. Coat chicken with flour. Brown lightly in oil in skillet. Arrange over broccoli. Mix soup, mayonnaise, milk, lemon juice and curry powder in bowl. Pour over chicken; sprinkle with cheese. Mix bread crumbs and melted butter in bowl. Sprinkle over cheese. Bake at 350 degrees for 30 minutes or until chicken is tender.

Cheesy Chicken Divan

Yield:
12 servings

Utensil:
3-quart casserole

Approx Per Serving:
Cal 481
Prot 34 g
Carbo 10 g
Fiber 2 g
T Fat 34 g
Chol 105 mg
Sod 1020 mg

6 whole chicken breasts, boned
1 medium onion, cut into quarters
2 stalks celery
2 10-ounce packages frozen broccoli
1 cup Parmesan cheese
2 cans cream of chicken soup
1 cup shredded sharp Cheddar cheese
1 cup sour cream
1 cup mayonnaise
1 tablespoon lemon juice
1 teaspoon curry powder
Salt and pepper to taste
Paprika to taste
3 tablespoons butter

Rinse chicken; pat dry. Cook chicken with onion and celery in water to cover in large saucepan until tender; drain. Cook broccoli using package directions; drain. Arrange in 3-quart casserole; sprinkle with 1/3 of the Parmesan cheese. Mix soup, Cheddar cheese, sour cream, mayonnaise, lemon juice, curry powder, salt and pepper in bowl. Layer chicken, half the remaining Parmesan cheese, soup mixture and remaining Parmesan cheese over broccoli. Sprinkle with paprika; dot with butter. Bake at 350 degrees for 30 to 40 minutes or until bubbly.

Chicken Jubilee

Yield:
8 servings

Utensil:
9x13-inch dish

Approx Per Serving:
Cal 305
Prot 25 g
Carbo 16 g
Fiber 4 g
T Fat 17 g
Chol 59 mg
Sod 374 mg

4 cups chopped cooked chicken
3/4 cup cooked rice
1 cup chopped mushrooms
1 onion, chopped
1 cup chopped celery
1 cup chopped pimento
1 cup slivered almonds
1 green bell pepper, chopped
1 can cream of mushroom soup

Combine chicken, rice, mushrooms, onion, celery, pimento, almonds and green pepper in bowl; mix well. Add soup; mix well. Pour into greased 9x13-inch baking dish. Bake at 350 degrees for 1 hour. May substitute turkey for chicken if preferred.

Chicken Lasagna

Yield:
4 servings

Utensil:
9x13-inch dish

Approx Per Serving:
Cal 554
Prot 40 g
Carbo 38 g
Fiber 3 g
T Fat 27 g
Chol 134 mg
Sod 728 mg

1 onion, chopped
1/2 cup sliced mushrooms
1/2 teaspoon basil
1 teaspoon oregano
Salt and pepper to taste
1 20-ounce can tomatoes, crushed
2 1/2 cups chopped cooked chicken
3 tablespoons butter
3 tablespoons flour
1 10-ounce can chicken broth
1/2 cup half and half
10 lasagna noodles, cooked
1 cup shredded mozzarella cheese
1/2 cup ricotta cheese

Sauté onion in large skillet sprayed with nonstick cooking spray until tender. Add mushrooms, basil, oregano, salt and pepper; mix well. Cook for 5 to 6 minutes or until mushrooms are tender, stirring constantly. Add tomatoes. Bring to a simmer; stir in chicken. Simmer until heated through, stirring constantly. Melt butter in saucepan. Stir in flour. Cook for 2 to 3 minutes. Add broth; mix well. Cook until thickened, stirring constantly. Stir in half and half. Layer noodles, chicken mixture, white sauce, mozzarella cheese and ricotta cheese 1/3 at a time in 9x13-inch baking dish. Bake at 350 degrees for 20 to 25 minutes or until hot and bubbly.

Chicken and Spinach Bake

Yield:
4 servings

Utensil:
2-quart dish

Approx Per Serving:
Cal 409
Prot 37 g
Carbo 24 g
Fiber 3 g
T Fat 19 g
Chol 145 mg
Sod 892 mg

1 can chicken noodle soup
4 chicken breast filets
1/2 cup Italian bread crumbs
1/2 cup sour cream
1 egg
1 clove of garlic, minced
1 tablespoon flour
1/3 cup chopped onion
1 10-ounce package frozen spinach, thawed, drained
4 ounces Swiss cheese, cut into strips

Drain soup, reserving broth and noodles. Rinse chicken; pat dry. Dip in reserved soup broth; coat with bread crumbs. Combine sour cream, egg, garlic and flour in bowl; mix well. Add reserved noodles, onion, spinach and half the cheese; mix well. Spread in 2-quart baking dish. Arrange chicken over top; sprinkle with remaining bread crumbs. Bake at 350 degrees for 35 minutes. Add remaining cheese. Bake for 10 to 15 minutes longer or until cheese is melted.

Chicken Pie

Yield:
6 servings

Utensil:
9x13-inch dish

Approx Per Serving:
Cal 642
Prot 39 g
Carbo 35 g
Fiber 1 g
T Fat 38 g
Chol 246 mg
Sod 1820 mg

2 1/2 pounds chicken, cooked, skinned, boned
Salt and pepper to taste
3 hard-boiled eggs, sliced
1 8-ounce can green peas
1/2 cup butter
2 cups chicken broth
1 can cream of celery soup
1 can cream of mushroom soup
1 1/2 cups baking mix
1 1/4 cups milk

Place chicken in 9x13-inch baking dish sprayed with nonstick cooking spray. Sprinkle with salt and pepper. Layer eggs and peas over chicken. Combine butter, broth and soups in medium saucepan; mix well. Cook until heated through, stirring constantly. Pour over chicken. Mix baking mix and milk in small bowl until smooth. Spoon over top. Bake at 350 degrees for 1 hour or until golden brown.

Chicken Spaghetti

Yield:
6 servings

Utensil:
saucepan

Approx Per Serving:
Cal 449
Prot 24 g
Carbo 52 g
Fiber 3 g
T Fat 16 g
Chol 55 mg
Sod 186 mg

1/2 cup chopped green bell pepper
1/2 cup chopped onion
1/4 cup margarine
1/3 cup flour
3 cups milk
4 teaspoons chicken bouillon
2 cups chopped cooked chicken
2 tablespoons chopped pimento
6 cups cooked spaghetti

Sauté green pepper and onion in margarine in 2-quart saucepan until tender. Stir in flour. Add milk and bouillon gradually. Bring mixture to a boil, stirring to dissolve bouillon. Stir in chicken and pimento. Cook until heated through, stirring constantly. Serve over hot cooked spaghetti.

Chicken with Stuffing

Yield:
4 servings

Utensil:
2-quart dish

Approx Per Serving:
Cal 182
Prot 15 g
Carbo 19 g
Fiber 1 g
T Fat 5 g
Chol 33 mg
Sod 1047 mg

2 chicken breasts
1 can cream of celery soup
1/4 cup chicken broth
2 cups stuffing mix
1 cup chicken broth
1 onion, chopped

Rinse chicken and pat dry. Cook in water to cover in saucepan until tender. Remove and discard skin and bones. Chop chicken. Combine with soup and 1/4 cup chicken broth in bowl; mix well. Spoon into buttered 2-quart baking dish. Mix stuffing mix, remaining 1 cup broth and onion in bowl. Spread over chicken mixture. Bake at 350 degrees for 35 minutes. May prepare ahead and chill, covered, until baking time. May substitute cream of chicken soup for cream of celery soup.

Chicken with Tarragon Sauce

Yield:
8 servings

Utensil:
skillet

Approx Per Serving:
Cal 285
Prot 21 g
Carbo 4 g
Fiber <1 g
T Fat 20 g
Chol 105 mg
Sod 212 mg

4 whole chicken breasts, boned, skinned
Salt and pepper to taste
2 tablespoons butter
1 tablespoon peanut oil
2 tablespoons chopped scallions
1/4 cup Brandy
1 cup chicken broth
2 teaspoons tarragon
1 cup whipping cream
1/2 teaspoon lemon juice
2 tablespoons butter

Rinse chicken; pat dry. Cut into halves. Sprinkle with salt and pepper. Cook in 2 tablespoons butter and oil in large skillet for 10 to 12 minutes or until tender; remove to platter. Add scallions, Brandy, chicken broth and tarragon to skillet; mix well. Cook until thickened, stirring constantly. Add cream; mix well. Cook until thickened, stirring constantly. Stir in lemon juice and remaining 2 tablespoons butter. Pour over chicken. May substitute canola oil for peanut oil.

Creamy Chicken and Bows

Yield:
2 servings

Utensil:
skillet

Approx Per Serving:
Cal 605
Prot 39 g
Carbo 51 g
Fiber 4 g
T Fat 27 g
Chol 117 mg
Sod 1401 mg

8 ounces chicken breast filets, cut into strips
2 tablespoons butter
1/4 cup chopped red bell pepper
2 envelopes 1-serving cream of chicken soup
1 1/2 cups milk
1/2 cup frozen peas
1/3 cup Parmesan cheese
1/2 teaspoon garlic powder
6 ounces cooked bow noodles

Rinse chicken; pat dry. Melt butter in large skillet. Add chicken and red pepper. Sauté for 3 minutes. Mix soup and milk in small bowl. Add peas, cheese, garlic powder and soup mixture to skillet; mix well. Simmer for 5 minutes, stirring constantly. Toss with hot cooked noodles in serving bowl.

Drumsticks and Broccoli

Yield:
6 servings

Utensil:
skillet

Approx Per Serving:
Cal 230
Prot 27 g
Carbo 6 g
Fiber 2 g
T Fat 11 g
Chol 76 mg
Sod 175 mg

6 chicken drumsticks, skinned
2 tablespoons flour
1/4 teaspoon salt
1/8 teaspoon pepper
2 tablespoons oil
1 small clove of garlic, minced
1/4 cup water
1 10-ounce package frozen broccoli spears
1 tablespoon lemon juice
1 tomato, cut into wedges

Rinse chicken; pat dry. Coat with mixture of flour, salt and pepper. Brown in hot oil in large skillet over high heat. Reduce heat. Add garlic and water; mix well. Simmer, covered, for 20 to 25 minutes or until chicken is tender. Push chicken to 1 side of pan. Add broccoli. Bring to a full boil over medium-high heat, stirring with fork to separate spears. Reduce heat. Simmer, covered, for 5 minutes. Arrange chicken and broccoli on serving platter. Add lemon juice to pan drippings in skillet; mix well. Spoon over chicken and broccoli. Garnish with tomato wedges.

Hawaiian Chicken

Yield:
4 servings

Utensil:
skillet

Approx Per Serving:
Cal 239
Prot 21 g
Carbo 30 g
Fiber 1 g
T Fat 5 g
Chol 49 mg
Sod 495 mg

1 16-ounce can pineapple chunks
4 chicken breast filets
1 tablespoon flour
1/2 teaspoon salt
1 tablespoon oil
1 tablespoon honey
1 tablespoon teriyaki sauce
2 teaspoons dried chopped chives
1/4 teaspoon pepper
Fresh chives or parsley to taste

Drain pineapple, reserving 1/4 cup juice. Rinse chicken; pat dry. Coat with mixture of flour and salt. Brown chicken in hot oil in skillet over medium heat for 10 to 12 minutes or until golden brown and tender. Remove to platter. Add honey, teriyaki sauce, 2 teaspoons chives, pepper and reserved pineapple juice to pan drippings in skillet; mix well. Bring to a boil over high heat, stirring constantly. Boil for 30 seconds. Stir in pineapple. Cook until heated through, stirring constantly. Pour over chicken. Garnish with fresh chives or parsley.

North Star Chicken and Bean Bake

Yield:
6 servings

Utensil:
1½-quart dish

Approx Per Serving:
Cal 259
Prot 11 g
Carbo 32 g
Fiber 2 g
T Fat 10 g
Chol 40 mg
Sod 700 mg

1 cup uncooked wild rice
1 6-ounce jar sliced mushrooms, drained
¼ cup melted butter
2 tablespoons flour
½ teaspoon salt
⅛ teaspoon pepper
1 cup chicken broth
1 16-ounce can French-style green beans, drained
5 ounces cooked chicken, chopped

Cook rice using package directions. Sauté mushrooms in butter in skillet until light brown. Stir in flour, salt and pepper. Stir in broth gradually. Cook over low heat until thickened, stirring frequently. Add rice, green beans and chicken. Spoon into greased 1½-quart baking dish. Bake at 350 degrees for 30 minutes. Garnish with parsley, chopped carrots or peanuts. May substitute leftover turkey and broth or gravy for chicken and chicken broth.

Oven-Fried Honey Chicken

Yield:
6 servings

Utensil:
9x13-inch dish

Approx Per Serving:
Cal 433
Prot 34 g
Carbo 20 g
Fiber 1 g
T Fat 24 g
Chol 101 mg
Sod 381 mg

1 3-pound chicken, cut up, skinned
½ cup margarine
3 tablespoons honey
1½ cups crisp rice cereal, crushed
Salt and pepper to taste

Rinse chicken; pat dry. Melt margarine with honey in saucepan. Dip chicken in honey mixture; roll in cereal crumbs. Place meat side up in 9x13-inch baking dish. Sprinkle with salt and pepper. Bake at 325 degrees for 1½ hours. Cover with foil during last 30 minutes if chicken becomes too crisp.

PECAN CHICKEN

Yield:
4 servings

Utensil:
9x13-inch dish

Approx Per Serving:
Cal 368
Prot 23 g
Carbo 24 g
Fiber 2 g
T Fat 22 g
Chol 49 mg
Sod 252 mg

4 chicken breast filets
1/4 cup honey
1/4 cup Dijon mustard
1 cup finely chopped pecans

Rinse chicken; pat dry. Place between waxed paper. Pound to 1/4-inch thickness. Dip chicken in mixture of honey and mustard in shallow bowl; roll in pecans. Arrange in lightly greased 9x13-inch baking dish. Bake at 350 degrees for 35 to 40 minutes or until tender.

TUESDAY CHICKEN

Yield:
8 servings

Utensil:
9x13-inch dish

Approx Per Serving:
Cal 423
Prot 28 g
Carbo 50 g
Fiber 1 g
T Fat 12 g
Chol 63 mg
Sod 1084 mg

2 pounds chicken breasts, boned, skinned
2 soup cans milk
2 cans cream of mushroom soup
1 can cream of chicken soup
2 cups uncooked rice
1 envelope onion soup mix

Rinse chicken; pat dry. Cut each breast into 4 to 6 pieces. Mix milk, mushroom soup and chicken soup in bowl. Add rice; mix well. Spoon into 9x13-inch baking dish. Top with chicken; sprinkle with onion soup mix. Bake, covered with foil, at 325 degrees for 2 1/2 hours.

TURKEY CASSEROLE

Yield:
6 servings

Utensil:
2-quart casserole

Approx Per Serving:
Cal 413
Prot 28 g
Carbo 35 g
Fiber 2 g
T Fat 18 g
Chol 71 mg
Sod 828 mg

8 ounces uncooked spaghetti
2 cups chopped cooked turkey
1/4 cup chopped pimento
1/2 cup chopped green bell pepper
1/2 small onion, chopped
1 can cream of mushroom soup
1/2 soup can water
1/2 teaspoon salt
1/8 teaspoon pepper
1 3/4 cups shredded sharp Cheddar cheese

Cook spaghetti using package directions. Drain and cool. Cut spaghetti into pieces. Combine turkey, pimento, green pepper and onion in bowl. Add soup, water, salt and pepper; mix well. Add 1 1/4 cups cheese and spaghetti; mix well. Spoon into 2-quart casserole. Sprinkle with remaining 1/2 cup cheese. Bake, covered, at 350 degrees for 30 minutes. Bake, uncovered, for 15 minutes longer.

TURKEY TETRAZZINI

Yield:
6 servings

Utensil:
2-quart dish

Approx Per Serving:
Cal 493
Prot 37 g
Carbo 35 g
Fiber <1 g
T Fat 22 g
Chol 88 mg
Sod 1464 mg

1 can cream of mushroom soup
1 can cream of chicken soup
1 cup turkey broth
1 cup shredded American cheese
3 cups chopped cooked turkey
1 tablespoon parsley flakes
2 tablespoons chopped pimento
Salt and pepper to taste
8 ounces Kluski noodles, cooked
1/2 cup shredded American cheese
1/4 cup Parmesan cheese
Paprika to taste

Combine soups and broth in saucepan; mix well. Cook until heated through. Add 1 cup cheese. Cook until cheese melts, stirring constantly; remove from heat. Add turkey, parsley, pimento, salt, pepper and noodles; mix well. Pour into greased 2-quart baking dish. Sprinkle with mixture of remaining 1/2 cup American cheese, Parmesan cheese and paprika. Bake at 350 for 25 to 30 minutes or until hot and bubbly.

Johnny's Stuffed Calamary

Yield:
6 servings

Utensil:
9x13-inch dish

Approx Per Serving:
Cal 385
Prot 11 g
Carbo 15 g
Fiber 1 g
T Fat 30 g
Chol 132 mg
Sod 565 mg

12 4-inch squid
1 cup chopped onion
3 tablespoons chopped parsley
3/4 cup olive oil
1/2 cup cooked rice
2 tablespoons pine nuts
2 tablespoons tomato paste
1/4 cup currants
1 1/2 teaspoons salt
1/8 teaspoon pepper
1 cup dry red wine
1/4 cup water

Clean squid. Remove and chop fins and tentacles. Sauté onion and parsley in olive oil in skillet until onion is golden brown. Stir in chopped squid. Simmer until squid changes color. Add rice, pine nuts, tomato paste, currants, salt and pepper; mix well. Cook for 5 minutes. Let stand until cool. Stuff each squid with rice mixture. Close with toothpicks. Arrange in oiled 9x13-inch baking dish. Pour mixture of wine and water over top. Bake at 350 degrees for 1 hour or until squid are tender and sauce thickens. Serve hot or cold. May substitute chopped walnuts for pine nuts and white wine for red wine.

Company Crab Meat Casserole

Yield:
6 servings

Utensil:
6x8-inch dish

Approx Per Serving:
Cal 364
Prot 28 g
Carbo 16 g
Fiber 1 g
T Fat 21 g
Chol 223 mg
Sod 1149 mg

1 cup soft bread crumbs
1 1/2 cups milk, scalded
1 pound crab meat
1 cup shredded Cheddar cheese
1/4 cup melted butter
1/2 cup chopped pimento
2 tablespoons chopped green bell pepper
1 tablespoon grated onion
1 1/2 teaspoons salt
3 eggs, beaten

Soak bread crumbs in milk in bowl. Add crab meat, cheese, melted butter, pimento, green pepper, onion and salt; mix well. Stir in eggs. Pour into greased 6x8-inch baking dish or loaf pan. Place in pan of hot water. Bake at 375 degrees for 45 minutes or until knife inserted near center comes out clean.

Crab Meat Cakes

Yield:
6 servings

Utensil:
skillet

Approx Per Serving:
Cal 426
Prot 23 g
Carbo 31 g
Fiber 2 g
T Fat 34 g
Chol 160 mg
Sod 907 mg

1 pound crab meat
4 ounces spiced bulk sausage
3/4 cup fine fresh bread crumbs
1 egg, slightly beaten
1 tablespoon chopped scallion
1 tablespoon chopped fresh parsley
1 teaspoon Worcestershire sauce
3 tablespoons Tidewater Tartar Sauce
Salt and pepper to taste
1 3/4 cups fine fresh bread crumbs
1/2 cup clarified butter

Combine crab meat, sausage, 3/4 cup bread crumbs, egg, scallion, parsley and Worcestershire sauce in large bowl; mix well. Stir in 3 tablespoons Tidewater Tartar Sauce. Season with salt and pepper. Shape into twelve 3-inch cakes. Coat with remaining 1 3/4 cups bread crumbs. Chill, covered, for 1 hour. Sauté cakes in butter in skillet for 2 to 3 minutes on each side; drain. Serve with additional Tartar Sauce, lemon wedges and hot pepper sauce to taste.

Tidewater Tartar Sauce

Yield:
6 servings

Utensil:
blender

Approx Per Serving:
Cal 102
Prot <1 g
Carbo 1 g
Fiber <1 g
T Fat 11 g
Chol 8 mg
Sod 140 mg

6 tablespoons mayonnaise
1/2 cup finely chopped scallions
1/4 cup finely chopped parsley
1 tablespoon capers
2 tablespoons chopped dill pickle
2 teaspoons hot pepper sauce
1/2 teaspoon Worcestershire sauce

Combine mayonnaise, scallions, parsley, capers, pickle, hot pepper sauce and Worcestershire sauce in blender container. Pulse until blended. Chill, covered, for 24 hours.

Crab Meat Quiche

Yield: *8 servings*

Utensil: *pie plate*

Approx Per Serving: *Cal 311* *Prot 15 g* *Carbo 14 g* *Fiber 2 g* *T Fat 22 g* *Chol 125 mg* *Sod 539 mg*

1 6-ounce package frozen Alaskan king crab
1 cup shredded Swiss cheese
1 unbaked 11-inch pie shell
2 green onions with tops, sliced
3 eggs, beaten
1 cup half and half
1/2 cup toasted almonds
1 teaspoon salt
1 teaspoon grated lemon rind
1/4 teaspoon dry mustard

Thaw crab meat; drain. Sprinkle cheese in pie shell. Layer crab meat and green onions over cheese. Combine eggs, half and half, almonds, salt, lemon rind and dry mustard in bowl; mix well. Pour over layers. Bake at 350 degrees for 45 minutes. Let stand for 10 minutes.

Imperial Crab Meat

Yield: *4 servings*

Utensil: *baking sheet*

Approx Per Serving: *Cal 239* *Prot 25 g* *Carbo 2 g* *Fiber <1 g* *T Fat 14 g* *Chol 162 mg* *Sod 567 mg*

1 egg, beaten
1/4 cup chopped green bell pepper
1 tablespoon chopped pimento
1 tablespoon mayonnaise
1 tablespoon Worcestershire sauce
1/4 teaspoon hot pepper sauce
1 teaspoon dry mustard
1 teaspoon crab seasoning
1/4 teaspoon paprika
1 pound crab meat
3 tablespoons mayonnaise
1 tablespoon Worcestershire sauce
1 teaspoon prepared mustard
Paprika to taste

Combine first 9 ingredients in large bowl; mix well. Stir in crab meat. Scoop into 4 mounds on baking sheet with ice cream scoop. Combine remaining 3 tablespoons mayonnaise, 1 tablespoon Worcestershire sauce and prepared mustard in bowl; mix well. Spoon over mounds. Sprinkle with additional paprika. Bake at 350 degrees for 15 minutes or until golden brown.

Nutritional information for this recipe does not include crab seasoning.

Orange Roughy with Lemon Sauce ≈MW≈

Yield:
6 servings

Utensil:
pie plate

Approx Per Serving:
Cal 242
Prot 31 g
Carbo 3 g
Fiber <1 g
T Fat 11 g
Chol 86 mg
Sod 248 mg

6 4-ounce orange roughy filets
1/8 teaspoon salt
1/8 teaspoon pepper
1 tablespoon butter
2 tablespoons flour
1/4 teaspoon salt
2/3 cup half and half
1 tablespoon freshly squeezed lemon juice
1 teaspoon chopped fresh chives

Arrange fish in 9-inch glass pie plate. Sprinkle with 1/8 teaspoon salt and pepper. Microwave, loosely covered with plastic wrap, on High for 4 to 6 minutes, rotating dish 1/4 turn. Let stand, covered, for 5 minutes. Melt butter in 2-cup glass measure. Add flour and remaining 1/4 teaspoon salt; stir until smooth. Stir in half and half. Microwave on High for 3 to 4 minutes or until thickened and bubbly, stirring 2 or 3 times. Stir in lemon juice and chives. Spoon over fish. May substitute thinly sliced green onions for chives.

Salmon Loaf with Creamy Dijon Sauce

Yield:
4 servings

Utensil:
1 1/2-quart dish

Approx Per Serving:
Cal 313
Prot 16 g
Carbo 32 g
Fiber 3 g
T Fat 14 g
Chol 101 mg
Sod 206 mg

1 7-ounce can salmon, drained, flaked
2 cups chopped cooked potatoes
1/4 cup chopped celery
1/4 cup milk
1 egg, beaten
1/4 cup chopped chives
1/2 teaspoon grated lemon rind
Pepper to taste
2 tablespoons minced onion
1 tablespoon oil
1 tablespoon butter
1 tablespoon flour
1 cup milk
2 tablespoons Dijon mustard

Combine salmon, potatoes, celery, 1/4 cup milk, egg, chives, lemon rind and pepper in bowl; mix well. Press into lightly greased 1 1/2-quart baking dish. Bake at 350 degrees for 25 minutes or until set. Sauté onion in oil and butter in skillet until tender. Stir in flour and remaining 1 cup milk. Cook until thickened, stirring constantly. Stir in Dijon mustard. Serve with salmon loaf.

Scallops Provolone

Yield:
4 servings

Utensil:
9x13-inch dish

Approx Per Serving:
Cal 833
Prot 56 g
Carbo 14 g
Fiber 2 g
T Fat 63 g
Chol 239 mg
Sod 1221 mg

Juice of 1/2 lemon
1 1/2 pounds scallops
8 ounces fresh mushrooms, sliced
1 medium Vidalia onion, thinly sliced
2 cloves of garlic, minced
1/2 green bell pepper, thinly sliced
1 cup butter
Seafood seasoning to taste
8 ounces provolone cheese, sliced

Sprinkle lemon juice over scallops. Sauté mushrooms, onion, garlic and green pepper in 1/2 cup butter in skillet. Cut remaining 1/2 cup butter into pieces. Place in 9x13-inch baking dish. Add scallops, sautéed vegetables and seasoning. Bake at 425 degrees for 20 minutes. Top with cheese. Bake for 5 to 10 minutes longer or until cheese is melted. Serve over rice. May reduce butter to 1/2 cup or substitute margarine for fewer calories.

Scallop Thermidor

Yield:
4 servings

Utensil:
2-quart casserole

Approx Per Serving:
Cal 336
Prot 27 g
Carbo 16 g
Fiber 1 g
T Fat 18 g
Chol 58 mg
Sod 1116 mg

1 pound scallops
1 4-ounce can mushrooms, drained
1/4 cup melted margarine
1/4 cup flour
1 teaspoon salt
1/2 teaspoon dry mustard
Cayenne pepper to taste
2 cups milk
2 tablespoons chopped parsley
1/4 cup Parmesan cheese
Paprika to taste

Cut large scallops into halves. Sauté mushrooms in margarine in skillet for 5 minutes. Add flour, salt, dry mustard and cayenne pepper; mix well. Add milk gradually. Cook until thickened, stirring constantly. Stir in scallops and parsley. Spoon into greased 2-quart casserole. Sprinkle with cheese and paprika. Bake at 400 degrees for 15 minutes.

Thai Shrimp and Fried Rice

Yield:
6 servings

Utensil:
skillet

Approx Per Serving:
Cal 275
Prot 16 g
Carbo 47 g
Fiber 3 g
T Fat 2 g
Chol 109 mg
Sod 93 mg

1½ cups uncooked rice
9 ounces cooked small shrimp
Oil for frying
1 egg
8 green onions and tops, chopped
2 onions, chopped
2 cucumbers, peeled, chopped
2 tomatoes, chopped
Soy sauce to taste
Fish sauce to taste

Cook rice using package directions; drain. Brown rice and shrimp in a small amount of oil in large skillet. Push rice to sides of skillet. Place a small amount of oil in center of skillet. Scramble egg in oil. Chop into small pieces; mix with rice. Stir in green onions, onions, cucumbers and tomatoes. Add soy sauce and fish oil; mix well. Cook for 10 minutes, stirring frequently. Serve with additional sliced cucumbers, tomatoes and green onions. I acquired this recipe while stationed in Thailand with the U. S. Army. It is called "Kao Pot" in Thai.

Nutritional information for this recipe does not include oil for frying, soy sauce or fish sauce.

Shrimp in Wine Sauce

Yield:
4 servings

Utensil:
skillet

Approx Per Serving:
Cal 344
Prot 31 g
Carbo 16 g
Fiber <1 g
T Fat 15 g
Chol 265 mg
Sod 1516 mg

1 pound shrimp
2 cloves of garlic, crushed
1 tablespoon butter
2 cups milk
2 cans cream of shrimp soup
1/8 teaspoon paprika
1/2 cup dry white wine

Clean and devein shrimp. Sauté shrimp and garlic in butter in skillet just until transparent. Stir in milk and soup. Sprinkle with paprika. Simmer for 15 minutes or until shrimp are firm; do not overcook. Stir in wine. Cook until heated through. Serve over rice. Garnish with parsley. May substitute Sherry for white wine.

Shrimp Scampi

Yield:
6 servings

Utensil:
skillet

Approx Per Serving:
Cal 220
Prot 32 g
Carbo 1 g
Fiber <1 g
T Fat 9 g
Chol 316 mg
Sod 582 mg

2 pounds large shrimp
1/4 cup butter
1/2 teaspoon salt
1/4 teaspoon pepper
2 cloves of garlic, chopped
1/4 cup chopped parsley

Peel and devein shrimp. Melt butter in skillet. Add shrimp. Cook for 3 to 5 minutes or until pink. Remove shrimp to serving plate. Add salt, pepper, garlic and parsley to skillet. Sauté for 1 minute. Spoon over shrimp. Serve over rice. Garnish with lemon wedges.

Seafood Casserole

Yield:
6 servings

Utensil:
2-quart casserole

Approx Per Serving:
Cal 273
Prot 18 g
Carbo 17 g
Fiber 2 g
T Fat 15 g
Chol 117 mg
Sod 614 mg

8 ounces cooked peeled shrimp
1 7-ounce can crab meat, drained, flaked
4 medium stalks celery, chopped
2 medium onions, finely chopped
1/2 teaspoon salt
1/4 teaspoon pepper
1/8 teaspoon paprika
6 tablespoons mayonnaise
1 cup bread crumbs
1 tablespoon melted butter

Cut shrimp into halves. Combine with crab meat, celery, onions, salt, pepper, paprika and mayonnaise in large bowl; mix well. Spoon into buttered 2-quart casserole. Top with mixture of bread crumbs and melted butter. Bake at 350 degrees for 30 minutes or until bubbly and browned.

Seafood Casserole with Mushrooms

Yield:
8 servings

Utensil:
9x13-inch dish

Approx Per Serving:
Cal 505
Prot 22 g
Carbo 35 g
Fiber 2 g
T Fat 31 g
Chol 119 mg
Sod 615 mg

1 cup uncooked rice
1 cup chopped celery
1/4 cup chopped onion
1 green bell pepper, chopped
2 tablespoons margarine
2 tablespoons melted butter
3 tablespoons flour
1 1/2 cups milk
1 teaspoon Worcestershire sauce
1 cup mayonnaise
8 ounces shrimp
8 ounces crab meat
1 6-ounce can tuna, drained
1 4-ounce can mushrooms, drained
1 cup bread crumbs

Cook rice using package directions; drain. Spoon into greased 9x13-inch baking dish. Sauté celery, onion and green pepper in margarine in skillet until lightly browned. Blend butter and flour in saucepan. Cook for 1 minute. Stir in milk and Worcestershire sauce. Cook until thickened, stirring constantly. Add sautéed vegetables, mayonnaise, shrimp, crab meat, tuna and mushrooms; mix well. Pour over rice. Sprinkle with bread crumbs. Bake at 350 degrees for 40 minutes.

Tuna Burgers

Yield:
5 servings

Utensil:
skillet

Approx Per Serving:
Cal 206
Prot 14 g
Carbo 10 g
Fiber 1 g
T Fat 12 g
Chol 32 mg
Sod 400 mg

1 7-ounce can tuna
1/2 cup bread crumbs
1/2 cup finely chopped celery
2 tablespoons minced onion
1/3 cup mayonnaise
2 tablespoons chili sauce
1 teaspoon lemon juice

Drain and flake tuna. Combine with bread crumbs, celery and onion in large bowl; mix well. Stir in mixture of mayonnaise, chili sauce and lemon juice. Shape into 5 patties. Place in lightly oiled skillet. Cook over low to medium heat for 5 minutes or until light brown. Serve plain or on hamburger buns with lettuce and tomato.

Vegetables and Side Dishes

ASPARAGUS QUICHE

Yield:
6 servings

Utensil:
pie plate

Approx Per Serving:
Cal 341
Prot 14 g
Carbo 19 g
Fiber 1 g
T Fat 24 g
Chol 236 mg
Sod 483 mg

8 ounces fresh asparagus, cut into 1-inch pieces
1 unbaked 9-inch pie shell
1/2 cup shredded Swiss cheese
6 eggs, beaten
1 cup milk
1/2 cup sour cream
3 tablespoons finely chopped onion
1/2 teaspoon salt
Pepper to taste

Cook asparagus in 1 inch water in saucepan for 3 to 5 minutes or until tender; drain. Arrange in pie shell; sprinkle with cheese. Beat eggs, milk and sour cream in small mixer bowl until smooth. Add onion, salt and pepper; mix well. Pour over cheese layer. Bake at 375 degrees for 35 to 40 minutes or until knife inserted near center comes out clean. Let stand for 5 minutes. May substitute one 10-ounce package frozen cut asparagus for fresh asparagus if preferred.

BARBECUED BEANS CASSEROLE

Yield:
8 servings

Utensil:
1 1/2-quart dish

Approx Per Serving:
Cal 241
Prot 11 g
Carbo 43 g
Fiber 11 g
T Fat 5 g
Chol 13 mg
Sod 1049 mg

1 16-ounce can pork and beans
1 16-ounce can kidney beans, drained
1 12-ounce can Mexicorn, drained
1 16-ounce can chili without beans
3/4 cup catsup
1 medium onion, chopped

Combine pork and beans, kidney beans, corn, chili, catsup and onion in bowl; mix well. Spoon into 1 1/2-quart baking dish. Bake at 250 degrees for 2 1/2 hours.

Bean Bundles

Yield:
6 servings

Utensil:
9x13-inch dish

Approx Per Serving:
Cal 194
Prot 5 g
Carbo 8 g
Fiber 2 g
T Fat 16 g
Chol 10 mg
Sod 783 mg

8 ounces bacon
2 16-ounce cans whole green beans, drained
1/2 8-ounce bottle of French salad dressing

Cut bacon slices into halves. Wrap 8 whole green beans with 1/2 bacon slice; secure with toothpick. Repeat with remaining beans and bacon. Place bundles in 9x13-inch baking dish. Pour salad dressing over bundles. Marinate in refrigerator for 2 hours, basting once. Bake at 350 degrees for 40 minutes, turning bundles after 20 minutes.

Favorite Green Bean Casserole

Yield:
6 servings

Utensil:
2-quart casserole

Approx Per Serving:
Cal 135
Prot 4 g
Carbo 14 g
Fiber 1 g
T Fat 8 g
Chol 10 mg
Sod 673 mg

1 can cream of mushroom soup
3/4 cup milk
Salt and pepper to taste
4 cups drained canned green beans
1 3-ounce can French-fried onions

Mix soup, milk, salt and pepper in bowl. Add green beans; mix well. Fold in half the French-fried onions. Spoon into greased 2-quart casserole; sprinkle with remaining onions. Bake at 350 degrees for 1 hour.

Green Beans and Tomatoes

Yield:
8 servings

Utensil:
skillet

Approx Per Serving:
Cal 161
Prot 5 g
Carbo 18 g
Fiber 3 g
T Fat 9 g
Chol 29 mg
Sod 656 mg

1 medium onion, chopped
2 tablespoons bacon drippings
2 16-ounce cans French-style green beans, drained
2 16-ounce cans tomatoes
1/4 cup sugar
Salt and pepper to taste
12 slices crisp-fried bacon, crumbled

Sauté onion in bacon drippings in large skillet until tender. Add green beans and undrained tomatoes. Bring to a simmer, stirring constantly. Add sugar, salt and pepper; mix well. Simmer for 30 to 45 minutes or until most of liquid has evaporated, stirring occasionally. Spoon into serving dish; sprinkle with crumbled bacon.

Lima Bean and Onion Casserole

Yield:
4 servings

Utensil:
1-quart casserole

Approx Per Serving:
Cal 261
Prot 10 g
Carbo 31 g
Fiber 7 g
T Fat 12 g
Chol 29 mg
Sod 660 mg

1 10-ounce package frozen lima beans, thawed, drained
1 can cheese soup
1/2 cup milk
3/4 cup sliced celery
1/2 cup chopped parsley
1 3-ounce can French-fried onions

Place beans in 1-quart casserole. Mix soup and milk in bowl. Pour over beans. Stir in celery, parsley and half the onions. Bake at 350 degrees for 45 minutes. Sprinkle remaining onions around outer edge of casserole. Bake for 10 minutes longer.

Broccoli Casserole

Yield:
8 servings

Utensil:
9-inch casserole

Approx Per Serving:
Cal 380
Prot 10 g
Carbo 17 g
Fiber 3 g
T Fat 31 g
Chol 85 mg
Sod 771 mg

2 10-ounce packages frozen chopped broccoli
1 medium onion, chopped
1 cup mayonnaise
2 eggs, beaten
1 can cream of mushroom soup
1 cup shredded Cheddar cheese
1 1/2 cups corn bread stuffing mix

Cook broccoli using package directions; drain. Combine onion, mayonnaise, eggs and soup in bowl; mix well. Stir in broccoli. Spoon into 9-inch casserole. Sprinkle with cheese and stuffing mix. Bake at 350 degrees for 45 minutes or until brown and bubbly.

Broccoli and Cheese Casserole ≈*MW*≈

Yield:
8 servings

Utensil:
1 1/2-quart dish

Approx Per Serving:
Cal 170
Prot 8 g
Carbo 23 g
Fiber 2 g
T Fat 5 g
Chol 11 mg
Sod 594 mg

1 small onion, chopped
1 tablespoon water
1 10-ounce package frozen chopped broccoli
1 7-ounce package long grain and wild rice with mushrooms mix
1 tablespoon corn oil margarine
1/4 teaspoon salt
2 tablespoons flour
1 cup evaporated skim milk
3 ounces American cheese, shredded

Cook onion in water in skillet until transparent. Microwave broccoli using package directions for 6 minutes; drain. Prepare rice using package directions, omitting 2 teaspoons margarine. Melt margarine in large saucepan; remove from heat. Add salt and flour, stirring until smooth. Add milk gradually, stirring until mixed well. Bring to a boil, stirring constantly. Boil for 1 minute, stirring constantly. Stir in cheese. Cook until cheese melts, stirring constantly. Add onions, broccoli and rice; mix well. Pour into 1 1/2-quart baking dish sprayed with nonstick cooking spray. Bake at 350 degrees for 30 minutes.

Broccoli and Mushroom Casserole

Yield:
8 servings

Utensil:
2-quart casserole

Approx Per Serving:
Cal 230
Prot 10 g
Carbo 20 g
Fiber 3 g
T Fat 13 g
Chol 30 mg
Sod 681 mg

2 10-ounce packages frozen chopped broccoli
2 tablespoons butter
1/4 cup milk
1 can cream of chicken soup
1 8-ounce jar Cheez Whiz
1 cup uncooked minute rice
1 small onion, chopped
1 cup sliced mushrooms

Cook broccoli using package directions; drain. Combine butter, milk and soup in saucepan; mix well. Cook until blended, stirring constantly. Add Cheez Whiz, rice and onion; mix well. Combine with broccoli; mix well. Spoon into 2-quart casserole. Bake, covered, at 350 degrees for 45 minutes. Add mushrooms; mix well. Bake for 15 minutes longer.

Broccoli Quiche

Yield:
6 servings

Utensil:
pie plate

Approx Per Serving:
Cal 339
Prot 11 g
Carbo 19 g
Fiber 3 g
T Fat 25 g
Chol 148 mg
Sod 351 mg

1 unbaked 9-inch pie shell
2 tablespoons Dijon mustard
Flowerets of 1 bunch broccoli
3/4 cup milk
1/2 cup whipping cream
3 eggs
Salt and pepper to taste
Nutmeg to taste
2 tablespoons Madeira
1/2 cup shredded Gruyère cheese
Parmesan cheese to taste

Bake pie shell using package directions, decreasing baking time by 2 minutes. Brush Dijon mustard over bottom of pie shell. Bake for 2 minutes longer. Cut broccoli flowerets into quarters. Blanch in salted water for 5 minutes; drain. Let stand until cool. Beat milk, cream and eggs in bowl with wire whisk until smooth. Add salt, pepper, nutmeg and wine; mix well. Fold in Gruyère cheese and broccoli. Pour into prepared pie shell; sprinkle with Parmesan cheese. Bake at 375 degrees for 30 minutes.

Broccoli and Rice Casserole

Yield:
8 servings

Utensil:
2-quart casserole

Approx Per Serving:
Cal 392
Prot 12 g
Carbo 27 g
Fiber 3 g
T Fat 27 g
Chol 57 mg
Sod 1118 mg

2 10-ounce packages frozen chopped broccoli
1/2 cup melted butter
1 8-ounce jar Cheez Whiz
2 cans cream of mushroom soup
1 1/2 cups uncooked minute rice
1/2 cup chopped onion
1/2 cup chopped celery
1/2 cup shredded Cheddar cheese

Cook broccoli in large saucepan using package directions; drain. Add butter, Cheez Whiz, soup, rice, onion and celery; mix well. Spoon into well greased 2-quart casserole. Bake at 350 degrees for 25 minutes. Sprinkle with Cheddar cheese. Bake for 25 minutes longer.

Baked Sweet and Sour Brussels Sprouts

Yield:
4 servings

Utensil:
9x13-inch dish

Approx Per Serving:
Cal 116
Prot 4 g
Carbo 10 g
Fiber 3 g
T Fat 8 g
Chol 2 mg
Sod 330 mg

1 10-ounce package frozen Brussels sprouts
2 tablespoons oil
1/4 cup cider vinegar
1 tablespoon sugar
1/2 teaspoon salt
1/4 teaspoon pepper
2 tablespoons Parmesan cheese

Cook Brussels sprouts using package directions; drain. Arrange in 9x13-inch baking dish. Combine oil, vinegar, sugar, salt and pepper in small bowl; mix well. Pour over Brussels sprouts. Sprinkle with Parmesan cheese. Bake, covered, at 350 degrees for 15 minutes or until Brussels sprouts are tender. May use 1 pint fresh Brussels sprouts if preferred.

Cheesy Cauliflower

≈MW≈

Yield:
6 servings

Utensil:
2-quart dish

Approx Per Serving:
Cal 231
Prot 7 g
Carbo 6 g
Fiber 2 g
T Fat 21 g
Chol 31 mg
Sod 608 mg

1 head cauliflower
2 teaspoons prepared mustard
1 teaspoon salt
1/2 cup mayonnaise
1 small onion, finely chopped
1 cup shredded Cheddar cheese

Place cauliflower in 2-quart glass dish. Microwave on High for 12 minutes. Combine mustard, salt, mayonnaise, onion and cheese in glass dish; mix well. Microwave on High for 2 minutes; mix well. Pour over cauliflower.

Copper Penny Carrots

Yield:
8 servings

Utensil:
large bowl

Approx Per Serving:
Cal 244
Prot 2 g
Carbo 45 g
Fiber 4 g
T Fat 8 g
Chol 0 mg
Sod 312 mg

2 pounds carrots, sliced
1 medium onion, chopped
1 medium green bell pepper, chopped
1 can tomato soup
3/4 cup cider vinegar
1 cup sugar
1/4 cup oil
1 teaspoon dry mustard
1 teaspoon Worcestershire sauce

Cook carrots in water to cover in saucepan until tender; drain. Combine with onion and green pepper in large bowl. Combine tomato soup, vinegar, sugar, oil, dry mustard and Worcestershire sauce in bowl; mix well. Pour over carrots; toss to coat. Marinate in refrigerator overnight.

Corn au Gratin

Yield:
8 servings

Utensil:
9-inch casserole

Approx Per Serving:
Cal 419
Prot 17 g
Carbo 20 g
Fiber 1 g
T Fat 32 g
Chol 192 mg
Sod 573 mg

2 14-ounce cans whole kernel corn, drained
1 cup whipping cream
2 tablespoons melted margarine
4 eggs, beaten
12 ounces sharp Cheddar cheese, shredded
1/8 teaspoon pepper

Combine corn, whipping cream, margarine, eggs, cheese and pepper in bowl; mix well. Pour into greased 9-inch casserole. Bake at 300 degrees for 1 hour or until set.

Fried Corn

Yield:
4 servings

Utensil:
cast-iron skillet

Approx Per Serving:
Cal 207
Prot 4 g
Carbo 29 g
Fiber 5 g
T Fat 11 g
Chol 37 mg
Sod 103 mg

6 ears fresh sweet corn
2 tablespoons butter
1 tablespoon bacon drippings
Sugar to taste
Salt and pepper to taste

Cut kernels from corn with sharp knife; scrape cobs gently to remove liquid. Melt butter in bacon drippings in cast-iron skillet over medium heat. Add corn. Simmer for 8 to 10 minutes or until corn is tender, stirring frequently. Add a small amount of hot water during cooking if necessary for desired consistency. Sprinkle with sugar, salt and pepper; mix well.

Old-Fashioned Corn Pudding

Yield:
4 servings

Utensil:
1-quart casserole

Approx Per Serving:
Cal 208
Prot 9 g
Carbo 27 g
Fiber 3 g
T Fat 9 g
Chol 173 mg
Sod 683 mg

2 teaspoons sugar
1½ teaspoons cornstarch
1 cup milk
3 eggs
1 16-ounce can cream-style corn
2 teaspoons butter
½ teaspoon salt
Nutmeg to taste

Mix sugar and cornstarch in bowl. Add milk and eggs; mix well. Stir in corn, butter, salt and nutmeg. Pour into 1-quart casserole. Place casserole in baking pan half filled with hot water. Bake at 300 degrees for 1¾ hours.

Scalloped Corn

Yield:
6 servings

Utensil:
1½-quart dish

Approx Per Serving:
Cal 193
Prot 6 g
Carbo 32 g
Fiber 2 g
T Fat 6 g
Chol 14 mg
Sod 383 mg

1 20-ounce can whole kernel corn, drained
½ cup (or more) milk
½ small onion, chopped
1 cup dry bread crumbs
3 tablespoons chopped green bell pepper
Salt and pepper to taste
2 tablespoons butter

Mix corn and milk in bowl. Add onion, bread crumbs, green pepper, salt and pepper; mix well. Add additional milk if necessary. Pour into greased 1½-quart baking dish; dot with butter. Bake at 350 degrees for 30 minutes.

Spinach-Stuffed Mushrooms

Yield:
12 servings

Utensil:
9x13-inch dish

Approx Per Serving:
Cal 62
Prot 3 g
Carbo 3 g
Fiber 1 g
T Fat 5 g
Chol 40 mg
Sod 364 mg

1 12-ounce package frozen spinach soufflé
1 cup crumbled cheese-flavored crackers
2 teaspoons lemon juice
1 teaspoon chopped onion
1 teaspoon salt
Pepper to taste
12 large mushrooms, stems removed
Paprika to taste

Thaw spinach soufflé partially. Mash with fork in bowl. Add crumbs, lemon juice, onion, salt and pepper; mix well. Arrange mushroom caps in 9x13-inch baking dish. Spoon spinach mixture into caps. Sprinkle with paprika. Bake at 350 degrees for 15 minutes. May substitute Parmesan cheese for paprika. May substitute 24 medium mushrooms for 12 large mushrooms.

Okra and Tomatoes

Yield:
6 servings

Utensil:
large skillet

Approx Per Serving:
Cal 121
Prot 3 g
Carbo 15 g
Fiber 4 g
T Fat 6 g
Chol 16 mg
Sod 297 mg

2 medium onions, chopped
3 tablespoons butter
1 10-ounce package frozen chopped okra
1 green bell pepper, chopped
2 16-ounce cans tomatoes, drained
1/2 teaspoon cumin seed
1/2 teaspoon Wye River Seasonings Original Red Formula
1/2 teaspoon garlic powder
1 teaspoon Italian seasoning
5 dashes of Louisiana hot sauce

Sauté onions in butter in large skillet until soft. Add okra and green pepper. Sauté until tender. Push to side of skillet. Add tomatoes. Cover skillet. Bring to a simmer; mix well. Sprinkle with cumin, Red Formula, garlic powder, Italian seasoning and hot sauce; mix well. Simmer, covered, for 30 minutes or until most of the liquid has evaporated. May serve over brown or wild rice or with shrimp. Flavor improves when made in advance and reheated. May use 8 ounces fresh okra and substitute olive oil or bacon drippings for butter if preferred.

Cheesy Potato Casserole

Yield:
8 servings

Utensil:
2-quart casserole

Approx Per Serving:
Cal 371
Prot 9 g
Carbo 41 g
Fiber 4 g
T Fat 20 g
Chol 53 mg
Sod 461 mg

6 medium potatoes
1 cup shredded mild Cheddar cheese
1/2 cup milk
3 tablespoons butter
1 cup sour cream
1/4 cup chopped onion
1 teaspoon salt
1/4 teaspoon pepper
3 tablespoons butter
Paprika to taste

Cook potatoes in boiling salted water to cover in large saucepan for 30 minutes or until tender; drain. Chill in refrigerator. Peel and grate potatoes. Combine cheese, milk and 3 tablespoons butter in small saucepan; mix well. Cook over low heat until butter and cheese melt, stirring occasionally; remove from heat. Stir in sour cream, onion, salt and pepper. Combine with potatoes in bowl; mix gently. Pour into greased 2-quart casserole. Dot with remaining 3 tablespoons butter; sprinkle with paprika. Bake at 350 degrees for 45 minutes. May be frozen before baking.

Party Potatoes

Yield:
15 servings

Utensil:
9x13-inch dish

Approx Per Serving:
Cal 325
Prot 8 g
Carbo 29 g
Fiber 1 g
T Fat 21 g
Chol 34 mg
Sod 580 mg

2 cans cream of chicken soup
1 cup sour cream
1 32-ounce package frozen hashed brown potatoes
2 cups shredded mild Cheddar cheese
2 cups crushed cornflakes
1/4 cup melted butter

Combine soup and sour cream in large bowl; mix well. Fold in potatoes and cheese. Spoon into 9x13-inch baking dish. Sprinkle with cornflakes; drizzle with butter. Bake at 350 degrees for 1 hour.

Squash Bake

Yield:
4 servings

Utensil:
2-quart casserole

Approx Per Serving:
Cal 498
Prot 12 g
Carbo 52 g
Fiber 4 g
T Fat 28 g
Chol 57 mg
Sod 1078 mg

1/2 onion, chopped
2 cups mashed cooked summer squash
1 can cream of chicken soup
1 cup sour cream
1 carrot, shredded
Salt and pepper to taste
2 cups herb-seasoned bread crumbs
3 tablespoons butter, softened

Sauté onion in skillet sprayed with nonstick cooking spray. Mix squash, soup and sour cream in bowl. Add onion, carrot, salt and pepper; mix well. Fold in bread crumbs. Spoon into 2-quart casserole. Dot with butter. Bake at 350 degrees for 30 minutes.

Squash Casserole

Yield:
10 servings

Utensil:
9x13-inch dish

Approx Per Serving:
Cal 419
Prot 6 g
Carbo 29 g
Fiber 2 g
T Fat 31 g
Chol 21 mg
Sod 932 mg

1 16-ounce package corn bread stuffing mix
1 cup melted margarine
4 cups sliced squash
3 medium onions, chopped
1 can cream of mushroom soup
2 cups sour cream

Toss stuffing mix with margarine in bowl. Combine squash, onions, soup and sour cream in bowl; mix well. Spread 1/4 of the stuffing mixture in 9x13-inch baking dish. Layer with squash mixture and remaining stuffing mixture. Bake at 350 degrees for 1 1/4 hours or until brown and bubbly.

Sweet Potato Casserole

Yield:
6 servings

Utensil:
2-quart dish

Approx Per Serving:
Cal 739
Prot 8 g
Carbo 111 g
Fiber 4 g
T Fat 32 g
Chol 115 mg
Sod 451 mg

3 cups mashed cooked sweet potatoes
1 cup sugar
2 eggs
1/2 cup milk
1/4 cup butter, softened
1/2 teaspoon salt
1 teaspoon vanilla extract
1 cup packed brown sugar
1 cup chopped pecans
1/4 cup melted butter
1/2 cup flour

Combine sweet potatoes, sugar, eggs, milk, 1/4 cup butter, salt and vanilla in large bowl; mix well. Pour into buttered 2-quart baking dish. Mix brown sugar, pecans, 1/4 cup melted butter and flour in bowl until crumbly. Sprinkle over sweet potatoes. Bake at 350 degrees for 30 minutes.

Sweet Potato and Orange Casserole

Yield:
8 servings

Utensil:
2-quart casserole

Approx Per Serving:
Cal 262
Prot 2 g
Carbo 44 g
Fiber 4 g
T Fat 9 g
Chol 16 mg
Sod 203 mg

2 16-ounce cans sweet potatoes, drained
1/4 cup packed brown sugar
2 tablespoons melted butter
1/2 teaspoon salt
2 tablespoons rum
1 11-ounce can mandarin oranges, drained
1/4 cup chopped pecans
4 teaspoons brown sugar
2 tablespoons melted butter

Mash sweet potatoes in large mixer bowl. Add 1/4 cup brown sugar, 2 tablespoons melted butter, salt and rum; mix well. Fold in oranges. Spoon into buttered 2-quart casserole. Mix pecans, remaining 4 teaspoons brown sugar and 2 tablespoons melted butter in small bowl. Sprinkle over sweet potatoes. Bake at 375 degrees for 30 minutes.

Tomato and Corn Bake

Yield:
8 servings

Utensil:
9x13-inch dish

Approx Per Serving:
Cal 65
Prot 3 g
Carbo 9 g
Fiber 1 g
T Fat 2 g
Chol 6 mg
Sod 97 mg

4 small tomatoes
Salt to taste
1 9-ounce can whole kernel corn, drained
1/2 cup shredded Swiss cheese
1 tablespoon sliced green onions

Cut tomatoes into halves crosswise; remove and discard pulp, reserving shells. Sprinkle inside of tomato shells with salt. Invert onto paper towels to drain. Combine corn, cheese and green onions in bowl; mix well. Spoon into tomato shells. Place in 9x13-inch baking dish. Bake at 350 degrees for 20 to 25 minutes or until heated through. May reserve tomato pulp for another use.

Apple Mallow Yams

Yield:
6 servings

Utensil:
1 1/2-quart dish

Approx Per Serving:
Cal 407
Prot 3 g
Carbo 73 g
Fiber 6 g
T Fat 13 g
Chol 21 mg
Sod 103 mg

2 apples, sliced
1/3 cup chopped pecans
1/2 cup packed brown sugar
1/2 teaspoon cinnamon
2 17-ounce cans yams, drained
1/4 cup butter
2 cups miniature marshmallows

Toss apples and pecans with mixture of brown sugar and cinnamon in bowl. Alternate layers of apples and yams in 1 1/2-quart baking dish. Dot with butter. Bake, covered, at 350 degrees for 35 to 40 minutes or until bubbly. Sprinkle with marshmallows. Broil 6 inches from heat source until light brown.

Zucchini Quiche

Yield:
6 servings

Utensil:
pie plate

Approx Per Serving:
Cal 345
Prot 16 g
Carbo 22 g
Fiber 2 g
T Fat 21 g
Chol 135 mg
Sod 408 mg

1 unbaked 9-inch pie shell
3 eggs, beaten
1 cup plain yogurt
1½ cups shredded Swiss cheese
2 tablespoons flour
½ teaspoon dillweed
¼ teaspoon salt
Pepper to taste
2 cups finely chopped zucchini
1 medium onion, finely chopped

Bake pie shell at 450 degrees for 5 to 7 minutes or until edge is light brown. Combine eggs, yogurt, cheese, flour, dillweed, salt and pepper in medium mixer bowl; beat until smooth. Stir in zucchini and onion. Pour into hot pie shell. Reduce oven temperature to 350 degrees. Bake for 25 to 30 minutes or until brown and bubbly. Let stand for 10 minutes before serving. May sprinkle with additional cheese before baking if desired.

Vegetable Stir-Fry

Yield:
6 servings

Utensil:
large skillet

Approx Per Serving:
Cal 160
Prot 7 g
Carbo 11 g
Fiber 4 g
T Fat 12 g
Chol 0 mg
Sod 561 mg

8 ounces bacon substitute, chopped
4 yellow squash, chopped
4 zucchini, chopped
2 large tomatoes, chopped
1 bunch green onions, chopped
Crushed garlic to taste

Stir-fry bacon substitute in large skillet until nearly crisp. Add squash, zucchini, tomatoes, onions and garlic. Stir-fry for 5 minutes. Simmer, covered, over low heat for 10 to 12 minutes or until done to taste.

Baked Curried Fruit

Yield:
4 servings

Utensil:
1 1/2-quart dish

Approx Per Serving:
Cal 441
Prot 1 g
Carbo 80 g
Fiber 5 g
T Fat 15 g
Chol 0 mg
Sod 202 mg

1 16-ounce can sliced peaches, drained
1 16-ounce can pineapple chunks, drained
1/4 cup maraschino cherries, cut into halves
1 16-ounce can pear halves, drained, sliced
1/3 cup melted margarine
1/2 cup packed light brown sugar
1 1/2 teaspoons curry powder

Combine peaches, pineapple, cherries and pears in 1 1/2-quart baking dish; toss gently. Combine margarine, brown sugar and curry powder in small bowl; mix well. Pour over fruit. Bake at 350 degrees for 1 hour.

Hot Fruit Compote

Yield:
10 servings

Utensil:
9x13-inch dish

Approx Per Serving:
Cal 287
Prot 1 g
Carbo 46 g
Fiber 3 g
T Fat 10 g
Chol 25 mg
Sod 87 mg

1 16-ounce can pineapple chunks, drained
1 16-ounce can sliced peaches, drained
1 15-ounce jar spiced apple rings, drained
1 16-ounce can pear halves, drained
1 16-ounce can apricot halves, drained
1/2 cup butter
2 tablespoons flour
1/2 cup sugar
1 cup Sherry
12 maraschino cherries

Layer pineapple, peaches, apple rings,pear halves and apricot halves in 9x13-inch baking dish. Melt butter in top of double boiler over hot water. Add flour, sugar and Sherry, stirring until smooth. Cook for 15 minutes or until mixture is slightly thickened, stirring constantly. Pour over fruit layers. Arrange cherries on top of fruit. Bake at 350 degrees for 20 minutes. Serve immediately. May store in refrigerator and reheat when ready to serve. This recipe adds color and a sweet touch to your morning menus.

Baked Pineapple

Yield:
4 servings

Utensil:
1½-quart dish

Approx Per Serving:
Cal 389
Prot 4 g
Carbo 70 g
Fiber 1 g
T Fat 12 g
Chol 130 mg
Sod 110 mg

2 eggs
2 tablespoons cornstarch
¾ cup sugar
1 teaspoon vanilla extract
¼ cup water
1 20-ounce can crushed pineapple
3 tablespoons butter
Cinnamon to taste

Beat eggs in mixer bowl until foamy. Add cornstarch, sugar, vanilla and water; beat well. Stir in pineapple. Pour into greased 1½-quart baking dish. Dot with butter; sprinkle with cinnamon. Bake at 350 degrees for 1 hour. Serve warm.

Special Macaroni and Cheese

Yield:
12 servings

Utensil:
2-quart casserole

Approx Per Serving:
Cal 246
Prot 12 g
Carbo 19 g
Fiber 1 g
T Fat 14 g
Chol 55 mg
Sod 439 mg

1 8-ounce package macaroni
1 tablespoon margarine
1 egg, beaten
3 cups shredded sharp Cheddar cheese
1 teaspoon dry mustard
1 teaspoon salt
1 tablespoon hot water
1 cup milk
½ cup shredded sharp Cheddar cheese
½ cup dry bread crumbs

Cook macaroni using package directions; drain well. Stir in margarine, egg and 3 cups cheese. Spoon into buttered 2-quart casserole. Dissolve dry mustard and salt in hot water in bowl. Stir in milk. Pour over macaroni. Sprinkle with remaining ½ cup cheese and crumbs. Bake at 350 degrees for 45 minutes or until top is crusty and brown.

Noodle Kugle

Yield:
8 servings

Utensil:
9x13-inch dish

Approx Per Serving:
Cal 505
Prot 10 g
Carbo 58 g
Fiber 1 g
T Fat 27 g
Chol 57 mg
Sod 137 mg

1 16-ounce package egg noodles
1/2 cup butter
1/3 cup sugar
2 cups sour cream
1 16-ounce can crushed pineapple, drained
Cinnamon to taste

Cook noodles using package directions; drain. Combine noodles, butter and sugar in large bowl; stir until butter is melted and sugar is dissolved. Add sour cream and pineapple; mix well. Pour into 9x13-inch baking dish; sprinkle with cinnamon. Bake at 350 degrees for 30 minutes or until brown and bubbly.

Rice Casserole

Yield:
4 servings

Utensil:
1-quart casserole

Approx Per Serving:
Cal 309
Prot 7 g
Carbo 61 g
Fiber 3 g
T Fat 4 g
Chol 9 mg
Sod 874 mg

4 cups cooked rice
1 6-ounce can tiny green peas
1 can cream of celery soup
1 6-ounce can mushroom pieces, drained

Mix rice, peas, soup and mushroom pieces in bowl. Pour into greased 1-quart casserole. Bake at 350 degrees for 15 to 20 minutes or until hot and bubbly. May top with shredded Cheddar cheese if desired. May substitute cream of mushroom or chicken soup for cream of celery soup.

Tancy's Rice

Yield:
6 servings

Utensil:
2-quart casserole

Approx Per Serving:
Cal 226
Prot 3 g
Carbo 27 g
Fiber 1 g
T Fat 12 g
Chol <1 mg
Sod 495 mg

1 cup uncooked rice
1 small onion, chopped
6 tablespoons melted margarine
1 14-ounce can beef consommé
1 beef bouillon cube
1 consommé can boiling water

Sauté rice and onion in margarine in skillet until slightly brown. Add consommé, bouillon cube and boiling water; mix well. Pour into 2-quart casserole. Bake at 350 degrees for 1 hour.

Sage Stuffing

Yield:
20 servings

Utensil:
skillet

Approx Per Serving:
Cal 159
Prot 3 g
Carbo 14 g
Fiber 1 g
T Fat 10 g
Chol 25 mg
Sod 501 mg

3 cups chopped onions
3 cups minced celery
1/4 cup melted butter
16 slices white bread, dried, broken into small pieces
6 tablespoons minced fresh sage
1 cup minced fresh parsley
2 teaspoons salt
1 teaspoon freshly ground black pepper
3/4 cup melted butter
2 cups chicken broth

Sauté onions and celery in 1/4 cup melted butter in skillet just until soft. Combine bread, sage, parsley, salt and pepper in large bowl; toss to mix. Add sautéed vegetables and remaining 3/4 cup melted butter; toss to mix well. Stir in enough broth gradually to moisten. Mixture should not be too moist. Adjust seasonings if desired. May substitute 3 tablespoons dried sage leaves for fresh sage. This recipe will stuff a 16-pound turkey.

Breads

Linda Crow

Angel Biscuits

Yield:
60 servings

Utensil:
baking sheet

Approx Per Serving:
Cal 79
Prot 2 g
Carbo 10 g
Fiber <1 g
T Fat 4 g
Chol <1 mg
Sod 75 mg

1 envelope dry yeast
2 tablespoons warm water
5 1/2 cups flour
1/4 cup sugar
1 teaspoon soda
1 tablespoon baking powder
1 teaspoon salt
1 cup shortening
2 cups buttermilk

Dissolve yeast in warm water. Combine flour, sugar, soda, baking powder and salt in large bowl; mix well. Cut in shortening until crumbly. Add yeast and buttermilk; mix well. Knead until smooth. Chill, covered, overnight. Roll dough 1/2 inch thick on floured surface. Cut with biscuit cutter. Place with sides touching on baking sheet. Let rise for 45 minutes. Bake at 400 degrees for 10 minutes or until light brown.

Butter-Flavored Biscuits

Yield:
15 servings

Utensil:
9x13-inch pan

Approx Per Serving:
Cal 126
Prot 3 g
Carbo 14 g
Fiber <1 g
T Fat 7 g
Chol 1 mg
Sod 218 mg

2 tablespoons oil
2 cups self-rising flour
2/3 cup instant dry milk
1 teaspoon baking powder
1/3 cup butter-flavored shortening
1 cup water

Coat 9x13-inch baking pan with oil. Combine flour, dry milk and baking powder in bowl. Cut in shortening until crumbly. Add water, stirring until soft dough forms. Pat dough 1/2 inch thick on floured surface. Cut with biscuit cutter. Place in prepared pan. Bake at 500 degrees for 10 minutes.

Southern Raised Biscuits

Yield:
24 servings

Utensil:
baking sheet

Approx Per Serving:
Cal 191
Prot 4 g
Carbo 24 g
Fiber 1 g
T Fat 9 g
Chol 1 mg
Sod 209 mg

2 envelopes dry yeast
1/4 cup warm water
2 cups buttermilk
5 cups flour
1/3 cup sugar
1 tablespoon baking powder
1 teaspoon soda
1 1/4 teaspoons salt
1 cup shortening

Dissolve yeast in warm water in bowl. Let stand for 5 minutes or until bubbly. Add buttermilk; mix well. Combine flour, sugar, baking powder, soda and salt in large bowl. Cut in shortening until crumbly. Add buttermilk mixture gradually, stirring until soft dough forms. Knead dough 4 to 5 times on floured surface. Roll dough to 1/2-inch thickness. Cut with biscuit cutter; place on greased baking sheet. Let rise, covered, for 1 hour. Bake at 450 degrees for 10 to 12 minutes or until light brown. May be partially baked for 6 minutes, cooled and stored in airtight container in freezer. Bake at 450 degrees for 6 minutes or until brown.

Cranberry Coffee Cake

Yield:
16 servings

Utensil:
bundt pan

Approx Per Serving:
Cal 384
Prot 5 g
Carbo 55 g
Fiber 1 g
T Fat 17 g
Chol 50 mg
Sod 342 mg

3 cups flour
1 1/2 teaspoons baking powder
1 1/2 teaspoons soda
3/4 teaspoon salt
3/4 cup margarine, softened
1 1/2 cups sugar
3 eggs, at room temperature
1 1/2 teaspoons almond extract
1 1/2 cups sour cream
1 16-ounce can whole-berry cranberry sauce
1/2 cup chopped walnuts
3/4 cup confectioners' sugar
1 tablespoon warm water
1/2 teaspoon almond extract

Sift first 4 ingredients together. Cream margarine and sugar in large mixer bowl until light and fluffy. Add eggs 1 at a time, beating well after each addition. Add 1 1/2 teaspoons almond extract; beat well. Add flour mixture alternately with sour cream, beating well after each addition. Layer batter and cranberry sauce alternately 1/3 at a time in greased and floured bundt pan. Sprinkle with walnuts. Bake at 350 degrees for 1 hour or until coffee cake tests done. Cool in pan for 5 minutes. Remove to wire rack to cool completely. Drizzle mixture of remaining ingredients over top.

Coffee Cake

Yield:
16 servings

Utensil:
bundt pan

Approx Per Serving:
Cal 347
Prot 3 g
Carbo 45 g
Fiber 1 g
T Fat 18 g
Chol 53 mg
Sod 263 mg

1/2 cup sugar
1/4 cup packed brown sugar
1 teaspoon cinnamon
1/2 cup coconut
1/2 cup chopped pecans
1 2-layer package yellow cake mix
1 4-ounce package vanilla instant pudding mix
3/4 cup corn oil
3/4 cup water
4 eggs
1 teaspoon vanilla extract
1 teaspoon butter extract

Grease and flour bundt pan. Combine sugar, brown sugar, cinnamon, coconut and pecans in bowl; mix well. Combine cake mix and pudding mix in large mixer bowl; mix well. Add oil, water, eggs, vanilla and butter flavorings. Beat at high speed for 6 minutes. Layer batter and crumb mixture alternately 1/3 at a time in prepared pan. Cool in pan for 20 minutes. Invert onto serving plate. May drizzle with favorite glaze if desired.

Corn Bread

Yield:
8 servings

Utensil:
9x13-inch pan

Approx Per Serving:
Cal 440
Prot 4 g
Carbo 27 g
Fiber 1 g
T Fat 37 g
Chol 78 mg
Sod 603 mg

1 1/2 cups mayonnaise
2 eggs
1 16-ounce can cream-style yellow corn
1 12-ounce package corn muffin mix

Combine mayonnaise, eggs, corn and corn muffin mix in bowl; mix well. Pour into greased 9x13-inch baking pan. Bake at 350 degrees for 45 minutes.

Crackling Corn Bread

Yield:
9 servings

Utensil:
8x8-inch pan

Approx Per Serving:
Cal 243
Prot 4 g
Carbo 27 g
Fiber 2 g
T Fat 13 g
Chol 48 mg
Sod 426 mg

1 cup flour
1 teaspoon salt
1 tablespoon baking powder
2 tablespoons sugar
3/4 cup yellow cornmeal
2 eggs, beaten
3/4 cup cream-style corn
1/4 cup milk
1/2 cup cracklings
1/2 cup melted shortening

Sift flour, salt, baking powder and sugar into cornmeal in large bowl; mix well. Mix eggs, corn, milk, cracklings and shortening in bowl. Add to flour mixture, stirring just until moistened. Pour into 8-inch square baking pan. Bake at 350 degrees for 20 to 25 minutes or until corn bread tests done.

Nutritional information for this recipe does not include cracklings.

Spinach Corn Bread

Yield:
10 servings

Utensil:
pie plate

Approx Per Serving:
Cal 161
Prot 7 g
Carbo 10 g
Fiber 1 g
T Fat 11 g
Chol 107 mg
Sod 387 mg

1 10-ounce package frozen chopped spinach, thawed
1 6-ounce envelope buttermilk corn bread mix
4 eggs, beaten
6 tablespoons melted butter
1 medium onion, chopped
1 cup cottage cheese
1/2 teaspoon salt

Drain spinach; squeeze dry. Place in bowl. Add corn bread mix, eggs, butter, onion, cottage cheese and salt; stir just until moistened. Pour into greased 9-inch pie plate. Bake at 400 degrees for 25 minutes or until light brown.

Hush Puppies

Yield:
60 servings

Utensil:
deep saucepan

Approx Per Serving:
Cal 43
Prot 1 g
Carbo 8 g
Fiber <1 g
T Fat <1 g
Chol 8 mg
Sod 69 mg

3 cups flour
1/4 cup sugar
1 teaspoon salt
4 teaspoons baking powder
2 eggs
1 1/2 cups (or less) milk
1 cup corn
Oil for deep frying
1 cup confectioners' sugar

Combine flour, sugar, salt and baking powder in mixer bowl; mix well. Add eggs; beat well. Add enough milk to make soft batter. Fold in corn. Drop by 1/2 teaspoonfuls into hot deep oil. Fry until golden brown. Drain on paper towels. Sprinkle with confectioners' sugar.

Nutritional information for this recipe does not include oil for deep frying.

Apple Bread

Yield:
12 servings

Utensil:
loaf pan

Approx Per Serving:
Cal 292
Prot 4 g
Carbo 39 g
Fiber 1 g
T Fat 14 g
Chol 36 mg
Sod 129 mg

2 cups flour
1 teaspoon baking powder
1/2 teaspoon salt
1/2 teaspoon cloves
1/2 teaspoon cinnamon
1/2 cup shortening
1 cup sugar
2 eggs
2 cups chopped apples
2/3 cup chopped pecans
3 tablespoons confectioners' sugar

Sift flour, baking powder, salt, cloves and cinnamon together. Cream shortening and sugar in large mixer bowl until light and fluffy. Add eggs; beat well. Add flour mixture gradually, beating until smooth. Stir in apples and pecans. Pour into greased 5x9-inch loaf pan. Bake at 350 degrees for 1 hour. Sprinkle with confectioners' sugar. Remove to wire rack to cool completely. Cut into slices.

Beer Bread

Yield:
12 servings

Utensil:
loaf pan

Approx Per Serving:
Cal 114
Prot 2 g
Carbo 20 g
Fiber 1 g
T Fat 2 g
Chol 5 mg
Sod 243 mg

2 cups self-rising flour
3 tablespoons sugar
1 12-ounce can beer
2 tablespoons melted butter

Combine flour, sugar and beer in bowl; mix well. Batter will be thin. Pour into greased 4x7-inch loaf pan. Bake at 375 degrees for 30 to 35 minutes or until golden brown. Brush top with melted butter. Remove to wire rack to cool completely. May serve with favorite soup.

Date and Walnut Bread

Yield:
12 servings

Utensil:
loaf pan

Approx Per Serving:
Cal 302
Prot 6 g
Carbo 43 g
Fiber 2 g
T Fat 13 g
Chol 36 mg
Sod 133 mg

4 ounces dates, chopped
1 cup boiling water
2 cups flour
1 cup sugar
1 teaspoon baking powder
1 teaspoon soda
1/8 teaspoon salt
2 eggs
1 teaspoon vanilla extract
8 ounces walnuts, chopped

Soak dates in boiling water in bowl for several minutes. Let stand until cool. Combine flour, sugar, baking powder, soda and salt in large bowl; mix well. Add eggs and vanilla; mix well. Stir in undrained dates and walnuts. Pour into greased 5x9-inch loaf pan. Bake at 350 degrees for 1 hour.

Orange and Walnut Bread

Yield:
12 servings

Utensil:
loaf pan

Approx Per Serving:
Cal 204
Prot 4 g
Carbo 35 g
Fiber 1 g
T Fat 6 g
Chol 23 mg
Sod 208 mg

2 tablespoons butter
1/2 cup boiling water
2 tablespoons grated orange rind
Juice of 1 orange
1 cup sugar
2 teaspoons vanilla extract
1 egg, slightly beaten
2 cups flour
1 teaspoon soda
1 teaspoon baking powder
1/2 teaspoon salt
1/2 cup chopped walnuts
3 walnut halves

Melt butter in boiling water in large bowl. Add orange rind, orange juice, sugar, vanilla and egg; mix well. Sift flour, soda, baking powder and salt over orange mixture. Add 1/2 cup walnuts; mix well. Pour into greased 5x9-inch loaf pan. Top with walnut halves. Bake at 350 degrees for 1 hour. Remove to wire rack to cool. Wrap in waxed paper and store in zip-lock freezer bag.

Moist Pumpkin Bread

Yield:
24 servings

Utensil:
loaf pans

Approx Per Serving:
Cal 255
Prot 3 g
Carbo 41 g
Fiber 1 g
T Fat 9 g
Chol 36 mg
Sod 223 mg

3 1/3 cups flour
1/2 teaspoon baking powder
2 teaspoons soda
1 1/2 teaspoons salt
1 teaspoon ground cloves
1 teaspoon cinnamon
2/3 cup shortening
2 2/3 cups sugar
4 eggs
2 cups mashed cooked pumpkin
2/3 cup water
2/3 cup finely chopped pecans
2/3 cup raisins

Combine flour, baking powder, soda, salt, cloves and cinnamon in bowl; mix well. Cream shortening in large mixer bowl until light. Add sugar; beat until fluffy. Add eggs; beat well. Stir in pumpkin and water. Add flour mixture; mix well. Fold in pecans and raisins. Spoon into 2 well greased and floured 5x9-inch loaf pans. Bake at 350 degrees for 1 hour and 10 minutes or until bread tests done. Remove to wire racks to cool. May substitute finely chopped walnuts for pecans.

Sourdough Bread

Yield:
36 servings

Utensil:
loaf pans

Approx Per Serving:
Cal 132
Prot 2 g
Carbo 23 g
Fiber 1 g
T Fat 3 g
Chol 0 mg
Sod 180 mg

Starter:
1 envelope dry yeast
1/2 cup warm water
2 tablespoons sugar
2 cups water
2 1/2 tablespoons flour

Feeding Starter:
1 cup warm water
3/4 cup sugar
3 tablespoons instant potato flakes

Bread:
6 cups bread flour
1 tablespoon salt
1/4 cup sugar
1 1/2 cups warm water
1/2 cup corn oil
1 cup Sourdough Starter

Starter: Dissolve yeast in 1/2 cup warm water. Mix sugar, 2 cups water and flour in glass bowl. Add yeast; mix well. Let stand, loosely covered, for 5 days. Store in refrigerator for 5 days.

Feeding Starter: "Feed" the starter by adding warm water, sugar and potato flakes; mix well. Let stand, loosely covered, at room temperature for 8 to 12 hours. Remove 1 cup starter. Use to prepare bread, give to a friend or discard. Return remaining starter to refrigerator. Repeat "feeding" and removing 1 cup starter every 3 to 5 days.

Bread: Combine flour, salt and sugar in large bowl; mix well. Mix warm water, oil and Sourdough Starter in small bowl; mix well. Add to flour mixture, stirring until dough pulls away from side of bowl. Pat down with oiled fingertips. Let rise, covered with foil, for 8 to 12 hours or until doubled in bulk. Knead on floured surface until smooth and elastic. Shape into 3 loaves. Place in 3 greased 5x9-inch loaf pans. Let rise, covered with greased waxed paper, for 8 to 12 hours or until doubled in bulk. Bake at 350 degrees for 30 minutes or until golden brown. Invert onto wire racks to cool. May store baked loaves in freezer.

Nutritional information is for bread only.

Coffee Can Sweet Potato Bread

Yield:
48 servings

Utensil:
coffee cans

Approx Per Serving:
Cal 164
Prot 2 g
Carbo 25 g
Fiber 1 g
T Fat 7 g
Chol 18 mg
Sod 93 mg

3 1/3 cups flour
1 teaspoon salt
2 teaspoons soda
2 teaspoons nutmeg
1 tablespoon cinnamon
3 cups sugar
4 eggs
1 cup oil
2/3 cup water
2 cups mashed cooked sweet potatoes
1 cup chopped black walnuts
1 cup raisins

Sift flour, salt, soda, nutmeg and cinnamon together. Beat sugar and eggs in mixer bowl until light. Blend in oil. Add water and sweet potatoes; mix well. Add flour mixture gradually, stirring until smooth. Fold in walnuts and raisins. Pour into 4 greased and floured 1-pound coffee cans. Bake at 325 degrees for 1 hour. Remove to wire racks to cool. May substitute pecans for walnuts.

Sweet Potato Bread

Yield:
36 servings

Utensil:
loaf pans

Approx Per Serving:
Cal 224
Prot 3 g
Carbo 34 g
Fiber 1 g
T Fat 9 g
Chol 24 mg
Sod 124 mg

3 cups sugar
1 cup oil
4 eggs
2 cups mashed cooked sweet potatoes
3 1/2 cups flour
1 teaspoon salt
2 teaspoons soda
2 tablespoons cinnamon
2 teaspoons nutmeg
2/3 cup water
1 cup chopped pecans
1 cup raisins
1 teaspoon vanilla extract
2 tablespoons confectioners' sugar

Beat sugar and oil in large mixer bowl until light. Add eggs 1 at a time, beating well after each addition. Stir in sweet potatoes. Add flour, salt, soda, cinnamon and nutmeg; mix well. Stir in water, pecans and raisins. Add vanilla; mix well. Pour into 3 greased and floured 5x9-inch loaf pans. Bake at 325 degrees for 45 minutes. Sprinkle with confectioners' sugar. Remove to wire rack to cool. May bake in tube pan for 1 hour or in muffin cups for 15 to 20 minutes or until muffins test done.

Zucchini Bread

Yield:
24 servings

Utensil:
loaf pans

Approx Per Serving:
Cal 269
Prot 3 g
Carbo 36 g
Fiber 1 g
T Fat 13 g
Chol 27 mg
Sod 141 mg

3 eggs
1 cup oil
1 cup sugar
1 cup packed brown sugar
2 cups shredded zucchini
2 teaspoons vanilla extract
3 cups flour
1 teaspoon soda
1 teaspoon salt
1/4 teaspoon baking powder
1 tablespoon cinnamon
1 cup raisins
1 cup chopped walnuts

Beat eggs in mixer bowl until fluffy. Add oil, sugar, brown sugar, zucchini and vanilla; mix well. Combine flour, soda, salt, baking powder and cinnamon in bowl. Add to zucchini mixture; mix well. Stir in raisins and walnuts. Pour into 2 well-greased 5x9-inch loaf pans. Bake at 375 degrees for 1 hour. Cool in pans for 10 minutes. Remove to wire racks to cool completely.

Blueberry Muffins

Yield:
12 servings

Utensil:
muffin pan

Approx Per Serving:
Cal 249
Prot 4 g
Carbo 38 g
Fiber 1 g
T Fat 9 g
Chol 58 mg
Sod 227 mg

2 cups flour
2 teaspoons baking powder
1/2 teaspoon salt
1/2 cup butter
1 cup sugar
2 eggs
1/2 cup milk
1 teaspoon vanilla extract
2 1/2 cups blueberries
2 teaspoons sugar

Sift flour, baking powder and salt together. Cream butter and 1 cup sugar in mixer bowl until light and fluffy. Add eggs 1 at a time, beating well after each addition. Add flour mixture alternately with milk, beating well after each addition. Stir in vanilla. Fold in blueberries. Spoon into greased muffin cups; sprinkle with remaining 2 teaspoons sugar. Bake at 375 degrees for 30 minutes.

Crumble-Top Blueberry Muffins

Yield:
12 servings

Utensil:
muffin pan

Approx Per Serving:
Cal 262
Prot 4 g
Carbo 42 g
Fiber 1 g
T Fat 9 g
Chol 41 mg
Sod 279 mg

2 1/2 cups sifted cake flour
4 teaspoons baking powder
1/2 teaspoon salt
1/4 cup butter, softened
1/2 cup sugar
1 egg
1 cup milk
1 teaspoon vanilla extract
1 1/2 cups fresh blueberries, rinsed, drained
1/2 cup sugar
1/2 teaspoon cinnamon
2/3 cup all-purpose flour
1/4 cup cold butter

Combine cake flour, baking powder and salt in bowl; mix well. Cream 1/4 cup butter and 1/2 cup sugar in mixer bowl until light and fluffy. Add egg; beat well. Add flour mixture alternately with milk, beating well after each addition. Stir in vanilla. Fold in blueberries. Spoon into greased muffin cups. Mix remaining 1/2 cup sugar, cinnamon, all-purpose flour and 1/4 cup cold butter in small bowl until crumbly. Sprinkle over batter. Bake at 375 degrees for 20 to 25 minutes or until golden brown. Serve warm.

Cheddar Muffins

Yield:
12 servings

Utensil:
muffin pan

Approx Per Serving:
Cal 169
Prot 6 g
Carbo 17 g
Fiber 1 g
T Fat 8 g
Chol 41 mg
Sod 290 mg

2 cups flour
3 1/2 teaspoons baking powder
1/2 teaspoon salt
1 teaspoon paprika
1 cup shredded Cheddar cheese
1 egg, beaten
1 cup milk
1/4 cup melted butter

Combine flour, baking powder, salt, paprika and Cheddar cheese in bowl. Make well in center. Beat egg, milk and butter in mixer bowl until blended. Pour into well in center of flour mixture; stir just until moistened. Fill greased muffin cups 2/3 full. Bake at 425 degrees for 20 minutes. Remove from pans immediately.

Italian-Style Popovers

Yield:
6 servings

Utensil:
custard cups

Approx Per Serving:
Cal 137
Prot 5 g
Carbo 18 g
Fiber 1 g
T Fat 5 g
Chol 74 mg
Sod 254 mg

2 eggs
1/2 cup milk
1/2 cup water
1 cup flour
1 tablespoon Italian salad dressing mix
1/4 teaspoon salt
1 tablespoon oil

Combine eggs, milk, water, flour, salad dressing mix and salt in small mixer bowl. Beat at medium speed for 1 1/2 minutes. Add oil. Beat for 30 seconds longer. Pour into 6-ounce custard cups. Bake at 350 degrees for 25 minutes.

Cheesy Herb Rolls

Yield:
4 servings

Utensil:
baking sheet

Approx Per Serving:
Cal 231
Prot 5 g
Carbo 18 g
Fiber 1 g
T Fat 16 g
Chol 35 mg
Sod 384 mg

1 5-ounce package frozen Parker House-style rolls
1/4 cup melted butter
1/4 cup freshly grated Parmesan cheese
Chopped fresh thyme to taste
Chopped fresh sage to taste
Chopped fresh parsley to taste

Place rolls on greased baking sheet. Let rise at room temperature until doubled in bulk. Brush with melted butter; sprinkle with Parmesan cheese, thyme, sage and parsley. Bake at 375 degrees for 10 to 12 minutes or until light brown.

Yeast Rolls

Yield:
36 servings

Utensil:
baking sheet

Approx Per Serving:
Cal 91
Prot 2 g
Carbo 15 g
Fiber 1 g
T Fat 2 g
Chol 7 mg
Sod 96 mg

1 envelope dry yeast
1/3 cup warm water
6 tablespoons sugar
1/4 cup shortening
1 1/2 teaspoons salt
1 1/2 cups scalded milk
2 cups sifted flour
1 egg
3 1/4 cups sifted flour

Dissolve yeast in warm water. Combine sugar, shortening and salt in large bowl; mix well. Add milk; stir until shortening melts. Add 2 cups flour; mix well. Add yeast and egg; mix well. Add remaining 3 1/4 cups flour gradually, stirring until soft dough forms. Place in greased bowl, turning to coat surface. Let rise in warm place for 2 hours or until doubled in bulk. Punch dough down. Knead on floured surface until smooth and elastic. Shape into small balls; place on ungreased baking sheet. Let rise in warm place until doubled in bulk. Bake at 400 degrees until golden brown.

Hot Buns

Yield:
36 servings

Utensil:
baking sheet

Approx Per Serving:
Cal 142
Prot 3 g
Carbo 19 g
Fiber 1 g
T Fat 6 g
Chol 19 mg
Sod 116 mg

2 envelopes dry yeast
1 cup warm water
1/2 cup warm milk
1/2 cup shortening
1/2 cup sugar
1 1/2 teaspoons salt
2 eggs, beaten
4 to 6 cups flour
1/2 cup melted butter

Dissolve yeast in warm water and warm milk in large bowl. Add shortening, sugar, salt and eggs; mix well. Add enough flour to make soft dough. Knead on floured surface for 5 minutes. Place in greased bowl, turning to coat surface. Let rise, covered, in warm place for 1 hour or until doubled in bulk. Punch dough down. Knead 4 to 5 times. Shape into buns or dinner rolls. Place on ungreased baking sheet. Let rise, covered, in warm place for 45 minutes or until doubled in bulk. Bake at 400 degrees for 17 minutes or just until tops are golden brown. Brush with melted butter. Remove from baking sheet. Let stand, covered with clean cloth, for soft crust. Let stand, uncovered, for firm crust. May add 1/2 to 3/4 cup shredded Cheddar cheese with flour, brushing with egg white and sprinkling with sesame seed before baking.

Desserts

Linda Crow

Apple Crisp

Yield:
6 servings

Utensil:
9x9-inch pan

Approx Per Serving:
Cal 318
Prot 2 g
Carbo 44 g
Fiber 2 g
T Fat 16 g
Chol 41 mg
Sod 219 mg

4 cups sliced apples
2 tablespoons water
1 cup flour
1/2 cup sugar
1/2 teaspoon cinnamon
1/4 teaspoon nutmeg
1/4 teaspoon salt
1/2 cup butter

Place apples and water in 9-inch square baking pan. Combine flour, sugar, cinnamon, nutmeg and salt in bowl; mix well. Cut in butter until crumbly. Sprinkle over apples. Bake, covered, at 350 degrees for 15 minutes. Bake, uncovered, for 30 minutes longer. Serve with vanilla ice cream.

Apple Strudel

Yield:
24 servings

Utensil:
baking sheet

Approx Per Serving:
Cal 207
Prot 3 g
Carbo 30 g
Fiber 1 g
T Fat 9 g
Chol 13 mg
Sod 86 mg

3 cups flour
2 tablespoons sugar
3/4 cup margarine
1 cup sour cream
1 egg, beaten
3 apples, peeled, cut into slices
1 21-ounce can apple pie filling
3/4 cup packed brown sugar
1/2 teaspoon cinnamon
1/4 cup raisins
1/4 cup chopped walnuts

Combine flour and sugar in bowl; mix well. Cut in margarine until crumbly. Add sour cream; mix well. Knead lightly. Chill overnight. Preheat oven to 425 degrees. Roll dough into two 14x16-inch rectangles on lightly floured surface. Place on baking sheets. Brush lightly with beaten egg. Combine apples, pie filling, brown sugar and cinnamon in bowl; mix well. Stir in raisins and walnuts. Spread in center of rectangles. Fold sides over filling. Reduce temperature to 375 degrees. Bake for 30 minutes or until apples are tender and crust is golden brown. May brush warm strudel with jam or marmalade.

BANANA SPLIT CAKE

Yield:
15 servings

Utensil:
9x13-inch dish

Approx Per Serving:
Cal 622
Prot 4 g
Carbo 80 g
Fiber 2 g
T Fat 34 g
Chol 28 mg
Sod 415 mg

3/4 cup melted margarine
3 cups graham cracker crumbs
1 1-pound package confectioners' sugar
1 cup margarine, softened
1 1/2 teaspoons vanilla extract
2 eggs, beaten
1 16-ounce can crushed pineapple, drained
7 bananas, sliced
16 ounces whipped topping
1/4 cup chopped maraschino cherries
1/4 cup chopped pecans

Combine margarine and graham cracker crumbs in 9x13-inch serving dish. Combine confectioners' sugar, remaining 1 cup margarine, vanilla and eggs in mixer bowl. Beat for 15 minutes. Spread over crumbs. Layer pineapple and bananas on top. Spread whipped topping over fruit. Sprinkle with cherries and pecans.

BLUEBERRY DELIGHT

Yield:
8 servings

Utensil:
9x13-inch dish

Approx Per Serving:
Cal 407
Prot 1 g
Carbo 54 g
Fiber 1 g
T Fat 23 g
Chol 42 mg
Sod 157 mg

2/3 cup butter, softened
2 cups confectioners' sugar
2 tablespoons (or more) milk
1/4 cup chopped pecans
1 21-ounce can blueberry pie filling
2 cups whipped topping

Combine butter and confectioners' sugar in bowl. Add enough milk to form a soft dough. Stir in pecans. Press onto bottom and sides of greased 9x13-inch baking dish. Bake at 350 degrees for 15 minutes or until lightly browned. Let stand until cool. Spoon pie filling over crust. Top with whipped topping. Chill until serving time. May substitute apple, peach or cherry pie filling for blueberry pie filling.

Blueberry Glaze

Yield:
12 servings

Utensil:
saucepan

Approx Per Serving :
Cal 48
Prot <1 g
Carbo 12 g
Fiber 1 g
T Fat <1 g
Chol 0 mg
Sod 48 mg

1/2 cup sugar
2 teaspoons cornstarch
1/4 teaspoon salt
1/2 cup water
1 tablespoon lemon juice
2 cups blueberries

Combine sugar, cornstarch, salt, water and lemon juice in saucepan. Stir in blueberries. Cook over medium heat until thickened, stirring frequently. Serve glaze over cake, ice cream, pudding, pancakes or cheesecake.

Holiday Cheesecake

Yield:
12 servings

Utensil:
springform pan

Approx Per Serving:
Cal 396
Prot 7 g
Carbo 28 g
Fiber <1 g
T Fat 29 g
Chol 131 mg
Sod 281 mg

1 cup graham cracker crumbs
3 tablespoons sugar
3 tablespoons melted butter
24 ounces cream cheese, softened
1 tablespoon lemon juice
1 teaspoon grated lemon rind
3/4 cup sugar
3 eggs
1 cup sour cream
2 tablespoons sugar
1 teaspoon vanilla extract

Combine cracker crumbs, 3 tablespoons sugar and melted butter in bowl; mix well. Press over bottom of 9-inch springform pan. Bake at 325 degrees for 10 minutes. Reduce oven temperature to 300 degrees. Beat cream cheese, lemon juice, lemon rind and 3/4 cup sugar in mixer bowl until light and fluffy. Add eggs 1 at a time, beating well after each addition. Pour into prepared pan. Bake for 55 minutes. Combine sour cream, remaining 2 tablespoons sugar and vanilla in bowl; mix well. Spread carefully over cheesecake. Bake for 10 minutes longer. Loosen cheesecake from rim of pan. Let stand until cool. Place on serving plate; remove side of pan. Garnish with favorite topping. Chill until serving time.

Chocolate Éclair

Yield:
15 servings

Utensil:
9x13-inch dish

Approx Per Serving:
Cal 354
Prot 5 g
Carbo 58 g
Fiber 1 g
T Fat 13 g
Chol 16 mg
Sod 360 mg

1 16-ounce package graham crackers
2 4-ounce packages French vanilla instant pudding mix
3 cups milk
8 ounces whipped topping
1/4 cup evaporated milk
1/3 cup baking cocoa
1 cup sugar
1/8 teaspoon salt
1 teaspoon vanilla extract
1/4 cup butter, softened

Line 9x13-inch serving dish with 1/3 of the graham crackers. Combine pudding mix, milk and whipped topping in mixer bowl. Beat at medium speed for 2 minutes. Layer pudding mixture and remaining graham crackers 1/2 at a time in prepared dish. Combine evaporated milk, cocoa, sugar and salt in saucepan. Bring to a boil. Cook for 1 minute. Remove from heat. Beat in vanilla and butter. Pour over graham crackers. May substitute 1 can chocolate frosting for boiled frosting.

Three-Layer Chocolate Pudding Dessert

Yield:
15 servings

Utensil:
9x13-inch dish

Approx Per Serving:
Cal 366
Prot 4 g
Carbo 38 g
Fiber 1 g
T Fat 23 g
Chol 23 mg
Sod 244 mg

1 cup flour
1/2 cup melted margarine
1/2 cup chopped pecans
1 cup confectioners' sugar
8 ounces cream cheese, softened
12 ounces whipped topping
2 4-ounce packages chocolate instant pudding mix
3 cups cold milk
1/4 cup chopped pecans

Combine flour, margarine and 1/2 cup pecans in bowl; mix well. Press into 9x13-inch baking dish. Bake at 350 degrees for 12 to 15 minutes or until lightly browned. Let stand until cool. Cream confectioners' sugar, cream cheese and 1 cup whipped topping in mixer bowl until light and fluffy. Spread over crust. Combine pudding mix and milk in bowl; mix well. Spread over cream cheese mixture. Top with remaining whipped topping. Sprinkle with remaining 1/4 cup pecans. Chill for 2 hours.

Dirt

Yield:
16 servings

Utensil:
flower pot

Approx Per Serving:
Cal 455
Prot 5 g
Carbo 54 g
Fiber 1 g
T Fat 25 g
Chol 23 mg
Sod 399 mg

1/2 cup margarine, softened
8 ounces cream cheese, softened
1 cup confectioners' sugar
3 1/2 cups milk
2 4-ounce packages French vanilla instant pudding mix
12 ounces whipped topping
1 20-ounce package Oreo cookies, crushed

Cream margarine, cream cheese and confectioners' sugar in mixer bowl until light and fluffy. Add milk, pudding mix and whipped topping. Beat until smooth. Layer cookie crumbs and pudding mixture alternately in large, new plastic flowerpot until all ingredients are used, ending with cookie crumbs. Decorate with silk flower in center. Garnish with gummy worms. Serve with garden trowel.

Flower Garden Cake

Yield:
14 servings

Utensil:
tube pan

Approx Per Serving:
Cal 194
Prot 5 g
Carbo 39 g
Fiber <1 g
T Fat 3 g
Chol 91 mg
Sod 180 mg

1 tablespoon unflavored gelatin
1/4 cup cold water
6 egg yolks, beaten
3/4 cup sugar
1 1/2 teaspoons grated lemon rind
3/4 cup lemon juice
6 egg whites
3/4 cup sugar
1 15-ounce angel food cake, cut into bite-sized pieces

Soften gelatin in cold water. Combine egg yolks, 3/4 cup sugar, lemon rind and lemon juice in double boiler. Cook over hot water until custard coats a spoon, stirring constantly. Stir in gelatin mixture. Beat egg whites in bowl until soft peaks form. Add 3/4 cup sugar gradually, beating until stiff peaks form. Fold gently into custard. Fold in cake pieces; do not stir. Spoon into oiled 10-inch tube pan. Chill overnight. Unmold onto serving plate. Garnish with whipped cream or whipped topping and maraschino cherries or fresh strawberries. May add bits of pecans and cherries to custard mixture for flavor and color.

Easy Vanilla Ice Cream

Yield:
16 servings

Utensil:
ice cream freezer

Approx Per Serving:
Cal 200
Prot 6 g
Carbo 30 g
Fiber 0 g
T Fat 6 g
Chol 25 mg
Sod 89 mg

2 14-ounce cans sweetened condensed milk
4 cups milk
4 teaspoons vanilla extract

Combine condensed milk, milk and vanilla in bowl; mix well. Pour into ice cream freezer container. Freeze using manufacturer's instructions. Let stand, packed in ice and covered, for 1 hour to ripen. May add 1/2 cup chocolate syrup and 1 cup semisweet chocolate minichips to make double chocolate ice cream. May add 1 tablespoon butter extract and 2 cups chopped toasted pecans to make butter pecan ice cream. May add 1 1/2 cups "M & M's" Chocolate Candies to make rainbow ice cream. May dissolve 1 tablespoon instant coffee in 1 cup hot water and add with 1/2 cup chocolate syrup to make mocha ice cream.

Violet's Lemon Bisque

Yield:
15 servings

Utensil:
9x13-inch dish

Approx Per Serving:
Cal 244
Prot 4 g
Carbo 43 g
Fiber <1 g
T Fat 7 g
Chol 26 mg
Sod 156 mg

1 16-ounce package vanilla wafers
1 3-ounce package lemon gelatin
1 cup boiling water
Juice of 2 lemons
1 12-ounce can evaporated milk, chilled
1 cup sugar

Crush vanilla wafers, reserving a small amount of crumbs. Spread in 9x13-inch serving dish. Dissolve gelatin in boiling water in large bowl. Cool. Stir in lemon juice. Whip evaporated milk with sugar in bowl until soft peaks form. Fold into gelatin mixture. Pour into prepared dish. Sprinkle with reserved crumbs. Chill overnight.

Lemon Lush

Yield:
15 servings

Utensil:
9x13-inch pan

Approx Per Serving:
Cal 419
Prot 5 g
Carbo 42 g
Fiber 1 g
T Fat 27 g
Chol 23 mg
Sod 281 mg

1 1/2 cups flour
3/4 cup margarine, softened
1/2 cup chopped pecans
1 cup confectioners' sugar
8 ounces cream cheese, softened
16 ounces whipped topping
1 teaspoon vanilla extract
2 4-ounce packages lemon instant pudding mix
3 cups cold milk

Combine flour and margarine in bowl; mix well. Stir in pecans. Press into 9x13-inch baking pan. Bake at 350 degrees for 20 minutes. Cream confectioners' sugar, cream cheese, 1 cup whipped topping and vanilla in mixer bowl until light and fluffy. Spread in prepared pan. Chill for 1 hour. Combine pudding mix and milk in bowl; mix well. Chill until partially set. Spoon over creamed mixture. Top with remaining whipped topping. Chill until serving time.

Cool Lime Dessert

Yield:
15 servings

Utensil:
9x13-inch dish

Approx Per Serving:
Cal 239
Prot 4 g
Carbo 28 g
Fiber <1 g
T Fat 13 g
Chol 29 mg
Sod 174 mg

1 1/2 cups crushed chocolate wafers
6 tablespoons margarine, softened
1 3-ounce package lime gelatin
1 cup boiling water
3 tablespoons lime juice
8 ounces cream cheese, softened
1 cup sugar
1 teaspoon vanilla extract
1 12-ounce can evaporated milk, chilled

Combine crushed wafers and margarine in bowl; mix well. Press into buttered 9x13-inch serving dish. Dissolve gelatin in hot water in bowl. Stir in lime juice. Chill until partially set. Beat cream cheese in mixer bowl until light. Add sugar and vanilla; beat until fluffy. Stir into gelatin mixture. Beat evaporated milk until soft peaks form. Fold gently into gelatin mixture. Spread in prepared dish. Chill for 4 hours or longer.

Mountain Momma Mud Slide

Yield:
15 servings

Utensil:
9x13-inch pan

Approx Per Serving:
Cal 374
Prot 4 g
Carbo 39 g
Fiber 1 g
T Fat 23 g
Chol 22 mg
Sod 240 mg

1/2 cup margarine, softened
1 cup flour
1 cup chopped pecans
1 cup confectioners' sugar
8 ounces cream cheese, softened
8 ounces whipped topping
1 4-ounce package chocolate instant pudding mix
1 4-ounce package vanilla instant pudding mix
2 cups cold milk
1 3-ounce chocolate bar, grated

Combine margarine, flour and pecans in bowl; mix well. Press into 9x13-inch baking pan. Bake at 350 degrees for 20 minutes. Let stand until cool. Cream confectioners' sugar and cream cheese in mixer bowl until light and fluffy. Fold in whipped topping. Combine pudding mixes and milk in bowl; mix well. Layer half the creamed mixture, pudding mixture and remaining creamed mixture in prepared pan. Sprinkle with grated chocolate. Chill for 1 hour.

Chocolate Dream

Yield:
12 servings

Utensil:
9x13-inch pan

Approx Per Serving:
Cal 440
Prot 6 g
Carbo 46 g
Fiber 1 g
T Fat 27 g
Chol 50 mg
Sod 280 mg

1 cup flour
1/2 cup melted butter
1/2 cup chopped walnuts
1 cup confectioners' sugar
8 ounces cream cheese, softened
12 ounces whipped topping
2 4-ounce packages chocolate instant pudding mix
3 cups milk

Combine flour, melted butter and walnuts in bowl; mix well. Press into 9x13-inch baking pan. Bake at 350 degrees for 25 minutes. Let stand until cool. Cream confectioners' sugar, cream cheese and 1 cup whipped topping in mixer bowl until light and fluffy. Spread in prepared pan. Combine pudding mix and milk in bowl; mix well. Spread over creamed mixture. Top with remaining whipped topping. Garnish with additional chopped walnuts. Chill overnight.

Pavlova

Yield:
8 servings

Utensil:
baking sheet

Approx Per Serving:
Cal 210
Prot 2 g
Carbo 27 g
Fiber <1 g
T Fat 11 g
Chol 41 mg
Sod 37 mg

4 egg whites, at room temperature
1/8 teaspoon cream of tartar
1 cup sugar
2 teaspoons cornstarch
1 tablespoon cold water
1/4 teaspoon vanilla extract
1 cup whipping cream, whipped

Preheat oven to 400 degrees. Beat egg whites in mixer bowl at low speed until foamy. Add cream of tartar. Beat at high speed for 4 minutes or until stiff peaks form. Add sugar gradually, beating constantly at high speed until very stiff glossy peaks form. Add cornstarch, cold water and vanilla. Beat for 2 minutes or until smooth. Spoon onto foil-lined baking sheet. Spread into large circle. Reduce oven temperature to 250 degrees. Bake for 1 1/2 hours. Turn off oven. Let stand in closed oven until completely cooled. Place on serving plate. Spread with whipped cream. Garnish with fresh fruit or chocolate shavings. This is the "unofficial" dessert of Australia.

Peaches 'n' Cream

Yield:
15 servings

Utensil:
9x13-inch pan

Approx Per Serving:
Cal 281
Prot 3 g
Carbo 41 g
Fiber 1 g
T Fat 13 g
Chol 38 mg
Sod 277 mg

1/2 cup butter, softened
1 2-layer package yellow cake mix
1 29-ounce can sliced peaches, drained
1/4 cup sugar
1 teaspoon cinnamon
1 egg, slightly beaten
1 cup sour cream

Cut butter into cake mix in bowl until crumbly. Press into greased 9x13-inch baking pan. Bake at 350 degrees for 10 minutes. Let stand until cool. Arrange peaches over baked layer. Sprinkle with mixture of sugar and cinnamon. Combine egg and sour cream in bowl; mix well. Drizzle over peaches. Bake for 30 minutes. Let stand until cool. Cut into squares.

Bridal Pudding

Yield:
12 servings

Utensil:
springform pan

Approx Per Serving:
Cal 227
Prot 4 g
Carbo 17 g
Fiber 1 g
T Fat 17 g
Chol 54 mg
Sod 87 mg

1/2 cup flaked coconut
2 envelopes unflavored gelatin
1/2 cup cold water
1/3 cup boiling water
6 egg whites, at room temperature
1/4 teaspoon salt
3/4 cup sugar
2 cups whipping cream
1 teaspoon vanilla extract
1/2 cup flaked coconut

Sprinkle bottom and side of buttered 9-inch springform pan with 1/2 cup coconut. Soften gelatin in cold water. Add boiling water; stir until dissolved. Beat egg whites in mixer bowl at low speed until foamy. Add salt. Beat at medium speed until soft peaks form. Add sugar gradually, beating constantly at high speed until stiff peaks form. Fold gelatin mixture gently into egg whites. Beat whipping cream in mixer bowl until soft peaks form. Stir in vanilla. Fold gently into egg white mixture. Spoon into prepared pan. Sprinkle with remaining 1/2 cup coconut. Chill for 4 hours to overnight.

Fresh Peach Pudding

Yield:
9 servings

Utensil:
6x10-inch pan

Approx Per Serving:
Cal 308
Prot 3 g
Carbo 62 g
Fiber 4 g
T Fat 7 g
Chol 18 mg
Sod 87 mg

4 pounds peaches
3/4 cup sugar
7 1/2 teaspoons tapioca
1/8 teaspoon salt
1 cup sifted flour
1/2 cup sugar
1/3 cup butter

Peel and slice peaches. Combine with 3/4 cup sugar, tapioca and salt in bowl; mix well. Spoon into 6x10-inch baking pan. Combine flour and remaining 1/2 cup sugar in bowl; mix well. Cut in butter until crumbly. Sprinkle over peaches. Bake at 360 degrees for 1 hour and 20 minutes or until peaches are tender and topping is browned. Garnish with additional peach slices.

Rice Pudding

Yield:
10 servings

Utensil:
saucepan

Approx Per Serving:
Cal 244
Prot 7 g
Carbo 42 g
Fiber 1 g
T Fat 6 g
Chol 98 mg
Sod 177 mg

3 cups water
1/2 teaspoon salt
Rind of 1 lemon
1 cup rice
4 eggs, beaten
3/4 cup sugar
4 cups milk
1 tablespoon cinnamon
1/2 cup raisins
1 teaspoon cinnamon

Combine water, salt, lemon rind and rice in saucepan. Cook over low heat until water evaporates. Discard lemon rind. Combine eggs, sugar and milk in bowl; mix well. Pour over rice mixture; mix well. Cook for 1 to 2 minutes longer or until heated through. Stir in 1 tablespoon cinnamon and raisins. Tint with several drops of yellow food coloring if desired. Sprinkle with remaining 1 teaspoon cinnamon. Serve warm or chilled.

Pumpkin Roll

Yield:
8 servings

Utensil:
10x15-inch pan

Approx Per Serving:
Cal 453
Prot 8 g
Carbo 62 g
Fiber 2 g
T Fat 21 g
Chol 103 mg
Sod 289 mg

3 eggs
1 cup sugar
2/3 cup canned pumpkin
1 teaspoon lemon juice
3/4 cup flour
1 teaspoon baking powder
2 teaspoons cinnamon
1 teaspoon ginger
1/2 teaspoon salt
1 cup chopped walnuts
1/2 cup confectioners' sugar
4 teaspoons margarine, softened
1 cup confectioners' sugar
6 ounces cream cheese, softened
1/2 teaspoon vanilla extract

Beat eggs in mixer bowl at high speed for 5 minutes. Add sugar, pumpkin and lemon juice gradually, beating well after each addition. Add flour, baking powder, cinnamon, ginger and salt; mix well. Pour into greased and floured foil-lined 10x15-inch baking pan. Sprinkle with walnuts. Bake at 375 degrees for 15 minutes. Turn out on towel sprinkled with 1/2 cup confectioners' sugar. Roll up with towel. Chill in refrigerator. Cream margarine, remaining 1 cup confectioners' sugar, cream cheese and vanilla in mixer bowl until light and fluffy. Unroll cake. Spread with creamed mixture; roll up. Chill until serving time.

Strawberry Trifle

Yield:
10 servings

Utensil:
trifle dish

Approx Per Serving:
Cal 354
Prot 6 g
Carbo 42 g
Fiber 1 g
T Fat 15 g
Chol 70 mg
Sod 201 mg

1 10-ounce package frozen sliced strawberries
1 pound cake, cut into slices
1 cup Sherry
2 3-ounce packages strawberry gelatin
2 cups boiling water
1 cup whipping cream, whipped
1 pint fresh strawberries

Thaw and drain frozen strawberries. Line trifle dish or deep stemmed dish with cake slices. Add strawberries. Sprinkle with Sherry. Combine 1 package gelatin with 1 cup boiling water in bowl; mix well. Chill until partially set. Spoon over cake and strawberries. Chill until gelatin is set. Combine remaining 1 package gelatin and 1 cup boiling water in bowl. Cool slightly. Fold in whipped cream. Spoon over trifle. Chill until set. Arrange fresh strawberries in decorative pattern over top. Garnish with additional whipped cream. Do not use dry Sherry.

Yummy Dessert

Yield:
12 servings

Utensil:
7x11-inch dish

Approx Per Serving:
Cal 354
Prot 5 g
Carbo 40 g
Fiber 1 g
T Fat 20 g
Chol 28 mg
Sod 294 mg

1/2 cup melted margarine
1 cup flour
1/2 cup chopped pecans
1/2 cup whipped topping
1 cup confectioners' sugar
8 ounces cream cheese, softened
1 4-ounce package chocolate instant pudding mix
1 4-ounce package vanilla instant pudding mix
2 1/2 cups milk

Combine margarine, flour and pecans in bowl; mix well. Press into 7x11-inch glass baking dish. Bake at 350 degrees until lightly browned. Let stand until cool. Cream whipped topping, confectioners' sugar and cream cheese in mixer bowl until light and fluffy. Spread over crust. Combine pudding mixes and milk in bowl; mix well. Spread over cream cheese mixture. Garnish with additional whipped topping.

Almost Heaven Cake

Yield:
12 servings

Utensil:
9x13-inch pan

Approx Per Serving:
Cal 563
Prot 7 g
Carbo 80 g
Fiber 1 g
T Fat 26 g
Chol 26 mg
Sod 353 mg

1 2-layer package yellow cake mix
1 20-ounce can crushed pineapple
1 4-ounce package vanilla instant pudding mix
2 cups cold milk
8 ounces cream cheese, softened
12 ounces whipped topping

Prepare and bake cake mix using package directions for 9x13-inch cake pan. Pierce cake with fork. Pour undrained pineapple over hot cake. Combine pudding mix and milk in medium bowl; mix well. Blend in cream cheese. Spread over pineapple. Spread whipped topping over top. Chill for 6 hours. Garnish with chopped pecans or shredded coconut.

Angel Food Cake

Yield:
12 servings

Utensil:
tube pan

Approx Per Serving:
Cal 166
Prot 3 g
Carbo 38 g
Fiber <1 g
T Fat <1 g
Chol 0 mg
Sod 44 mg

1 1/2 cups sifted confectioners' sugar
1 cup sifted cake flour
1 1/2 cups egg whites, at room temperature
1 1/2 teaspoons cream of tartar
1 teaspoon vanilla extract
1 cup sugar

Sift confectioners' sugar and flour together 3 times. Beat egg whites, cream of tartar and vanilla in 3-quart mixer bowl at medium speed until soft peaks form. Add sugar 2 tablespoons at a time, beating constantly at high speed until stiff peaks form. Sift 1/4 of the flour mixture at a time over egg whites. Fold in gently with rubber spatula. Spoon into ungreased 10-inch tube pan. Cut through batter 1 inch from center of pan with knife. Place on lowest oven rack. Bake at 350 degrees for 40 to 45 minutes or until top springs back when touched lightly. Invert on funnel to cool. Loosen cake from side of pan. Invert onto serving plate. Slice with serrated knife.

Yellow Angel Food Cake

Yield:
16 servings

Utensil:
tube pan

Approx Per Serving:
Cal 141
Prot 3 g
Carbo 28 g
Fiber <1 g
T Fat 2 g
Chol 67 mg
Sod 62 mg

1 1/2 cups flour
1/2 teaspoon baking powder
1/4 teaspoon salt
5 egg yolks
1/2 cup cold water
1 1/2 cups sugar
5 egg whites, at room temperature
3/4 teaspoon cream of tartar
1 teaspoon vanilla extract

Sift flour, baking powder and salt together several times. Beat egg yolks in bowl. Add cold water; beat well. Add sugar; beat well. Beat flour mixture into egg mixture. Beat egg whites in mixer bowl at low speed until foamy. Add cream of tartar and vanilla. Beat at high speed until stiff peaks form. Fold egg whites into batter gently. Spoon into ungreased tube pan. Cut through batter 1 inch from center of pan with knife. Bake at 325 degrees for 1 hour or until top is brown and dry. Invert on funnel to cool. Loosen cake from side of pan. Invert onto serving plate.

Fresh Apple Cake

Yield:
16 servings

Utensil:
tube pan

Approx Per Serving:
Cal 425
Prot 5 g
Carbo 49 g
Fiber 2 g
T Fat 24 g
Chol 40 mg
Sod 208 mg

3 cups flour
2 cups sugar
1 teaspoon salt
1 teaspoon soda
1 1/2 cups oil
2 teaspoons vanilla extract
3 large eggs, beaten
3 cups chopped Golden Delicious apples
3/4 cup coconut
1 cup chopped walnuts

Combine flour, sugar, salt and soda in large bowl. Add oil, vanilla and eggs; mix well. Batter will be stiff. Stir in apples. Add coconut and walnuts; mix well. Spoon into greased and floured tube pan. Bake at 350 degrees for 1 hour and 20 minutes. Cool in pan for several minutes. Invert cake onto serving plate.

Apple Cake and Topping

Yield:
15 servings

Utensil:
9x13-inch pan

Approx Per Serving:
Cal 464
Prot 4 g
Carbo 54 g
Fiber 1 g
T Fat 27 g
Chol 43 mg
Sod 287 mg

3 eggs
1$^3/_4$ cups sugar
1 cup oil
2 cups flour
1 teaspoon soda
1 teaspoon salt
1 teaspoon cinnamon
2 cups chopped apples
1 cup chopped walnuts
$^1/_2$ cup sugar
1 tablespoon cornstarch
$^1/_2$ cup packed brown sugar
1 cup water
$^1/_2$ cup margarine, softened
1 teaspoon vanilla extract

Beat eggs, 1$^3/_4$ cups sugar and oil in mixer bowl until foamy. Sift flour, soda, salt and cinnamon into bowl; mix well. Stir into egg mixture. Stir in apples and walnuts. Pour into greased 9x13-inch cake pan. Bake at 350 degrees for 40 to 50 minutes or until cake tests done. Combine remaining $^1/_2$ cup sugar, cornstarch and brown sugar in saucepan. Add water, margarine and vanilla. Cook until thickened, stirring constantly. Serve warm over cake.

Spicy Apple Cake

Yield:
16 servings

Utensil:
tube pan

Approx Per Serving:
Cal 377
Prot 5 g
Carbo 49 g
Fiber 2 g
T Fat 19 g
Chol 27 mg
Sod 194 mg

2 cups sugar
4 apples, chopped
3 cups flour
1 teaspoon cinnamon
1 teaspoon cloves
1 teaspoon nutmeg
1 teaspoon salt
1 teaspoon soda
1 cup oil
2 eggs, beaten
1 cup chopped black walnuts

Sprinkle sugar over apples in large bowl. Let stand for 10 minutes. Add flour, cinnamon, cloves, nutmeg, salt and soda; mix well. Stir in oil and eggs. Add walnuts; mix well. Pour into greased and floured tube pan. Bake at 350 degrees for 1 hour. Cool in pan for several minutes. Invert onto serving plate.

Jewish Apple Cake

Yield:
16 servings

Utensil:
bundt pan

Approx Per Serving:
Cal 398
Prot 4 g
Carbo 62 g
Fiber 2 g
T Fat 15 g
Chol 53 mg
Sod 214 mg

2 1/2 cups sugar
1 cup oil
4 eggs
1/3 cup orange juice
2 1/2 teaspoons vanilla extract
1 tablespoon baking powder
3 cups flour
1 teaspoon salt
6 apples, peeled, cored, cut into slices
1/4 cup flour
1/4 cup sugar
2 teaspoons cinnamon

Cream 2 1/2 cups sugar and oil in mixer bowl until light and fluffy. Add eggs 1 at a time, beating well after each addition. Add orange juice and vanilla; mix well. Add baking powder, 3 cups flour and salt; mix well. Batter will be thick. Mix apples, remaining 1/4 cup flour, remaining 1/4 cup sugar and cinnamon in bowl. Alternate layers of batter and apple mixture in greased and floured bundt pan until all ingredients are used, ending with apple mixture. Bake at 350 degrees for 1 1/2 hours or until top is brown and dry. Cool in pan for several minutes. Invert onto serving plate.

Applesauce Cake

Yield:
16 servings

Utensil:
tube pan

Approx Per Serving:
Cal 380
Prot 4 g
Carbo 69 g
Fiber 3 g
T Fat 12 g
Chol 29 mg
Sod 170 mg

1 15-ounce package seedless raisins
1 cup chopped pecans
3 cups flour
Pinch of salt
1/2 teaspoon baking powder
1 teaspoon cinnamon
1 teaspoon allspice
1 teaspoon cloves
1/2 cup butter, softened
2 cups sugar
1 egg
2 teaspoons soda
2 cups applesauce

Coat raisins and pecans with a small amount of flour. Sift remaining flour, salt, baking powder, cinnamon, allspice and cloves together. Cream butter, sugar and egg in mixer bowl until light and fluffy. Add flour mixture and mixture of soda and applesauce alternately to creamed mixture; mix well. Stir in pecans and raisins. Pour into greased and floured tube pan. Bake at 275 degrees for 2 hours. Cool in pan for several minutes. Invert onto serving plate.

Carrot Cake

Yield:
12 servings

Utensil:
2 cake pans

Approx Per Serving:
Cal 853
Prot 7 g
Carbo 99 g
Fiber 2 g
T Fat 50 g
Chol 112 mg
Sod 337 mg

2 cups flour
1 teaspoon baking powder
1 teaspoon soda
1 teaspoon cinnamon
1/2 teaspoon salt
1 1/2 cups oil
2 cups sugar
4 eggs
2 cups grated carrots
1/2 cup butter, softened
8 ounces cream cheese, softened
1 1-pound package confectioners' sugar
1 teaspoon vanilla extract
1 cup chopped walnuts

Sift first 5 ingredients together. Combine oil and sugar in bowl; mix well. Add eggs 1 at a time, beating well after each addition. Stir in carrots. Pour into 2 greased and floured 9-inch round cake pans. Bake at 350 degrees for 30 minutes. Cool in pans for 3 minutes. Remove to wire racks to cool completely. Cream butter and cream cheese in mixer bowl until light and fluffy. Beat in confectioners' sugar gradually. Stir in vanilla and walnuts. Spread between layers and over top and side of cake.

Carrot Cake with Irish Cream Frosting

Yield:
12 servings

Utensil:
2 cake pans

Approx Per Serving:
Cal 652
Prot 6 g
Carbo 84 g
Fiber 2 g
T Fat 33 g
Chol 154 mg
Sod 423 mg

2 1/2 cups flour
4 1/2 teaspoons baking powder
2 teaspoons cinnamon
1/8 teaspoon nutmeg
1/8 teaspoon allspice
1 cup butter, softened
1 cup packed brown sugar
4 eggs
2 1/2 cups grated carrots
3/4 cup raisins
2 teaspoons grated orange rind
1/4 cup orange juice
1 cup butter, softened
3 1/4 cups confectioners' sugar
1/4 cup Irish cream liqueur

Sift first 5 ingredients together. Cream 1 cup butter and brown sugar in mixer bowl until light and fluffy. Add eggs 1 at a time, beating well after each addition. Stir in carrots, raisins and orange rind. Add flour mixture and orange juice alternately to creamed mixture; mix well. Pour into 2 greased and floured 8-inch round cake pans. Bake at 350 degrees for 40 to 45 minutes or until layers test done. Cool in pans for 20 minutes. Remove to wire racks to cool completely. Beat remaining 1 cup butter in mixer bowl until smooth. Beat in confectioners' sugar gradually. Add liqueur. Beat until light and fluffy. Spread between layers and over top and side of cake.

Divine Decadence

Yield:
8 servings

Utensil:
9-inch round pan

Approx Per Serving:
Cal 590
Prot 6 g
Carbo 69 g
Fiber 2 g
T Fat 35 g
Chol 115 mg
Sod 150 mg

1/2 cup corn syrup
1/2 cup butter
5 ounces semisweet chocolate
3/4 cup sugar
3 eggs
1 cup flour
1 cup chopped pecans
1 teaspoon vanilla extract
3 ounces semisweet chocolate
1 tablespoon butter
2 tablespoons corn syrup
1 teaspoon milk

Combine 1/2 cup corn syrup and 1/2 cup butter in saucepan. Bring to a boil over medium heat, stirring occasionally. Remove from heat. Add 5 ounces chocolate; stir until melted. Add sugar; stir until dissolved. Add eggs 1 at a time, beating well after each addition. Stir in flour, pecans and vanilla. Pour into greased and floured 9-inch round cake pan. Bake at 350 degrees or until knife inserted near center comes out clean. Cool in pan for 10 minutes. Remove to wire rack to cool completely. Melt remaining 3 ounces chocolate and 1 tablespoon butter in saucepan over low heat, stirring constantly. Stir in remaining 2 tablespoons corn syrup and milk. Spread over top and side of cake.

Chocolate Chip Cake

Yield:
16 servings

Utensil:
tube pan

Approx Per Serving:
Cal 333
Prot 4 g
Carbo 43 g
Fiber 1 g
T Fat 17 g
Chol 55 mg
Sod 269 mg

1 2-layer package yellow cake mix
1 4-ounce package vanilla instant pudding mix
4 eggs, beaten
1 cup milk
1/2 cup oil
3 ounces German's chocolate, grated
1 cup chocolate chips

Combine cake mix, pudding mix, eggs, milk, oil and grated chocolate in mixer bowl. Beat for 5 minutes. Stir in chocolate chips gently. Pour into greased and floured tube pan. Bake at 350 degrees for 1 hour. Cool in pan for several minutes. Invert onto serving plate. May drizzle with favorite glaze if desired.

Miniature Tollhouse Cupcakes

Yield:
20 servings

Utensil:
cupcake pan

Approx Per Serving:
Cal 224
Prot 3 g
Carbo 25 g
Fiber 1 g
T Fat 14 g
Chol 34 mg
Sod 86 mg

1 cup plus 2 tablespoons sifted flour
1/2 teaspoon soda
1/8 teaspoon salt
1/2 cup butter, softened
6 tablespoons sugar
6 tablespoons packed brown sugar
1 egg
1/2 teaspoon vanilla extract
1/2 cup packed brown sugar
1 teaspoon vanilla extract
1 egg
1 cup semisweet chocolate chips
1 1/2 cups chopped walnuts

Sift flour, soda and salt together. Cream butter, sugar and 6 tablespoons brown sugar in mixer bowl at medium speed until light and fluffy. Add 1 egg. Beat for 1 minute longer. Stir in flour mixture and 1/2 teaspoon vanilla. Spoon 1 rounded teaspoonful into miniature paper-lined cups. Bake at 375 degrees for 12 minutes. Beat 1/2 cup brown sugar, 1 teaspoon vanilla and 1 egg in mixer bowl at medium speed until thickened. Stir in chocolate chips and walnuts. Spoon over cupcakes. Bake for 15 minutes longer. Cool in pan for 3 minutes. Remove to wire racks to cool completely.

Brown Sugar Devil's Food Cake

Yield:
16 servings

Utensil:
2 cake pans

Approx Per Serving:
Cal 264
Prot 4 g
Carbo 46 g
Fiber 1 g
T Fat 8 g
Chol 56 mg
Sod 134 mg

1/2 cup butter, softened
2 cups packed brown sugar
3 eggs
1/2 cup baking cocoa
1/2 cup hot water
1/2 cup buttermilk
1 teaspoon soda
3 cups flour
1 teaspoon vanilla extract

Cream butter and brown sugar in mixer bowl until light and fluffy. Add eggs 1 at a time, beating well after each addition. Stir in mixture of cocoa and hot water. Add mixture of buttermilk and soda; mix well. Stir in flour and vanilla. Pour into 2 greased and floured 9-inch round cake pans. Bake at 350 degrees for 45 minutes to 1 hour or until layers test done. Cool in pan for several minutes. Invert onto serving plate.

Hershey Cake

Yield:
15 servings

Utensil:
9x13-inch pan

Approx Per Serving:
Cal 395
Prot 5 g
Carbo 55 g
Fiber 1 g
T Fat 19 g
Chol 92 mg
Sod 154 mg

1/2 cup butter, softened
1 cup sugar
4 eggs
1 16-ounce can chocolate syrup
1 teaspoon vanilla extract
1 cup flour
1/2 cup butter
1/3 cup evaporated milk
1 cup sugar
1/2 cup chocolate chips
1/2 cup chopped pecans (optional)

Cream 1/2 cup butter and 1 cup sugar in mixer bowl until light and fluffy. Add eggs 1 at a time, beating well after each addition. Add chocolate syrup, vanilla and flour; mix well. Pour into greased and floured 9x13-inch cake pan. Bake at 350 degrees for 30 to 40 minutes or until cake tests done. Combine remaining 1/2 cup butter, evaporated milk and remaining 1 cup sugar in saucepan. Bring to a boil over medium heat, stirring frequently. Simmer for 3 minutes. Add chocolate chips and pecans. Cook until chocolate is melted, stirring constantly. Spread on cake immediately; frosting will harden fast.

Coconut-Sour Cream Layer Cake

Yield:
12 servings

Utensil:
2 cake pans

Approx Per Serving:
Cal 676
Prot 6 g
Carbo 102 g
Fiber 3 g
T Fat 30 g
Chol 17 mg
Sod 238 mg

1 2-layer package butter-recipe yellow cake mix
2 cups sugar
2 cups sour cream
1 12-ounce package frozen coconut, thawed
1 1/2 cups whipped topping

Prepare and bake cake mix using package directions for two 9-inch round cake pans. Cool in pans for several minutes. Remove to wire racks to cool completely. Combine sugar, sour cream and coconut in bowl; mix well. Chill in refrigerator. Split each layer horizontally. Combine 1 cup coconut mixture and whipped topping in bowl; mix gently. Spread remaining coconut mixture between layers. Spread whipped topping mixture over top and side. Store in airtight container in refrigerator for 3 days before serving.

GRAHAM CRACKER CAKE

Yield:
16 servings

Utensil:
tube pan

Approx Per Serving:
Cal 628
Prot 6 g
Carbo 86 g
Fiber 2 g
T Fat 31 g
Chol 113 mg
Sod 382 mg

1 cup butter, softened
2 cups sugar
5 eggs
2 teaspoons vanilla extract
1 16-ounce package graham crackers, crushed
2 teaspoons baking powder
1 cup milk
1 cup chopped pecans
1 cup coconut
1 1-pound package confectioners' sugar
3 ounces cream cheese, softened
1/4 cup butter, softened
2 teaspoons vanilla extract
1/2 cup chopped pecans

Cream 1 cup butter and sugar in mixer bowl until light and fluffy. Add eggs 1 at a time, beating well after each addition. Stir in 2 teaspoons vanilla. Add mixture of cracker crumbs and baking powder alternately with milk, beating well after each addition. Stir in 1 cup pecans and coconut. Pour into greased and floured 10-inch tube pan. Bake at 375 degrees for 1 hour. Cool in pan for several minutes. Invert onto serving plate. Cream confectioners' sugar, cream cheese, remaining 1/4 cup butter and 2 teaspoons vanilla in mixer bowl until light and fluffy. Stir in remaining 1/2 cup pecans. Spread on cooled cake.

MOCHA TORTE

Yield:
8 servings

Utensil:
serving plate

Approx Per Serving:
Cal 353
Prot 4 g
Carbo 30 g
Fiber <1 g
T Fat 23 g
Chol 42 mg
Sod 203 mg

1 pound cake
1 envelope whipped topping mix
6 Heath candy bars
1 teaspoon instant coffee

Slice cake horizontally into 3 layers. Place on serving plate. Prepare whipped topping using package directions. Chop candy into fine pieces, reserving 2 tablespoons. Fold candy into whipped topping. Stir in coffee powder. Spread between layers and over top and side of cake. Sprinkle with reserved candy.

Mandarin Orange Cake

Yield:
12 servings

Utensil:
2 cake pans

Approx Per Serving:
Cal 490
Prot 5 g
Carbo 65 g
Fiber 1 g
T Fat 24 g
Chol 71 mg
Sod 360 mg

1 2-layer package butter-recipe yellow cake mix
1 11-ounce can mandarin oranges
1/2 cup corn oil
4 eggs, beaten
16 ounces whipped topping
1 16-ounce can crushed pineapple
1 4-ounce package vanilla instant pudding mix

Combine cake mix, undrained oranges, oil and eggs in bowl; mix well. Pour into 2 greased and floured 9-inch round cake pans. Bake at 350 degrees for 25 minutes or until layers spring back when touched lightly. Cool in pans for several minutes. Remove to wire racks to cool completely. Combine whipped topping, undrained pineapple and pudding mix in bowl; mix well. Spread between layers and over top and side of cooled cake. Chill until serving time.

Peanut Butter Fudge Cake

Yield:
32 servings

Utensil:
9x13-inch pan

Approx Per Serving:
Cal 307
Prot 5 g
Carbo 38 g
Fiber 1 g
T Fat 16 g
Chol 14 mg
Sod 187 mg

2 cups sugar
2 cups flour
1 teaspoon soda
1 cup margarine
1/4 cup baking cocoa
1 cup water
1/2 cup buttermilk
2 eggs, beaten
1 teaspoon vanilla extract
1 1/2 cups creamy peanut butter
4 1/2 teaspoons peanut oil
1/2 cup margarine
1/4 cup baking cocoa
6 tablespoons buttermilk
1 1-pound package confectioners' sugar
1 teaspoon vanilla extract

Mix sugar, flour and soda in bowl. Bring 1 cup margarine and next 5 ingredients to a boil in saucepan, stirring frequently. Pour over flour mixture; mix well. Pour into greased 9x13-inch cake pan. Bake at 350 degrees for 25 minutes. Cool in pan. Spread mixture of peanut butter and oil over cake. Bring 1/2 cup margarine and next 2 ingredients to a boil in saucepan, stirring frequently. Pour over confectioners' sugar in bowl; mix well. Stir in 1 teaspoon vanilla. Spread over peanut butter mixture. Cut into squares.

Penny Candy Cake

Yield:
16 servings

Utensil:
tube pan

Approx Per Serving:
Cal 660
Prot 8 g
Carbo 109 g
Fiber 4 g
T Fat 24 g
Chol 85 mg
Sod 338 mg

1 cup butter, softened
2 cups sugar
4 eggs
1 cup buttermilk
1 teaspoon soda
1/2 cup buttermilk
4 cups flour
1 teaspoon salt
1 pound chopped dates
2 cups chopped pecans
1 16-ounce package orange slice candy, chopped
1 6-ounce can frozen orange juice concentrate, thawed
1/2 cup packed brown sugar

Cream butter and sugar in mixer bowl until light and fluffy. Add eggs 1 at a time, beating well after each addition. Add 1 cup buttermilk; mix well. Add mixture of soda and remaining 1/2 cup buttermilk; mix well. Add mixture of flour and salt; mix well. Stir in dates, pecans and candy. Pour into greased and floured tube pan. Bake at 275 degrees for 2 1/2 to 3 hours or until cake tests done. Combine orange juice concentrate and brown sugar in bowl; mix well. Pour over hot cake. Cool in pan. Invert onto serving plate.

Pineapple Dream Cake

Yield:
12 servings

Utensil:
3 cake pans

Approx Per Serving:
Cal 497
Prot 5 g
Carbo 55 g
Fiber 1 g
T Fat 29 g
Chol 125 mg
Sod 365 mg

1 2-layer package yellow cake mix
1 11-ounce can mandarin oranges
1/2 cup oil
4 eggs
2 cups whipping cream
1 4-ounce package vanilla instant pudding mix
1 16-ounce can crushed pineapple, drained

Combine cake mix, undrained mandarin oranges, oil and eggs in large mixer bowl. Beat for 2 minutes. Pour into 3 greased and floured 9-inch round cake pans. Bake at 350 degrees for 20 minutes or until layers test done. Cool in pans on wire racks for 20 minutes. Remove to wire racks to cool completely. Beat whipping cream in mixer bowl until soft peaks form. Add pudding mix. Beat until stiff peaks form. Fold in pineapple. Spread between layers and over top and sides of cooled cake.

Lemon Pound Cake

Yield:
16 servings

Utensil:
tube pan

Approx Per Serving:
Cal 426
Prot 5 g
Carbo 56 g
Fiber 1 g
T Fat 21 g
Chol 69 mg
Sod 230 mg

1 cup margarine, softened
3 cups sugar
3 cups flour
1/2 teaspoon salt
5 eggs, beaten
1/2 cup oil
1 cup milk
1 tablespoon lemon extract

Combine margarine, sugar, flour, salt, eggs, oil, milk and flavoring in bowl; mix well. Pour into greased and floured tube pan. Bake at 325 degrees for 1 hour and 20 minutes. Cool in pan for several minutes. Invert onto serving plate.

Favorite Pound Cake

Yield:
16 servings

Utensil:
tube pan

Approx Per Serving:
Cal 434
Prot 5 g
Carbo 58 g
Fiber 1 g
T Fat 20 g
Chol 99 mg
Sod 202 mg

1 cup butter, softened
1/2 cup shortening
3 cups sugar
5 eggs
3 cups flour
1/2 teaspoon baking powder
1/2 teaspoon salt
3/4 cup milk
1/4 cup almond liqueur
1 teaspoon mace extract
1/2 teaspoon lemon extract

Cream butter, shortening and sugar in mixer bowl until light and fluffy. Add eggs 1 at a time, beating well after each addition. Stir in mixture of flour, baking powder and salt. Add milk, liqueur and flavorings; beat well. Pour into greased and floured tube pan. Bake at 325 degrees for 1 1/4 hours. Cool in pan for several minutes. Invert onto serving plate.

Old-Fashioned Pound Cake

Yield:
16 servings

Utensil:
tube pan

Approx Per Serving:
Cal 407
Prot 4 g
Carbo 55 g
Fiber 1 g
T Fat 20 g
Chol 110 mg
Sod 148 mg

1 cup butter, softened
3 cups sugar
5 eggs
1/2 teaspoon vanilla extract
1/2 teaspoon lemon extract
1/4 teaspoon soda
2 cups sour cream
3 cups cake flour

Cream butter and sugar in large mixer bowl until light and fluffy. Add eggs 1 at a time, beating well after each addition. Stir in flavorings and soda. Blend in sour cream. Add flour gradually, beating well after each addition. Spoon into greased and floured tube pan. Bake at 325 degrees for 1 hour or until cake tests done. Let stand for 1 hour. Invert on funnel to cool completely. Loosen cake from side of pan with sharp knife. Invert onto serving plate. Serve with fresh fruit and whipped cream.

Rhubarb Cake

Yield:
12 servings

Utensil:
9x13-inch pan

Approx Per Serving:
Cal 307
Prot 4 g
Carbo 53 g
Fiber 1 g
T Fat 9 g
Chol 19 mg
Sod 109 mg

1 1/2 cups packed brown sugar
1/2 cup shortening
1 egg
1 cup buttermilk
2 cups flour
1 teaspoon soda
1 teaspoon vanilla extract
2 cups chopped rhubarb
1/2 cup sugar
1 teaspoon cinnamon

Cream brown sugar and shortening in mixer bowl until light and fluffy. Beat in egg. Add buttermilk, flour, soda and vanilla; mix well. Stir in rhubarb. Pour into greased and floured 9x13-inch cake pan. Sprinkle with mixture of sugar and cinnamon. Bake at 350 degrees for 35 minutes. Cool in pan for 2 hours. Serve with whipped topping or vanilla ice cream.

Ricotta Cheese Cake

Yield:
12 servings

Utensil:
9x13-inch pan

Approx Per Serving:
Cal 501
Prot 14 g
Carbo 64 g
Fiber 0 g
T Fat 22 g
Chol 109 mg
Sod 296 mg

1 2-layer package marble cake mix
32 ounces ricotta cheese
4 eggs
1/2 cup sugar
1 teaspoon vanilla extract

Prepare cake mix using package directions for 9x13-inch cake pan; do not bake. Combine cheese, eggs, sugar and vanilla in mixer bowl. Beat until smooth. Spoon over batter. Mixture will sink to bottom of pan. Bake at 350 degrees for 1 1/2 hours. Cool in pan.

Rum Cake

Yield:
16 servings

Utensil:
tube pan

Approx Per Serving:
Cal 423
Prot 4 g
Carbo 47 g
Fiber 1 g
T Fat 22 g
Chol 69 mg
Sod 310 mg

1 cup chopped pecans
1 2-layer package yellow cake mix
1 4-ounce package vanilla instant pudding mix
4 eggs, beaten
1/2 cup cold water
1/2 cup oil
1/2 cup rum
1/2 cup butter
1/4 cup water
1 cup sugar
1/2 cup rum

Sprinkle pecans in bottom of greased and floured 10-inch tube pan. Combine cake mix, pudding mix, eggs, cold water, oil and 1/2 cup rum in bowl; mix well. Pour over pecans. Bake at 325 degrees for 55 minutes to 1 hour or until cake tests done. Cool in pan for 10 minutes. Invert onto serving plate. Pierce cake with fork. Melt butter in saucepan. Stir in water and sugar. Bring to a boil. Simmer for 5 minutes, stirring constantly. Remove from heat. Stir in remaining 1/2 cup rum. Drizzle a small amount of glaze over top and side of cake. Let stand until glaze is absorbed into cake. Repeat process until all glaze is used.

Sauerkraut Cake

Yield:
15 servings

Utensil:
9x13-inch pan

Approx Per Serving:
Cal 238
Prot 4 g
Carbo 35 g
Fiber 2 g
T Fat 10 g
Chol 65 mg
Sod 264 mg

2/3 cup butter, softened
1 1/2 cups sugar
3 eggs
1 teaspoon vanilla extract
2 1/4 cups sifted flour
1/2 cup baking cocoa
1 teaspoon soda
1 teaspoon baking powder
1/4 teaspoon salt
1 cup water
2/3 cup chopped sauerkraut, rinsed, drained

Cream butter and sugar in mixer bowl until light and fluffy. Add eggs 1 at a time, beating well after each addition. Stir in vanilla. Sift flour, cocoa, soda, baking powder and salt together. Add to creamed mixture alternately with water, beating well after each addition. Stir in sauerkraut. Pour into greased and floured 9x13-inch cake pan. Bake at 350 degrees for 30 minutes. Garnish with confectioners' sugar or serve with whipped cream or mocha cream.

Spice Cake

Yield:
16 servings

Utensil:
bundt pan

Approx Per Serving:
Cal 238
Prot 3 g
Carbo 44 g
Fiber 2 g
T Fat 6 g
Chol 40 mg
Sod 183 mg

2 cups self-rising flour
2 cups sugar
3 eggs, beaten
2 4-ounce jars baby food prunes
1 teaspoon nutmeg
1 teaspoon cinnamon
1 teaspoon allspice
1 cup chopped pecans
1/4 cup confectioners' sugar

Combine flour, sugar, eggs, prunes, nutmeg, cinnamon and allspice in mixer bowl; beat well. Stir in pecans. Pour into greased and floured bundt pan. Bake at 350 degrees for 55 minutes. Cool in pan for several minutes. Invert onto serving plate. Sprinkle with confectioners' sugar. May substitute baby food plums, carrots or applesauce for prunes. May substitute 1/2 cup chopped pecans and 1/2 cup raisins for 1 cup pecans.

Tropical Dream Cake

Yield:
16 servings

Utensil:
tube pan

Approx Per Serving:
Cal 387
Prot 4 g
Carbo 61 g
Fiber 2 g
T Fat 15 g
Chol 40 mg
Sod 220 mg

2 cups sugar
1 cup oil
3 eggs
1 8-ounce can juice-pack crushed pineapple
1 1/2 teaspoons vanilla extract
2 cups all-purpose flour
1 cup whole wheat flour
1 teaspoon salt
1 teaspoon soda
1 teaspoon baking powder
1 teaspoon cinnamon
2 cups finely chopped bananas
1 3/4 cups sifted confectioners' sugar
2 to 3 tablespoons orange juice

Beat sugar and oil in mixer bowl until foamy. Add eggs 1 at a time, beating well after each addition. Stir in undrained pineapple and vanilla. Sift flours, salt, soda, baking powder and cinnamon together. Add to pineapple mixture; beat well. Stir in bananas. Pour into greased 10-inch fluted tube pan. Bake at 350 degrees for 1 hour to 1 hour and 10 minutes or until cake tests done. Cool in pan for 10 minutes. Remove to wire rack to cool completely. Mix confectioners' sugar and enough orange juice to make of glaze consistency. Drizzle over cooled cake.

Apple Butter Bars

Yield:
36 servings

Utensil:
9x13-inch pan

Approx Per Serving:
Cal 140
Prot 2 g
Carbo 22 g
Fiber 1 g
T Fat 6 g
Chol 14 mg
Sod 53 mg

1 1/2 cups flour
2 1/2 cups quick-cooking oats
1 1/2 cups sugar
1 teaspoon soda
1 cup melted butter
1 1/2 cups apple butter

Combine flour, oats, sugar and soda in large bowl; mix well. Stir in melted butter. Press half the mixture into greased 9x13-inch baking pan. Top with apple butter. Spoon remaining oat mixture over apple butter. Press down lightly with spoon. Bake at 350 degrees for 55 minutes or until browned. Let stand until cool. Cut into bars. May substitute peach preserves for apple butter.

Best Chocolate Syrup Brownies

Yield:
18 servings

Utensil:
9x9-inch pan

Approx Per Serving:
Cal 188
Prot 3 g
Carbo 25 g
Fiber 1 g
T Fat 9 g
Chol 49 mg
Sod 81 mg

1/2 cup butter, softened
1 cup sugar
3 eggs, beaten
1/8 teaspoon salt
1 cup flour
3/4 cup chocolate syrup
2 teaspoons vanilla extract
3/4 cup chopped walnuts

Cream butter, sugar and eggs in mixer bowl until light and fluffy. Add salt and flour; mix well. Stir in syrup, vanilla and walnuts. Spoon into greased and lightly floured 9-inch square baking pan. Smooth top. Bake at 350 degrees for 35 minutes or until brownies test done. Loosen from sides of pan. Cool in pan on wire rack. Garnish with walnut halves or dust with confectioners' sugar. May substitute pecans for walnuts.

Candy-Like Brownies

Yield:
16 servings

Utensil:
8x8-inch pan

Approx Per Serving:
Cal 256
Prot 2 g
Carbo 36 g
Fiber 1 g
T Fat 13 g
Chol 45 mg
Sod 104 mg

1/2 cup butter
2 ounces baking chocolate
1 cup sugar
1/2 cup sifted flour
2 eggs
1/2 cup chopped pecans
1/8 teaspoon salt
1 teaspoon vanilla extract
1 tablespoon butter
1 ounce baking chocolate
1/2 cup packed light brown sugar
1/4 cup evaporated milk
1 1/2 cups (or more) confectioners' sugar
1/2 teaspoon vanilla extract
1/8 teaspoon salt

Melt 1/2 cup butter and 2 ounces chocolate in saucepan. Combine sugar and flour in bowl; mix well. Add eggs 1 at a time, mixing well after each addition. Stir in chocolate mixture. Add pecans, 1/8 teaspoon salt and 1 teaspoon vanilla; mix well. Pour into buttered 8-inch square glass baking pan. Bake at 350 degrees for 25 minutes or until brownies spring back when lightly touched. Cool in pan. Heat remaining 1 tablespoon butter and next 3 ingredients in saucepan until butter and chocolate are melted, stirring constantly. Stir in confectioners' sugar and remaining ingredients. Spread over cooled brownies.

Butter Cookies

Yield:
72 servings

Utensil:
cookie sheet

Approx Per Serving:
Cal 94
Prot 1 g
Carbo 10 g
Fiber <1 g
T Fat 5 g
Chol 20 mg
Sod 44 mg

2 cups butter, softened
1 1/3 cups sugar
2 egg yolks, beaten
1 egg white, beaten
1 tablespoon rum
1/2 teaspoon vanilla extract
5 cups flour

Cream butter and sugar in mixer bowl until light and fluffy. Add egg yolks and egg white; beat well. Stir in rum and vanilla. Add flour gradually, beating well after each addition. Spoon into cookie press. Press onto ungreased cookie sheet. Decorate as desired. Bake at 350 degrees for 10 to 15 minutes or until lightly browned. Remove to wire rack to cool. May substitute Brandy for rum.

Chocolate Chip Cookies

Yield:
96 servings

Utensil:
cookie sheet

Approx Per Serving:
Cal 154
Prot 2 g
Carbo 21 g
Fiber 1 g
T Fat 8 g
Chol 20 mg
Sod 87 mg

5 cups oats
4 cups flour
2 teaspoons soda
2 teaspoons baking powder
1 teaspoon salt
2 cups butter, softened
2 cups sugar
2 cups packed brown sugar
4 eggs, beaten
2 teaspoons vanilla extract
4 cups chocolate chips
1 8-ounce chocolate bar, grated

Process oats in blender until of flour consistency. Combine with flour, soda, baking powder and salt in bowl; mix well. Cream butter, sugar, brown sugar, eggs and vanilla in mixer bowl until light and fluffy. Add flour mixture; beat well. Stir in chocolate chips and grated chocolate. Shape into golf ball-sized balls. Place 2 inches apart on ungreased cookie sheet. Bake at 375 degrees for 8 minutes. Remove to wire rack to cool. These cookies are very similar to Mrs. Fields' Cookies.

"Coconot" Cookies

Yield:
36 servings

Utensil:
cookie sheet

Approx Per Serving:
Cal 128
Prot 2 g
Carbo 19 g
Fiber <1 g
T Fat 5 g
Chol 6 mg
Sod 254 mg

1/2 cup margarine, softened
1 cup sugar
1 egg
1 2-ounce package instant potatoes
1 20-ounce package baking mix
2 teaspoons coconut extract

Cream margarine and sugar in mixer bowl until light and fluffy. Beat in egg. Add instant potatoes and baking mix; beat well. Stir in flavoring. Chill dough for 1 hour. Shape into marble-sized balls. Place 2 inches apart on nonstick cookie sheet. Bake at 375 degrees for 10 to 15 minutes or until lightly browned. Remove to wire rack to cool.

Congo Squares

Yield:
15 servings

Utensil:
9x13-inch pan

Approx Per Serving:
Cal 435
Prot 5 g
Carbo 61 g
Fiber 2 g
T Fat 21 g
Chol 59 mg
Sod 208 mg

2 3/4 cups flour
2 1/2 teaspoons baking powder
1/2 teaspoon salt
1 1-pound package brown sugar
1/2 cup butter, softened
3 eggs
2 cups chocolate chips
1 cup chopped pecans

Sift flour, baking powder and salt together. Cream brown sugar and butter in mixer bowl until light and fluffy. Add eggs 1 at a time, beating well after each addition. Add flour mixture; beat well. Stir in chocolate chips and pecans. Spread in greased 9x13-inch baking pan. Bake at 350 degrees for 30 to 35 minutes or until done. Let stand until cool. Cut into squares. May serve warm.

ONE-PAN GRANOLA BARS

Yield:
36 servings

Utensil:
9x13-inch pan

Approx Per Serving:
Cal 127
Prot 2 g
Carbo 17 g
Fiber 2 g
T Fat 6 g
Chol 10 mg
Sod 36 mg

1¼ cups packed brown sugar
¾ cup butter
4 cups quick-cooking oats
¾ cup chopped prunes
½ cup sliced almonds
½ cup chopped pecans
1 tablespoon cinnamon

Combine brown sugar and butter in 9x13-inch baking pan. Heat at 350 degrees for 5 minutes or until butter is melted, stirring occasionally. Remove from oven. Add oats, prunes, almonds, pecans and cinnamon; mix well. Press firmly into even layer. Bake for 25 to 30 minutes or just until golden brown. Cool in pan for 15 minutes. Cut into bars. Cool completely. May substitute raisins or dates for prunes and use 1 cup pecans for ½ cup almonds and ½ cup pecans.

LEMON BARS DELUXE

Yield:
18 servings

Utensil:
9x13-inch pan

Approx Per Serving:
Cal 267
Prot 3 g
Carbo 39 g
Fiber <1 g
T Fat 12 g
Chol 75 mg
Sod 111 mg

2 cups sifted flour
½ cup confectioners' sugar
1 cup butter
½ teaspoon baking powder
¼ cup flour
4 eggs, beaten
2 cups sugar
⅓ cup lemon juice
¼ cup confectioners' sugar

Sift 2 cups flour and ½ cup confectioners' sugar together. Cut in butter until mixture clings together. Press into 9x13-inch nonstick baking pan. Bake at 350 degrees for 20 to 25 minutes or until lightly browned. Sift baking powder and remaining ¼ cup flour together. Combine eggs, sugar and lemon juice in bowl; mix well. Add flour mixture; mix well. Pour over crust. Bake for 25 minutes longer. Sprinkle with remaining ¼ cup confectioners' sugar. Let stand until cool. Cut into bars.

Lemon Love Notes

Yield:
81 servings

Utensil:
9x9-inch pan

Approx Per Serving:
Cal 31
Prot <1 g
Carbo 5 g
Fiber <1 g
T Fat 1 g
Chol 8 mg
Sod 13 mg

1/2 cup butter, softened
1/4 cup confectioners' sugar
1 cup flour
2 eggs, beaten
1 cup sugar
2 tablespoons flour
1/2 teaspoon baking powder
2 tablespoons lemon juice
Grated rind of 1 lemon
1/4 cup confectioners' sugar

Cream butter, 1/4 cup confectioners' sugar and 1 cup flour in mixer bowl until light and fluffy. Spread in 9-inch square nonstick baking pan. Bake at 350 degrees for 15 minutes. Let stand until cool. Combine eggs, sugar, remaining 2 tablespoons flour, baking powder, lemon juice and lemon rind in bowl; mix well. Pour over crust. Bake for 25 minutes. Sprinkle with remaining 1/4 cup confectioners' sugar. Cut into 1-inch squares.

Lemon Whippersnaps

Yield:
48 servings

Utensil:
cookie sheet

Approx Per Serving:
Cal 62
Prot 1 g
Carbo 11 g
Fiber 0 g
T Fat 2 g
Chol 4 mg
Sod 68 mg

1 2-layer package lemon cake mix
2 cups whipped topping
1 egg, beaten
1/2 cup sifted confectioners' sugar

Combine cake mix, whipped topping and egg in bowl; mix well. Drop by teaspoonfuls into confectioners' sugar; roll to coat. Place 1 1/2 inches apart on greased cookie sheet. Bake at 350 degrees for 10 to 15 minutes or until golden brown. Remove from cookie sheet. Let stand until cool.

Old-Fashioned Soft Molasses Cookies

Yield:
72 servings

Utensil:
cookie sheet

Approx Per Serving:
Cal 80
Prot 1 g
Carbo 14 g
Fiber <1 g
T Fat 2 g
Chol 0 mg
Sod 89 mg

6 cups sifted flour
2 teaspoons soda
2 teaspoons salt
1 cup sugar
1½ cups molasses
¾ cup oil
¾ cup warm water
1½ teaspoons vanilla extract

Sift flour, soda and salt together. Combine sugar, molasses, oil, water and vanilla in bowl; mix well. Add flour mixture gradually. Stir until mixture forms soft dough. Chill for 1 hour. Roll on floured surface. Cut with cookie cutter. Place on greased cookie sheet. Bake at 375 degrees for 10 to 12 minutes or until lightly browned. Remove to wire rack to cool. Store in tightly covered jar with an apple slice for softness and freshness. May drop by teaspoonfuls onto greased cookie sheet instead of using cookie cutter.

Soft Molasses Cookies

Yield:
36 servings

Utensil:
cookie sheet

Approx Per Serving:
Cal 84
Prot 1 g
Carbo 13 g
Fiber <1 g
T Fat 3 g
Chol 6 mg
Sod 66 mg

3 cups flour
1½ teaspoons ginger
1 teaspoon cinnamon
¾ teaspoon salt
½ teaspoon soda
½ cup shortening
1 cup sorghum molasses
1 egg, beaten

Sift flour, ginger, cinnamon, salt and soda together. Cream shortening in mixer bowl until light and fluffy. Add molasses and egg; beat well. Stir in flour mixture. Chill in refrigerator. Roll ¼ inch thick on floured surface. Cut with cookie cutter. Place on greased cookie sheet. Bake at 350 degrees for 8 to 10 minutes or until lightly browned. Remove to wire rack to cool.

Oatmeal Cookies

Yield:
36 servings

Utensil:
cookie sheet

Approx Per Serving:
Cal 120
Prot 2 g
Carbo 17 g
Fiber 1 g
T Fat 5 g
Chol 12 mg
Sod 32 mg

2 cups flour
1 teaspoon cloves
1 teaspoon cinnamon
1 teaspoon soda
3/4 cup melted shortening
2 cups oats
1/2 cup sugar
1/4 cup milk
1/2 cup sorghum molasses
2 eggs, beaten
1 cup chopped raisins

Sift flour, cloves, cinnamon and soda into large bowl; mix well. Stir in melted shortening. Add oats, sugar, milk, molasses and eggs; mix well. Stir in raisins. Drop by teaspoonfuls onto greased cookie sheet. Bake at 350 degrees for 10 to 15 minutes or until lightly browned. Remove to wire rack to cool.

Party Cookies

Yield:
72 servings

Utensil:
cookie sheet

Approx Per Serving:
Cal 69
Prot 1 g
Carbo 9 g
Fiber <1 g
T Fat 4 g
Chol 6 mg
Sod 46 mg

2 1/4 cups sifted flour
1 teaspoon soda
1 teaspoon salt
1 cup shortening
1 cup packed brown sugar
1/2 cup sugar
2 teaspoons vanilla extract
2 eggs, beaten
1 1/2 cups "M & M's" Plain Chocolate Candies

Sift flour, soda and salt together. Combine shortening, brown sugar and sugar in large bowl; mix well. Beat in vanilla and eggs. Stir in flour mixture. Add 1/2 cup candy; mix well. Drop by teaspoonfuls onto ungreased cookie sheet. Decorate with remaining 1 cup candy. Bake at 375 degrees for 10 minutes or until golden brown. Remove to wire rack to cool.

PEANUT BUTTER COOKIES

Yield:
36 servings

Utensil:
cookie sheet

Approx Per Serving:
Cal 139
Prot 3 g
Carbo 11 g
Fiber 1 g
T Fat 10 g
Chol 6 mg
Sod 50 mg

2 cups flour
1 cup sorghum molasses
1 cup peanut butter
1 cup shortening
1/2 teaspoon baking powder
1/4 teaspoon soda
1 egg, beaten

Combine flour, molasses, peanut butter, shortening, baking powder, soda and egg in large bowl; mix well. Chill overnight. Shape into walnut-sized balls. Place on nonstick cookie sheet. Bake at 350 degrees for 15 minutes or until lightly browned. Remove to wire rack to cool. May substitute corn syrup for molasses.

PRALINE THUMBPRINT COOKIES

Yield:
36 servings

Utensil:
cookie sheet

Approx Per Serving:
Cal 176
Prot 1 g
Carbo 20 g
Fiber <1 g
T Fat 10 g
Chol 22 mg
Sod 78 mg

1 cup butter, softened
1 cup sifted confectioners' sugar
2 cups flour
1 cup finely chopped pecans
1 tablespoon vanilla extract
1/2 cup butter
1 cup packed brown sugar
1/8 teaspoon salt
1/2 cup evaporated milk
2 cups sifted confectioners' sugar
1/2 teaspoon vanilla extract

Cream 1 cup butter in mixer bowl until light and fluffy. Add 1 cup confectioners' sugar and flour; beat well. Stir in pecans and 1 tablespoon vanilla. Shape into 1-inch balls. Place 2 inches apart on nonstick cookie sheet. Make indentation in each cookie with thumb. Bake at 375 degrees for 15 minutes; do not brown. Melt remaining 1/2 cup butter in saucepan. Add brown sugar and salt; mix well. Bring to a boil, stirring constantly. Remove from heat. Stir in evaporated milk. Bring to a boil. Remove from heat. Add remaining 2 cups confectioners' sugar and 1/2 teaspoon vanilla; stir until smooth. Spoon into indentations on cookies. Cool on wire racks.

Quick Pudding Cookies

Yield:
24 servings

Utensil:
cookie sheet

Approx Per Serving:
Cal 99
Prot 1 g
Carbo 12 g
Fiber <1 g
T Fat 6 g
Chol 9 mg
Sod 102 mg

1 4-ounce package chocolate instant pudding mix
1 cup baking mix
1/4 cup oil
1 egg, slightly beaten
3 tablespoons water
1 cup chocolate chips

Combine pudding mix and baking mix in bowl. Stir in oil, egg, water and chocolate chips. Drop by teaspoonfuls 2 inches apart onto ungreased cookie sheet. Bake at 375 degrees for 12 minutes or until lightly browned. Remove to wire racks to cool. Store in tightly covered container. May use any flavor pudding mix.

Ricotta Cheese Cookies

Yield:
48 servings

Utensil:
cookie sheet

Approx Per Serving:
Cal 126
Prot 2 g
Carbo 19 g
Fiber <1 g
T Fat 5 g
Chol 11 mg
Sod 114 mg

1 cup margarine, softened
2 cups sugar
2 cups ricotta cheese
2 eggs, beaten
2 teaspoons vanilla extract
4 cups flour, sifted
1 teaspoon soda
1 teaspoon salt
1 cup confectioners' sugar
1 tablespoon milk

Cream margarine and sugar in mixer bowl until light and fluffy. Add cheese, eggs and vanilla; mix well. Stir in flour, soda and salt. Drop by teaspoonfuls onto greased cookie sheet. Bake at 350 degrees for 15 to 20 minutes or until lightly browned. Combine confectioners' sugar and milk in bowl; mix well. Spread on cookies. Remove to wire racks to cool. May use a small amount of food coloring to tint frosting.

Russian Tea Cakes

Yield:
36 servings

Utensil:
cookie sheet

Approx Per Serving:
Cal 104
Prot 1 g
Carbo 10 g
Fiber <1 g
T Fat 7 g
Chol 14 mg
Sod 58 mg

1 cup butter, softened
1/2 cup confectioners' sugar
2 1/2 cups sifted flour
1 teaspoon vanilla extract
1/4 teaspoon salt
3/4 cup finely chopped pecans
1/2 cup confectioners' sugar

Combine butter, 1/2 cup confectioners' sugar, flour, vanilla and salt in bowl; mix well. Stir in pecans. Shape into 1-inch balls. Place on nonstick cookie sheet. Bake at 400 degrees for 14 to 17 minutes or until lightly browned. Roll hot cookies in 1/4 cup confectioners' sugar. Let stand until cool. Roll in remaining 1/4 cup confectioners' sugar.

Spritz Pressed Cookies

Yield:
72 servings

Utensil:
cookie sheet

Approx Per Serving:
Cal 44
Prot 1 g
Carbo 4 g
Fiber <1 g
T Fat 3 g
Chol 13 mg
Sod 23 mg

1 cup butter, softened
2/3 cup sifted confectioners' sugar
1 egg
1 egg yolk
1 teaspoon almond extract
2 3/4 cups sifted flour

Cream butter and confectioners' sugar in mixer bowl until light and fluffy. Beat in egg, egg yolk, and flavoring. Add flour gradually, beating well after each addition. Spoon into cookie press. Press 1 inch apart onto ungreased cookie sheet. Bake at 400 degrees for 7 to 10 minutes or until set but not browned. Remove to wire rack to cool. Decorate as desired.

Caramel Corn

Yield:
20 servings

Utensil:
roasting pan

Approx Per Serving:
Cal 216
Prot 1 g
Carbo 34 g
Fiber 1 g
T Fat 10 g
Chol 0 mg
Sod 162 mg

1 cup margarine
2 cups packed brown sugar
1/8 teaspoon cream of tartar
1/2 cup corn syrup
1 teaspoon soda
5 quarts popped popcorn

Bring margarine, brown sugar, cream of tartar and corn syrup to a boil in saucepan. Cook for 5 minutes, stirring constantly. Remove from heat. Stir in soda. Pour over popcorn in roasting pan. Bake at 250 degrees for 1 hour, stirring 4 times. Let stand until cool. Store in airtight containers.

Easy Chocolate Fudge

Yield:
60 servings

Utensil:
saucepan

Approx Per Serving:
Cal 155
Prot 1 g
Carbo 22 g
Fiber <1 g
T Fat 8 g
Chol 2 mg
Sod 43 mg

1 cup margarine
5 cups sugar
1 12-ounce can evaporated milk
1 cup chopped pecans
3 cups semisweet chocolate chips
1 teaspoon vanilla extract

Bring margarine, sugar and evaporated milk to a rolling boil in saucepan. Cook for 6 minutes, stirring constantly. Stir in pecans, chocolate chips and vanilla. Pour into buttered 9x13-inch dish. Let stand until firm. Cut into squares.

Peanut Butter Fudge

Yield:
36 servings

Utensil:
saucepan

Approx Per Serving:
Cal 135
Prot 3 g
Carbo 21 g
Fiber 1 g
T Fat 5 g
Chol 1 mg
Sod 44 mg

1 1-pound package confectioners' sugar
1/2 cup milk
1 12-ounce jar peanut butter
1 7-ounce jar marshmallow creme
1 teaspoon butter

Bring confectioners' sugar and milk to a boil in heavy aluminum saucepan. Cook for 3 1/2 minutes, stirring constantly. Remove from heat. Add peanut butter, marshmallow creme and butter. Stir until smooth and well-blended. Pour into buttered 9-inch square glass dish. Chill in refrigerator. Cut with pizza cutter. Store in a covered tin in a cool place.

Velvety Fudge

Yield:
36 servings

Utensil:
saucepan

Approx Per Serving:
Cal 240
Prot 2 g
Carbo 35 g
Fiber 1 g
T Fat 12 g
Chol 13 mg
Sod 45 mg

4 1/2 cups sugar
1 12-ounce can evaporated milk
3 cups chocolate chips
1 cup chopped pecans
3 tablespoons vanilla extract
3/4 cup butter

Bring sugar and evaporated milk to a rolling boil in large saucepan. Cook for 6 minutes, stirring constantly. Remove from heat. Stir in chocolate chips, pecans, vanilla and butter. Pour into buttered serving dish.

Peanut Butter Puppy Chow

Yield:
20 servings

Utensil:
saucepan

Approx Per Serving:
Cal 379
Prot 6 g
Carbo 54 g
Fiber 2 g
T Fat 18 g
Chol 0 mg
Sod 298 mg

1/2 cup margarine
1 cup peanut butter
2 cups miniature semisweet chocolate chips
1 15-ounce package Crispix cereal
4 cups confectioners' sugar

Melt margarine, peanut butter and chocolate chips in saucepan over low heat, stirring constantly. Pour over cereal in large bowl; stir gently until coated. Place confectioners' sugar in large paper bag. Add cereal mixture to bag 1/4 at a time; shake until coated. Spread on tray to cool and dry. Store in airtight container.

Preacher "Cookies"

Yield:
24 servings

Utensil:
saucepan

Approx Per Serving:
Cal 164
Prot 3 g
Carbo 23 g
Fiber 2 g
T Fat 7 g
Chol 1 mg
Sod 69 mg

1/2 cup margarine
2 cups sugar
1/2 cup milk
1/2 cup baking cocoa
1/2 cup peanut butter
2 cups quick-cooking oats
1 teaspoon vanilla extract (optional)

Combine margarine, sugar, milk and cocoa in saucepan. Bring to a boil. Cook for 2 minutes, stirring constantly. Remove from heat. Stir in peanut butter, oats and vanilla. Drop by teaspoonfuls onto waxed paper. Let stand until cool. May increase amount of peanut butter to taste and amount of oats for thickness.

Apple Pie

Yield:
8 servings

Utensil:
pie plate

Approx Per Serving:
Cal 442
Prot 3 g
Carbo 61 g
Fiber 3 g
T Fat 17 g
Chol 8 mg
Sod 333 mg

1 recipe 2-crust pie pastry
7 tart apples, peeled, cored, cut into slices
1 cup sugar
2 tablespoons flour
1 teaspoon cinnamon
1/4 teaspoon nutmeg
1/8 teaspoon salt
2 tablespoons butter

Fit half the pastry into pie plate. Mix apples with sugar, flour, cinnamon, nutmeg and salt in bowl. Spoon into pastry-lined pie plate. Dot with butter. Top with remaining pastry, sealing edge and cutting vents. Bake at 400 degrees for 50 minutes. Add 1 tablespoon lemon juice or grated lemon rind to apples if apples are not tart.

Brandy and Raisin Apple Pie

Yield:
8 servings

Utensil:
pie plate

Approx Per Serving:
Cal 446
Prot 3 g
Carbo 63 g
Fiber 4 g
T Fat 15 g
Chol 4 mg
Sod 325 mg

1/4 cup raisins
1/4 cup Brandy
1 recipe 2-crust pie pastry
1/2 cup sugar
1/4 cup packed brown sugar
1 1/4 teaspoons cinnamon
2 tablespoons flour
1/2 teaspoon cloves
1/8 teaspoon salt
7 Granny Smith apples, peeled, cored, cut into slices
1 tablespoon butter
1 tablespoon sugar

Combine raisins and Brandy in tightly covered jar. Chill overnight; drain. Fit half the pastry into pie plate. Combine 1/2 cup sugar, brown sugar, cinnamon, flour, cloves and salt in bowl. Stir until smooth. Stir in raisins and apples. Spoon into pastry-lined pie plate. Dot with butter. Top with remaining pastry, sealing and fluting edge and cutting vents. Sprinkle with remaining 1 tablespoon sugar. Bake at 400 degrees for 50 minutes.

Cherry Cheese Pie

Yield:
8 servings

Utensil:
pie plate

Approx Per Serving:
Cal 537
Prot 8 g
Carbo 73 g
Fiber 2 g
T Fat 25 g
Chol 48 mg
Sod 408 mg

8 ounces cream cheese, softened
1 14-ounce can sweetened condensed milk
1/3 cup lemon juice
1 teaspoon vanilla extract
1 9-inch graham cracker pie shell
1 21-ounce can cherry pie filling, chilled

Beat cream cheese in mixer bowl until light and fluffy. Add condensed milk. Beat until smooth. Stir in lemon juice and vanilla. Spoon into pie shell. Chill for 3 hours or until set. Spoon chilled pie filling over top.

Chocolate Chip Pies

Yield:
16 servings

Utensil:
2 pie plates

Approx Per Serving:
Cal 386
Prot 4 g
Carbo 43 g
Fiber 1 g
T Fat 23 g
Chol 53 mg
Sod 230 mg

1 cup sugar
1 cup packed brown sugar
1/2 cup melted margarine
4 eggs, beaten
1 cup chopped pecans
1 cup chocolate chips
2 unbaked 9-inch pie shells

Combine sugar, brown sugar, margarine and eggs in bowl. Stir in pecans and chocolate chips. Spoon into pie shells. Bake at 350 degrees for 40 minutes.

Chocolate Mousse Pie

Yield:
6 servings

Utensil:
pie plate

Approx Per Serving:
Cal 653
Prot 6 g
Carbo 69 g
Fiber 2 g
T Fat 41 g
Chol 9 mg
Sod 368 mg

1 8-ounce Hershey's chocolate bar
1/4 cup milk
12 ounces whipped topping
1 9-inch chocolate crumb pie shell

Break chocolate bars into squares. Reserve 2 squares of chocolate bar. Combine remaining chocolate squares and milk in saucepan. Heat over medium heat until chocolate is melted, stirring constantly. Pour over whipped topping in bowl; mix well. Spoon into pie shell. Grate reserved chocolate. Sprinkle over filling. Freeze, covered, for 4 hours to overnight.

Silk Pie

Yield:
8 servings

Utensil:
pie plate

Approx Per Serving:
Cal 330
Prot 3 g
Carbo 30 g
Fiber 1 g
T Fat 23 g
Chol 41 mg
Sod 63 mg

2 egg whites
1/8 teaspoon salt
1/8 teaspoon cream of tartar
1/2 teaspoon vanilla extract
1/2 cup sugar
1/4 cup ground walnuts
8 ounces German's chocolate
3 tablespoons water
1 cup whipping cream
1/2 teaspoon vanilla extract

Beat egg whites in mixer bowl at low speed until foamy. Add salt, cream of tartar and 1/2 teaspoon vanilla. Beat at medium speed until soft peaks form. Add sugar gradually, beating constantly at high speed until stiff peaks form. Fold in walnuts. Spread in buttered 8 or 9-inch pie plate. Bake at 350 degrees for 55 minutes. Melt chocolate in water in saucepan. Cool until slightly thickened. Beat whipping cream and remaining 1/2 teaspoon vanilla in bowl until soft peaks form. Fold gently into chocolate mixture. Pour into prepared shell. Chill until serving time.

Coconut Pie

Yield:
8 servings

Utensil:
pie plate

Approx Per Serving:
Cal 335
Prot 4 g
Carbo 42 g
Fiber 2 g
T Fat 17 g
Chol 69 mg
Sod 228 mg

1 cup sugar
1 tablespoon (scant) flour
2 eggs, beaten
3 tablespoons melted butter
1 cup milk
1 teaspoon vanilla extract
1 cup coconut
1 unbaked 9-inch pie shell

Combine sugar, flour, eggs, melted butter, milk and vanilla in bowl; mix well. Stir in coconut. Spoon into pie shell. Bake at 350 degrees for 45 minutes or until set.

French Coconut Pie

Yield:
8 servings

Utensil:
pie plate

Approx Per Serving:
Cal 413
Prot 4 g
Carbo 46 g
Fiber 2 g
T Fat 25 g
Chol 111 mg
Sod 263 mg

1 1/4 cups sugar
1/2 cup melted butter
3 eggs, beaten
1 teaspoon vanilla extract
1 tablespoon vinegar
1 3-ounce can flaked coconut
1 unbaked 9-inch pie shell

Combine sugar, melted butter, eggs, vanilla and vinegar in bowl; mix well. Stir in coconut. Spoon into pie shell. Bake at 350 degrees for 45 to 50 minutes or until set.

CRÈME DE MENTHE PIE

Yield:
8 servings

Utensil:
pie plate

Approx Per Serving:
Cal 514
Prot 5 g
Carbo 52 g
Fiber 1 g
T Fat 31 g
Chol 7 mg
Sod 281 mg

2 cups yogurt
16 ounces whipped topping
1/3 cup Crème de Menthe
1 9-inch chocolate crumb pie shell
1/2 cup chocolate sprinkles

Combine yogurt, whipped topping and Crème de Menthe in large bowl; mix well. Spoon into pie shell. Sprinkle with chocolate sprinkles. Freeze until firm.

FRUIT SALAD PIE

Yield:
8 servings

Utensil:
pie plate

Approx Per Serving:
Cal 385
Prot 4 g
Carbo 78 g
Fiber 3 g
T Fat 8 g
Chol 0 mg
Sod 177 mg

1 16-ounce can sour cherries
1 16-ounce can crushed pineapple
1 3-ounce package cherry gelatin
1 cup sugar
1/3 cup flour
4 bananas, mashed
1 baked 9-inch deep-dish pie shell

Combine undrained cherries and undrained pineapple in saucepan. Bring to a boil. Add mixture of gelatin, sugar and flour; mix well. Cook until thickened, stirring constantly. Stir in bananas. Spoon into pie shell. Serve with whipped topping.

Japanese Fruit Pie

Yield:
8 servings

Utensil:
pie plate

Approx Per Serving:
Cal 451
Prot 4 g
Carbo 51 g
Fiber 2 g
T Fat 27 g
Chol 84 mg
Sod 255 mg

1/2 cup melted butter
1 cup sugar
2 eggs, slightly beaten
1/2 cup chopped pecans
1/2 cup coconut
1/2 cup raisins
3/4 cup crushed pineapple
1 tablespoon vinegar
1 unbaked 8-inch pie shell

Combine melted butter, sugar, eggs, pecans, coconut, raisins, pineapple and vinegar in bowl; mix well. Spoon into pie shell. Bake at 325 degrees for 35 to 40 minutes or until set.

Lemon Fluff Pie

Yield:
6 servings

Utensil:
pie plate

Approx Per Serving:
Cal 636
Prot 9 g
Carbo 63 g
Fiber 2 g
T Fat 41 g
Chol 104 mg
Sod 189 mg

1/3 cup butter
3/4 cup flour
1/4 cup packed brown sugar
3/4 cup finely chopped pecans
Juice of 4 lemons
1 14-ounce can sweetened condensed milk
1 cup whipping cream, whipped

Melt butter in heavy skillet. Stir in flour, brown sugar and pecans. Cook over medium heat until crumbs are toasted and golden brown, stirring constantly. Let stand until cool. Reserve 2 tablespoons crumbs. Press remaining crumbs into 9-inch pie plate. Combine lemon juice and condensed milk in large bowl; mix well. Fold in whipped cream. Spoon into prepared crust. Sprinkle with reserved crumbs. Chill until serving time.

Key Lime Pie

Yield:
8 servings

Utensil:
pie plate

Approx Per Serving:
Cal 494
Prot 6 g
Carbo 70 g
Fiber 1 g
T Fat 22 g
Chol 17 mg
Sod 309 mg

1 14-ounce can sweetened condensed milk
1 6-ounce can frozen limeade concentrate, thawed
8 ounces whipped topping
1 9-inch graham cracker pie shell

Combine condensed milk, limeade concentrate and whipped topping in bowl; mix well. Spoon into pie shell. Chill for 10 minutes or until serving time. May substitute lemonade concentrate for limeade concentrate.

Frozen Peanut Butter Pie

Yield:
8 servings

Utensil:
pie plate

Approx Per Serving:
Cal 492
Prot 9 g
Carbo 45 g
Fiber 2 g
T Fat 32 g
Chol 12 mg
Sod 345 mg

3/4 cup sifted confectioners' sugar
3 ounces cream cheese, softened
1/2 cup peanut butter
2 tablespoons milk
8 ounces whipped topping
1 9-inch chocolate crumb pie shell
1/4 cup chopped peanuts

Cream confectioners' sugar and cream cheese in mixer bowl until light and fluffy. Add peanut butter and milk. Beat until smooth. Fold in whipped topping. Spoon into pie shell. Sprinkle with peanuts. Freeze until firm. Serve frozen.

Crunchy Pecan and Raisin Pie

Yield:
8 servings

Utensil:
pie plate

Approx Per Serving:
Cal 411
Prot 4 g
Carbo 45 g
Fiber 2 g
T Fat 26 g
Chol 84 mg
Sod 251 mg

1/2 cup butter, softened
1 cup sugar
2 egg yolks
1/2 cup chopped pecans
1/2 cup raisins
1 teaspoon vinegar
1/2 teaspoon cinnamon
2 egg whites, beaten
1 unbaked 9-inch pie shell

Cream butter, sugar and egg yolks in mixer bowl until light and fluffy. Add pecans, raisins, vinegar and cinnamon; mix well. Fold in egg whites. Spoon into pie shell. Bake at 325 degrees for 25 to 30 minutes or until set.

Grand's Pecan Pie

Yield:
8 servings

Utensil:
pie plate

Approx Per Serving:
Cal 472
Prot 4 g
Carbo 69 g
Fiber 1 g
T Fat 22 g
Chol 61 mg
Sod 241 mg

2 eggs, beaten
1 cup dark corn syrup
1 cup sugar
1/8 teaspoon salt
2 tablespoons melted butter
1/2 teaspoon vanilla extract
1 cup chopped pecans
1 unbaked 9-inch pie shell

Combine eggs, corn syrup, sugar, salt, butter and vanilla in bowl; mix well. Stir in pecans. Spoon into pie shell. Bake at 400 degrees for 15 minutes. Reduce temperature to 350 degrees. Bake for 30 minutes longer or until knife inserted in center comes out clean.

Layered Pecan Pie

Yield:
8 servings

Utensil:
pie plate

Approx Per Serving:
Cal 548
Prot 8 g
Carbo 60 g
Fiber 2 g
T Fat 33 g
Chol 137 mg
Sod 342 mg

1/3 cup sugar
8 ounces cream cheese, softened
1/4 teaspoon salt
1 egg
1 teaspoon vanilla extract
1 unbaked 9-inch pie shell
1 1/4 cups chopped pecans
3 eggs
1 cup light corn syrup
1/4 cup sugar
1 teaspoon vanilla extract

Cream 1/3 cup sugar, cream cheese and salt in mixer bowl until light and fluffy. Beat in 1 egg and 1 teaspoon vanilla. Spoon into pie shell. Sprinkle with pecans. Combine remaining 3 eggs, corn syrup, 1/4 cup sugar and 1 teaspoon vanilla in bowl; beat well. Pour over pecans. Bake at 375 degrees for 35 to 40 minutes or until set.

Pudding Pecan Pie

Yield:
8 servings

Utensil:
pie plate

Approx Per Serving:
Cal 420
Prot 5 g
Carbo 59 g
Fiber 2 g
T Fat 20 g
Chol 34 mg
Sod 285 mg

1 4-ounce package vanilla instant pudding mix
1 cup corn syrup
3/4 cup evaporated milk
1 egg, slightly beaten
1 cup chopped pecans
1 unbaked 8-inch pie shell

Beat pudding mix with corn syrup in mixer bowl. Add evaporated milk and egg gradually, beating well after each addition. Stir in pecans. Spoon into pie shell. Bake at 375 degrees for 45 to 50 minutes or until top is firm and begins to crack. Cool on wire rack for 3 hours. Garnish with whipped topping and additional pecans. May substitute butter pecan pudding mix for vanilla and reduce pecans to 1/2 cup.

Pineapple Chess Pie

Yield:
6 servings

Utensil:
pie plate

Approx Per Serving:
Cal 472
Prot 4 g
Carbo 54 g
Fiber 1 g
T Fat 27 g
Chol 112 mg
Sod 337 mg

1 8-ounce can crushed pineapple
2 eggs, beaten
1 cup sugar
1/2 cup melted butter
1 teaspoon vanilla extract
1 unbaked 8-inch pie shell

Combine pineapple, eggs, sugar, melted butter and vanilla in bowl; mix well. Spoon into pie shell. Bake at 350 degrees for 30 minutes.

French Strawberry Glacé Pie

Yield:
8 servings

Utensil:
pie plate

Approx Per Serving:
Cal 341
Prot 4 g
Carbo 43 g
Fiber 2 g
T Fat 18 g
Chol 31 mg
Sod 223 mg

1 quart fresh strawberries
2/3 cup water
1 cup sugar
3 tablespoons cornstarch
1/3 cup water
8 ounces cream cheese, softened
1 unbaked 9-inch pie shell

Rinse strawberries; remove green tops. Reserve 8 strawberries. Slice remaining strawberries. Combine 1 cup strawberries and 2/3 cup water in saucepan. Bring to a boil. Simmer for 5 minutes. Stir in mixture of sugar, cornstarch and remaining 1/3 cup water. Cook until thickened, stirring constantly. Let stand until cool. Spread cream cheese over bottom of pie shell. Spoon 3 cups strawberries over cream cheese. Pour glaze over strawberries. Arrange reserved strawberries over top. Garnish with whipped cream. Chill for 2 hours.

Fresh Strawberry Pie

≈*MW*≈

Yield:
8 servings

Utensil:
pie plate

Approx Per Serving:
Cal 369
Prot 4 g
Carbo 53 g
Fiber 3 g
T Fat 17 g
Chol 1 mg
Sod 137 mg

1/2 cup oil
2 tablespoons milk
1 1/2 cups flour
1 tablespoon sugar
1/4 teaspoon salt
1/4 cup finely chopped pecans (optional)
1 quart large fresh strawberries
3 tablespoons cornstarch
1/3 cup water
1 cup sugar
1 tablespoon lemon juice
1/4 teaspoon salt

Mix oil and milk in bowl. Add mixture of flour, sugar, salt and pecans; mix well. Pat pastry into 9-inch pie plate. Prick with fork at least 6 times on bottom and in bend of plate. Microwave on High for 3 minutes. Rotate 1/4 turn. Microwave for 3 to 4 minutes longer or until firm. Rinse strawberries; remove green tops. Arrange half the strawberries over pie crust. Purée remaining strawberries, cornstarch and water in blender. Combine strawberry mixture, sugar, lemon juice and salt in microwave-safe bowl. Microwave on High for 6 minutes or until thickened, stirring 6 times. Let stand until cool. Pour over strawberries. Chill until set. Garnish with whipped cream.

Jarret House Vinegar Pie

Yield:
8 servings

Utensil:
pie plate

Approx Per Serving:
Cal 401
Prot 4 g
Carbo 50 g
Fiber 1 g
T Fat 21 g
Chol 111 mg
Sod 261 mg

1 1/2 cups sugar
3 eggs, beaten
1/2 cup melted butter
2 tablespoons vinegar
2 tablespoons flour
1 tablespoon vanilla extract
1 unbaked 9-inch pie shell

Combine sugar, eggs, melted butter, vinegar, flour and vanilla in large mixer bowl. Beat at high speed until smooth. Spoon into pie shell. Bake at 300 degrees for 50 minutes or until top forms a light golden crust.

Glossary of Cooking Terms

Bake: To cook by dry heat in an oven, or under hot coals.

Bard: To cover lean meats with bacon or pork fat before cooking to prevent dryness.

Baste: To moisten, especially meats, with melted butter, pan drippings, sauce, etc. during cooking time.

Beat: To mix ingredients by vigorous stirring or with electric mixer.

Blanch: To immerse, usually vegetables or fruit, briefly into boiling water to inactivate enzymes, loosen skin, or soak away excess salt.

Blend: To combine 2 or more ingredients, at least 1 of which is liquid or soft, to produce a mixture that is of smooth and uniform consistency.

Boil: To heat liquid until bubbly; the boiling point for water is about 212 degrees Fahrenheit, depending on altitude and atmospheric pressure.

Braise: To cook, especially meats, covered, in a small amount of liquid.

Brew: To prepare a beverage by allowing boiling water to extract flavor and/or color from certain substances.

Broil: To cook by direct exposure to intense heat such as a flame or an electric heating unit.

Caramelize: To melt sugar in heavy pan over low heat until golden, stirring constantly.

Chill: To cool in the refrigerator or in cracked ice.

Clarify: To remove impurities from melted butter by allowing the sediment to settle, then pouring off clear yellow liquid. Other fats may be clarified by straining.

Cream: To blend butter, margarine, shortening, usually softened, or sometimes oil, with a granulated or crushed ingredient until the mixture is soft and creamy. Usually described in method as light and fluffy.

Curdle: To congeal milk with rennet or heat until solid lumps or curds are formed.

Cut in: To disperse solid shortening into the dry ingredients with a knife or pastry blender. Texture of the mixture should resemble coarse cracker meal. Described in the method as crumbly.

Decant: To pour a liquid such as wine or melted butter carefully from 1 container into another leaving the sediment in the original container.

Deep-fry: To cook in a deep pan or skillet containing hot cooking oil. Deep-fried foods are generally completely immersed in the hot oil.

Deglaze: To heat stock, wine or other liquid in the pan in which meat has been cooked, mixing with pan juices and sediment to form a gravy or sauce base.

Degorger: To remove strong flavors or impurities before cooking, i.e. soaking ham in cold water or sprinkling vegetables with salt, then letting stand for a period of time and pressing out excess fluid.

Degrease: To remove accumulated fat from the surface of hot liquids.

Dice: To cut into small cubes about 1/4-inch in size. Do not use dice unless ingredient can truly be cut into cubes.

Dissolve: To create a solution by thoroughly mixing a solid or granular substance with a liquid until there is no remaining sediment.

Dredge: To coat completely with flour, bread crumbs, etc.

Filet: To remove bones from meat or fish. (Pieces of meat, fish, or poultry from which bones have been removed are called filets.)

Flambé: To pour warmed Brandy or other spirits over food in a pan, then ignite and continue cooking briefly.

Fold in: To blend a delicate frothy mixture into a heavier one so that none of the lightness or volume is lost. Using a rubber spatula, turn under and bring up and over, rotating bowl 1/4 turn after each folding motion.

Fry: To cook in a pan or skillet containing hot cooking oil. The oil should not totally cover the food.

Garnish: To decorate food before serving.

Glaze: To cover or coat with sauce, syrup, egg white, or a jellied substance. After applying, it becomes firm; adding color and flavor.

Grate: To rub food against a rough, perforated utensil to produce slivers, chunks, curls, etc.

Gratiné: To top a sauced dish with crumbs, cheese or butter, then brown under a broiler.

Grill: To broil, usually over hot coals or charcoal.

Grind: To cut, crush, or force through a chopper to produce small bits.

Infuse: To steep herbs or other flavorings in a liquid until liquid absorbs flavor.

Julienne: To cut vegetables, fruit, etc. into long thin strips.

Knead: To press, fold, and stretch dough until smooth and elastic. Method usually notes time frame or result.

Lard: To insert strips of fat or bacon into lean meat to keep it moist and juicy during cooking. Larding is an internal basting technique.

Leaven: To cause batters and doughs to rise, usually by means of a chemical leavening agent. This process may occur before or during baking.

Marinate: To soak, usually in a highly seasoned oil-acid solution, to flavor and/or tenderize food.

Melt: To liquefy solid foods by the action of heat.

Mince: To cut or chop into very small pieces.

Mix: To combine ingredients to distribute uniformly.

Mold: To shape into a particular form.

Panbroil: To cook in a skillet or pan using a very small amount of fat to prevent sticking.

Panfry: To cook in a skillet or pan containing only a small amount of fat.

Parboil: To partially cook in boiling water. Most parboiled foods require additional cooking with or without other ingredients.

Parch: To dry or roast slightly through exposure to very intense heat.

Pit: To remove the hard inedible seed from peaches, plums, etc.

Plank: To broil and serve on a board or wooden platter.

Plump: To soak fruits, usually dried, in liquid until puffy and softened.

Poach: To cook in a small amount of gently simmering liquid such as water.

Preserve: To prevent food spoilage by pickling, salting, dehydrating, smoking, boiling in syrup, etc. Preserved foods have excellent keeping qualities when they have been properly prepared.

Purée: To reduce the pulp of cooked fruit and vegetables to a smooth and thick liquid by straining or blending.

Reduce: To boil stock, gravy or other liquid until volume is reduced, liquid is thickened and flavor is intensified.

Refresh: To place blanched drained vegetables or other food in cold water to halt cooking process.

Render: To cook meat or meat trimmings at low temperature until fat melts and can be drained and strained.

Roast: (1) To cook by dry heat either in an oven or over hot coals. (2) To dry or parch by intense heat.

Sauté: To cook in a skillet or wok containing a small amount of hot cooking oil. Sautéed foods should never be immersed in the oil. They should be stirred frequently.

Scald: (1) To heat a liquid almost to the boiling point. (2) To soak; usually vegetables or fruit; in boiling water until the skins are loosened; see blanch, which is our preferred term.

Scallop: To bake with a sauce in a casserole. The food may either be mixed or layered with the sauce.

Score: To make shallow cuts diagonally in parallel lines.

Scramble: To cook and stir simultaneously, especially eggs.

Shirr: To crack eggs into individual buttered baking dishes, then bake or broil until whites are set. Chopped meats or vegetables, cheese, cream, or bread crumbs may also be added.

Shred: To cut food into slivers.

Shuck: To remove the husk from corn or the shell from oysters, clams, etc.

Sieve: To press a mixture through a closely meshed metal utensil to make it homogeneous.

Sift: To pass, usually dry ingredients, through a fine wire mesh in order to produce a uniform consistency.

Simmer: To cook in or with a liquid at or just below the boiling point.

Skewer: (1) To thread; usually meat and vegetables; onto a sharpened rod (as in shish kabob). (2) To fasten the opening of stuffed fowl closed with small pins.

Skim: To ladle or spoon off the excess fat or scum from the surface of a liquid.

Smoke: To preserve or cook through continuous exposure to wood smoke for a long time.

Steam: To cook with water vapor in a closed container, usually in a steamer, on a rack, or in a double boiler.

Sterilize: To cleanse and purify through exposure to very intense heat.

Stew: To simmer; usually meats and vegetables; for a long period of time. Also used to tenderize meats.

Stir-fry: To cook small pieces of vegetables and/or meat in a small amount of oil in a wok or skillet over high heat, stirring constantly, until tender-crisp.

Strain: To pass through a strainer, sieve, or cheesecloth in order to break down or remove solids or impurities.

Stuff: To fill or pack cavities especially those of meats, vegetables and poultry.

Toast: To brown and crisp, usually by means of direct heat or to bake until brown.

Toss: To mix lightly with lifting motion using 2 forks or spoons.

Truss: To bind poultry legs and wings close to body before cooking.

Whip: To beat a mixture until air has been thoroughly incorporated and the mixture is light and fluffy, volume is greatly increased, and mixture holds its shape.

Wilt: To apply heat to cause dehydration, and a droopy appearance.

Equivalent Chart

	When the recipe calls for	Use
Baking	1/2 cup butter	4 ounces
	2 cups butter	1 pound
	4 cups all-purpose flour	1 pound
	4 1/2 to 5 cups sifted cake flour	1 pound
	1 square chocolate	1 ounce
	1 cup semisweet chocolate chips	6 ounces
	4 cups marshmallows	1 pound
	2 1/4 cups packed brown sugar	1 pound
	4 cups confectioners' sugar	1 pound
	2 cups granulated sugar	1 pound
Cereal – Bread	1 cup fine dry bread crumbs	4 to 5 slices
	1 cup soft bread crumbs	2 slices
	1 cup small bread cubes	2 slices
	1 cup fine cracker crumbs	28 saltines
	1 cup fine graham cracker crumbs	15 crackers
	1 cup vanilla wafer crumbs	22 wafers
	1 cup crushed cornflakes	3 cups uncrushed
	4 cups cooked macaroni	8 ounces uncooked
	3 1/2 cups cooked rice	1 cup uncooked
Dairy	1 cup shredded cheese	4 ounces
	1 cup cottage cheese	8 ounces
	1 cup sour cream	8 ounces
	1 cup whipped cream	1/2 cup heavy cream
	2/3 cup evaporated milk	1 small can
	1 2/3 cups evaporated milk	1 13-ounce can
Fruit	4 cups sliced or chopped apples	4 medium
	1 cup mashed bananas	3 medium
	2 cups pitted cherries	4 cups unpitted
	3 cups shredded coconut	8 ounces
	4 cups cranberries	1 pound
	1 cup pitted dates	1 8-ounce package
	1 cup candied fruit	1 8-ounce package
	3 to 4 tablespoons lemon juice plus 1 tablespoon grated lemon rind	1 lemon
	1/3 cup orange juice plus 2 teaspoons grated orange rind	1 orange
	4 cups sliced peaches	8 medium
	2 cups pitted prunes	1 12-ounce package
	3 cups raisins	1 15-ounce package

	When the recipe calls for	Use
Meats	4 cups chopped cooked chicken 3 cups chopped cooked meat 2 cups cooked ground meat	1 5-pound chicken 1 pound, cooked 1 pound, cooked
Nuts	1 cup chopped nuts	4 ounces shelled 1 pound unshelled
Vegetables	2 cups cooked green beans 2½ cups lima beans or red beans 4 cups shredded cabbage 1 cup grated carrot 8 ounces fresh mushrooms 1 cup chopped onion 4 cups sliced or chopped potatoes 2 cups canned tomatoes	½ pound fresh or 1 16-ounce can 1 cup dried, cooked 1 pound 1 large 1 4-ounce can 1 large 4 medium 1 16-ounce can

Measurement Equivalents

1 tablespoon = 3 teaspoons 2 tablespoons = 1 ounce 4 tablespoons = ¼ cup 5⅓ tablespoons = ⅓ cup 8 tablespoons = ½ cup 12 tablespoons = ¾ cup 16 tablespoons = 1 cup 1 cup = 8 ounces or ½ pint 4 cups = 1 quart 4 quarts = 1 gallon	1 6½ to 8-ounce can = 1 cup 1 10½ to 12-ounce can = 1¼ cups 1 14 to 16-ounce can = 1¾ cups 1 16 to 17-ounce can = 2 cups 1 18 to 20-ounce can = 2½ cups 1 20-ounce can = 3½ cups 1 46 to 51-ounce can = 5¾ cups 1 6½ to 7½-pound can or Number 10 = 12 to 13 cups

Metric Equivalents

Liquid	Dry
1 teaspoon = 5 milliliters 1 tablespoon = 15 milliliters 1 fluid ounce = 30 milliliters 1 cup = 250 milliliters 1 pint = 500 milliliters	1 quart = 1 liter 1 ounce = 30 grams 1 pound = 450 grams 2.2 pounds = 1 kilogram

NOTE: The metric measures are approximate benchmarks for purposes of home food preparation.

Substitution Chart

	Instead of	Use
Baking	1 teaspoon baking powder	1/4 teaspoon soda plus 1/2 teaspoon cream of tartar
	1 tablespoon cornstarch (for thickening)	2 tablespoons flour or 1 tablespoon tapioca
	1 cup sifted all-purpose flour	1 cup plus 2 tablespoons sifted cake flour
	1 cup sifted cake flour	1 cup minus 2 tablespoons sifted all-purpose flour
	1 cup dry bread crumbs	3/4 cup cracker crumbs
Dairy	1 cup buttermilk	1 cup sour milk or 1 cup yogurt
	1 cup heavy cream	3/4 cup skim milk plus 1/3 cup butter
	1 cup light cream	7/8 cup skim milk plus 3 tablespoons butter
	1 cup sour cream	7/8 cup sour milk plus 3 tablespoons butter
	1 cup sour milk	1 cup milk plus 1 tablespoon vinegar or lemon juice or 1 cup buttermilk
Seasoning	1 teaspoon allspice	1/2 teaspoon cinnamon plus 1/8 teaspoon cloves
	1 cup catsup	1 cup tomato sauce plus 1/2 cup sugar plus 2 tablespoons vinegar
	1 clove of garlic	1/8 teaspoon garlic powder or 1/8 teaspoon instant minced garlic or 3/4 teaspoon garlic salt or 5 drops of liquid garlic
	1 teaspoon Italian spice	1/4 teaspoon each oregano, basil, thyme, rosemary plus dash of cayenne
	1 teaspoon lemon juice	1/2 teaspoon vinegar
	1 tablespoon mustard	1 teaspoon dry mustard
	1 medium onion	1 tablespoon dried minced onion or 1 teaspoon onion powder
Sweet	1 1-ounce square chocolate	1/4 cup cocoa plus 1 teaspoon shortening
	1 2/3 ounces semisweet chocolate	1 ounce unsweetened chocolate plus 4 teaspoons granulated sugar
	1 cup honey	1 to 1 1/4 cups sugar plus 1/4 cup liquid or 1 cup corn syrup or molasses
	1 cup granulated sugar	1 cup packed brown sugar or 1 cup corn syrup, molasses or honey minus 1/4 cup liquid

Index

You may order as many ***Pioneer Potpourri*** cookbooks as you wish for the price of $10.00 each plus $2.00 postage and handling per book ordered. Mail form and check for $12.00 for each cookbook ordered to:

GEORGE WASHINGTON CHAPTER
4121 COX ROAD
SUITE 210
GLEN ALLEN VA 23060

Number of Cookbooks Ordered: ____________________

Check Enclosed for Amount of: ____________________

Please Make Checks Payable To:
George Washington Chapter 102, TPA

Please Print:

Name: ____

Address: ____

City, State, Zip: ____________________________________

Daytime Telephone Number: (   ) ____________________